PILOTING
PALM

PILOTING PALM

THE INSIDE STORY OF PALM, HANDSPRING, AND THE BIRTH OF THE BILLION-DOLLAR HANDHELD INDUSTRY

ANDREA BUTTER
& DAVID POGUE

John Wiley & Sons, Inc.

Published by John Wiley & Sons, Inc., New York.
Published simultaneously in Canada.

ISBN 0-471-08965-6

Printed in the United States of America.

10 9 8 7 6 5 4 3 2 1

To Dagmar, Julia, and Matthias Butter

CONTENTS

ACKNOWLEDGMENTS

Above all, our gratitude goes to Jeff Hawkins, Donna Dubinsky, and Ed Colligan, who generously and incautiously consented to cooperate with many hours of interviews, which they endured with patience, good humor, and complete frankness. In a very concrete way, they made the book possible.

We also owe thanks to these people for sharing their time and recollections in interviews (sometimes many of them): Robin Abrams, Al Ahmed, David Anderson, Vicki Barklow, Randy Battat, Eric Benhamou, Mark Bercow, Monty Boyer, Markus Bregler, Stephen K. Brown, Bill Campbell, Elizabeth Cardinale, Marian Cauwet, David Christopher, Byron Connell, Chuck Corbett, Casey Cowell, Bruce Dunlevie, Martin Eastwood, Bob Ebert, Howard Elias, Shawn Ford, Donna Gafford, Mike Gallucci, Jean Louis Gassée, Rob Haitani, Doug Haslam, Ray Ivins, Joel Jewitt, Andrea Johnson, Doris Kanemura, Alan Kessler, Randy Komisar, Doug Kraul, Art Lamb, David T. Lee, Bill MacKenzie, Carolyn Malestic, Ron Marianetti, John McCartney, Pat McVeigh, Bruce Mendel, Jack Miller, Daniel Pifko, Kate Purmal, Frank Quattrone, Chris Raff, Dinesh Raghavan, Janice Roberts, Michael Seedman, Andy Simms, Joe Sipher, Bill Slakey, Caitlin Spaan, Janet Strauss, J Tempesta, Karl Townsend, Dave

Vadasz, Carl Yankowski, and Jon Zakin. We also appreciate the comments of those who have spoken off the record.

We are indebted to many others who responded quickly and ably to myriad ad hoc questions: Maria Amundson, Anne-Marie Bourcier, Allen Bush, Jim Chapman, Roger Flores, Dawn Hannah, Bob Ingols, Claudia Knight, Vitaly Kruglikov, Renee Lakatos, Scott Logsdon, Michael Mace, Rachel Martin, Mike Plasterer, Greg Shirai, Geordie Stewart, Chris Weasler, and Bill Woodruff.

Myra Hart of Harvard Business School provided, with Donna Dubinsky's approval, transcripts of interviews she conducted in 1993, 1994, and 1997, which helped jog memories on long-forgotten details and chronology.

Terry Desser gave helpful input to early parts of the manuscript. Bob Baxley and Mike Tobias provided their considerable photography skills on a moment's notice. Pamela Sklar at 3Com, and Marlene Somsak and Yvette Lorenz-Machlan at Palm, assisted in interviews with executives, photography, and information. Jennifer Funk gave friendly and frequent scheduling support at Handspring.

Of the original 28 Palm employees, the names of Cathy Cain, Carl Chen, Ed Hackett, Greg Kucala, Laura Quirke, Jody Schreiber, and Jenny Williams didn't make it into this book, but their contributions to the company, and this story, should not be overlooked.

Our agent, Jim Levine, proved that he truly walks on water. We could not have done without him and his team at James Levine Communications. Thanks also are due to the staff at Wiley, including executive editor Airié Dekidjiev, who provided enthusiasm and direction from the very first phone call, and her efficient, cheerful assistant, Jessica Noyes. Our copy editor, Tom Laughman, prevented us from embarrassing slips. Sabrina Rood-Sinker transcribed endless hours of interviews, which she not only turned around quickly but also pronounced interesting.

David Pogue: I'd like to offer my gratitude, thanks, and complimentary car-washing services to Andrea Butter, a brilliant collaborator who let me climb aboard the exciting project that was originally her inspired idea alone. Thanks and love, too, to Jennifer (for the support, the time, and the book's title), and to

Kelly and Tia, who stood by me (or crawled by me, as the case may be) during the many months of this book's creation.

Andrea Butter: I wish to thank David Pogue for joining me on this adventure. Without his instant enthusiasm (and exquisite outline), this book would not exist. Tristan and Isolde were my near constant companions during the many months of work. Their unquestioning love for even a tired writer brightened my life as it always does. Last, but not least, my tremendous appreciation goes to Chris. His unending support made this process possible.

NOTE TO THE READER

One of us, Andrea Butter, was a marketing executive at Palm from 1993 to 1999. Writing this book therefore posed a fascinating challenge: How should two authors refer to the one who appears in the story—as "she" or as "me"?

We have chosen to use the first person whenever Andrea Butter appears in the narrative. When you read "I" and "me," we hope you'll recognize that it's Andrea Butter talking, writing about herself in the story.

We also faced the challenge of documenting a moving target; the stories of Palm and Handspring didn't end, of course, when this book was published. It's our intention to follow their continuing adventures with periodic updates at *www.pilotingpalm.com,* where you'll also find links, downloadable chapters in Palm format, and additional anecdotes and behind-the-scenes material.

PROLOGUE

"That's it—I've got it!"

Breathless with excitement, Jeff Hawkins pushed his chair back from the desk and started pacing in the small room that served as his home office.

Only six months earlier, in December 1985, Hawkins would have been considered fairly typical for a Silicon Valley techie. Tall, lanky, and affable in the manner of an introverted guy who's learned to be sociable, he had a wife, an undergraduate degree in electrical engineering from Cornell, and a promising career at a high-tech firm. But that was before he abandoned his job to pursue a quixotic dream: to solve the mystery of the human brain. Over the years, Hawkins's interest in the workings of the brain had become an obsession: He became driven to decipher the enigma of human intelligence, to learn how the brain understood its environment. In his spare time, he read every book and journal he could lay his hands on, but found only partial answers.

He needed more time to focus, time that a nine-to-five job didn't afford, and a good library. Finally, leaving his steady job and income behind, Hawkins enrolled in a graduate-level bio-physics program at UC Berkeley.

1

His wife Janet worried about the decision. Hawkins's father Robert, a prolific inventor, had spent a lifetime chasing dreams. When he quit his engineering job to work on his inventions, the family had to scrape by on Mrs. Hawkins's teacher's salary.

Robert Hawkins's inventions found little commercial success, but left an indelible impression on Jeff. One creation, designed to decipher the communication of dolphins, won Robert modest fame. Another creative spark led to a line of folding houseboats.

And then there was the huge, 16-sided boat with eight retractable legs that Robert spent years building, with his three sons' assistance. On land, it looked like a gigantic, hulking spider, 51 feet in diameter and weighing 50 tons. Officially called SeaSpace but nicknamed the Bubble Monster, the boat was the world's largest air-cushion craft at the time—and probably the only one kept afloat by a vacuum-cleaner fan. In the end, the Hawkins family sold it to a touring orchestra, whose leader hired Jeff and his brothers as first mates during summers.

Jeff Hawkins couldn't escape this legacy. He thrived on solving mental problems like those in the mathematical puzzle books he'd read as a teenager, and could solve those that stymied others. By the time he reached adulthood, Jeff Hawkins had also developed his father's thick skin; he didn't particularly care what other people thought of his ideas, and had no problem swimming against the tide of consensus.

Between classes at UC Berkeley, most of Hawkins's time was spent in the library. "It was like a big puzzle," he says. "I was tracking down what scientists had written, I found who was doing interesting work, what else they'd written about, what other people thought about that person, trying to piece it all together. It was like trying to solve a murder mystery with thousands of clues."

As it turned out, plenty of people had researched the brain, but nobody had nailed an overarching theory of what brains do and how they work. None could account for how a human brain really understands, learns, and remembers.

The idea that would change his life forever struck Hawkins six months into his studies, while reading in his home office one night. "Our intuition about what brains do is wrong," he says. "All the research ignores the role that time and prediction play."

"People think that our perception of the world is like looking at a picture. You take a picture and analyze it, then you look at another picture, and you analyze it, and so on. But the way we experience the world is more like listening to a song. All our inputs, whether they're sound or touch or vision, change over time. We can only experience them through time; we can only recall them through time. You can't recall a memory all at once; you can only recall it sequentially—like a song. If I say, Do you know 'Yellow Submarine' or 'Mary Had a Little Lamb?' you'll say yes, but you can't imagine the whole song all at once. You can start it and you can play it back piece by piece; the role of time is essential."

So is the role of prediction, Hawkins says. If the shape of your doorknob were altered, slightly and without leaving a visual trace, you would still know that something had changed the instant you touched it. "We are constantly making predictions about what we will experience next, much as we anticipate the next part of a song while we listen to it," he says. "Prediction of time-changing patterns is the key to intelligence."

When it dawned on Hawkins that he might have found the missing link to an overarching theory of the brain function, excitement drove him from his desk. If his idea were right, it could lead to discovering, at last, how a human brain works.

Then trepidation set in. What if he were wrong?

Hawkins spent the next year and a half questioning his own theory from every possible angle, weighing it against every piece of data he came across, but he could find no flaw.

In fact, he became convinced that his insights about how the brain worked were just the beginning. He foresaw that machines could work on the same principles—devices that could understand the world around them. "There will be a big business building intelligent memory systems that work the same way brains work," he told his wife.

They would be nothing like the robots or androids of science fiction. Instead, he envisioned machines that could translate languages accurately because they understood the context of each word the way people do; vehicles that could drive themselves because they "understood" cars and traffic; and security surveillance systems that could distinguish between roaming dogs, late-night workers, and real burglars, knowing how to react to each one.

The impact of technology with human-like intelligence could be enormous—perhaps as dramatic as the invention of the transistor in 1948. The transistor ultimately became the basis for all electronic equipment; most people use millions of transistors in their homes, jobs, and cars without even knowing it. The "brain business," as Hawkins called it, could generate a similar avalanche of useful tools. And he knew one thing: The resulting industry would dwarf the PC business.

His department's chairman liked the idea. There was just one hitch: Hawkins would have to spend another six years in standard graduate and postdoctoral programs, studying topics he wasn't especially interested in, before he could focus on the research he was passionate about. The corporate world was far more attractive. In the role of a product creator, he had a better shot at what he really needed: the credibility and financial independence to fund the research he wanted to pursue.

And so, at 31, Jeff Hawkins had a master plan for his life:

Step 1. Quit UC Berkeley to return to the high-tech corporate world.

Step 2. Earn enough money and prominence to finish the brain work.

Step 3. Go into the "brain business."

With that, he called up his previous employer and asked to come back to his job. He wasn't sure how the road before him might twist or turn, but at least he had a plan for where he was going.

ONE

IN THE VALLEY OF DREAMS

B y 1998, Jeff Hawkins would be called the "father of handheld computing." But in 1991, he had no intentions of launching an entire industry, or even founding a company. He only set out to create a new kind of computer.

In Silicon Valley, where Hawkins lived, this attitude was bordering on eccentric. Over four decades of technology booms and occasional busts, the Valley had consistently spawned a petri dish of ideas from which new start-up high-tech companies were created. Since the arrival of venture capitalists (VCs) in the 1960s, a techie with a good idea didn't even have to risk his life's savings on his dream. Instead, he'd find a VC to fund his scheme, then he'd quit his job and voilà: A start-up was born.

Driving from his home in Redwood City, Jeff Hawkins passed the office towers of Silicon Valley legends. To the south, there was Intel, the computer chip company that was on the verge of becoming a household name with its new "Intel Inside" campaign. To the north, Oracle, which Larry Ellison had founded in 1977 with a mere $2,000, had turned into a software juggernaut with $1 billion in annual sales. On the west side of the Valley, Apple Computer's sprawling campus alongside Highway 280 teemed with the enthusiasm of a company that hadn't yet lost its mortal struggle with Microsoft.

Everywhere in between, the nondescript offices of unknown start-ups dotted the roads that crisscross the high-tech Mecca between San Francisco and San Jose. Only 1 in every 10 new companies would survive, but that didn't keep hundreds of entrepreneurs each year from striking out on their own.

For Hawkins, it wasn't the business odds that kept him at his job as a high-tech executive. It was the personal toll life as an entrepreneur might take.

"I'm not a start-up kind of guy," he says. "I don't like to work super-long hours. I knew that a lot of people who had started companies had failed marriages. Just observation said: This is a very stressful thing to do."

Nevertheless, in the late spring of 1991, Hawkins, like so many entrepreneurs before him, was in the grip of an idea for a new type of a computer. He couldn't get the concept out of his head.

At 34, Hawkins worked at GRiD Systems, a small computer company on the east side of the San Francisco Bay. It was his second stint there; he'd left his first GRiD job in 1986 in order to attend grad school. When he left UC Berkeley, GRiD was happy to welcome him back, this time as vice president of research.

It was a job that was tailor-made to his interests, which included managing the development of new products, not people. Without employees of his own, he didn't have to deal with the drudgery of the day-to-day administrative tasks common to VPs with large staffs (or to CEOs of start-ups).

One of the first ideas he presented to GRiD's management upon his return to the company was a new type of computer based on a concept called *pen computing*. Pen computing meant that you could write, using an inkless pen (stylus), directly on the computer screen.

It wasn't a new idea by any means. Very likely the first pair to think of the idea was Jerry Kaplan, a technology executive, and Mitch Kapor, the founder of Lotus Development. In a cross-country February 1987 flight in Kapor's private plane, they hit on the notion of a computer that could be used like a paper notepad. Using a pen rather than a keyboard, they thought, would be attractive to people who aren't conveniently seated at a desk every time they need to use a computer, such as delivery drivers, claims adjusters, or sales reps in the field.

Kaplan, an inspired salesman, pitched the idea to John Doerr, a partner at the elite venture capital firm Kleiner Perkins Caulfield and Byers. Doerr convinced his partners to invest in the idea, and Kaplan promptly got $1.5 million in start-up money for a new pen computing company called GO.

Pen computers seemed tailor-made for GRiD, though. Not only did the company pride itself in being a technology leader, but it had experience in designing portable machines, and its customers already included companies who most needed portable, tablet-style machines.

One of the keys to making a pen-based computer was, of course, handwriting recognition technology, which GRiD lacked—until now. Jeff's studies at Berkeley had provided an important asset to both him and his employer. He was the proud owner of a patent on an invention that stemmed, in part, from his brain studies. By taking the approach that a computer could mimic the brain's pattern recognition, he had written software that could recognize hand-printed characters.

GRiD's management green-lighted the project and agreed to license Hawkins's handwriting recognition software, later to be called PalmPrint, for use in the new machine. Jeff would oversee the creation of a tablet computer called the GRiDPad.

The GRiDPad was ready for prime time in 1989—and, in the specialized markets for which it was designed, it was a hit, even at 4.5 pounds and $2,500. To control costs and streamline the development time, Hawkins had bucked the high-tech trend of relying on expensive and unproven custom-designed parts and instead built the device from off-the-shelf components.

GRiDPad's success gave him the confidence to express his views even when they differed from the industry's conventional wisdom—which they often did. Among GRiD's executives and technical staff, he had gained a reputation as a self-assured and brilliant product designer, which allowed him the luxury of plucking GRiD's best engineers to work on his projects. Most of the other GRiD executives respected him, though some considered him stubborn, the kind of guy who was likely to say, about one engineering issue or another, "I don't care what you say; I *know* I'm right." Even those put off by his self-confidence, however, had to admit that his intuitions generally *were* right.

By early 1991, the pen-based computing wave was the Next Big Thing. John Doerr's 1987 investment in GO had triggered a high-tech gold rush by other investors, who poured nearly $100 million into pen computing start-ups. The press added to the buzz with breathless articles about the high-profile start-ups, including GO and a free-spending company called Momenta. IBM, Toshiba, Canon, and NCR had each announced plans to bring pen computers to market.

Where there's hardware, there's software, and a half-dozen small companies had sprung up to write programs running on the new computers. In March, Microsoft got into the game by announcing an operating system it called Microsoft Windows for Pen Computing.

Yet, despite all of this pen computing frenzy, only a single pen computer was commercially available: Jeff's GRiD machines. Despite the spending and the flashy press events, no other models had even reached the market.

The success of his product designs gave Hawkins a modest amount of fame as a pioneer of the fledgling pen computer industry. GRiD often asked him to meet with potential customers, journalists called him for his observations on new pen technologies, and he became a staple speaker at computer industry conferences.

But even as his public star was rising, privately, Jeff had begun to change his mind about the whole affair. He considered pen computers—even his own GRiDPad—too big, heavy, and expensive for everyday people to contemplate carrying around. Niche-market workers such as claims adjusters or meter readers may have found them useful, but these machines would never gain mass acceptance.

What the world really needed, he thought, was a pen computer for *consumers*. He asked his GRiDPad customers at every opportunity: Would they use a similar computer for their personal use? The answer was always the same: only if it were a lot smaller and less expensive—under $1,000.

The more he thought about it, the more obvious it seemed. Millions and millions of consumers would buy a small, inexpensive computer.

Hawkins presented the idea to his employer, but knew that GRiD would have no interest in the concept; GRiD was firmly focused on the corporate market, and couldn't afford to divert its resources to a consumer business. His consumer product would never see the light of day unless he struck out on his own.

He hoped to interest Tandy, GRiD's corporate parent for the last three years, in his idea. After all, Tandy had long been one of the giants in American consumer electronics sales. As the corporate owner of Radio Shack, Tandy operated nearly 7,000 consumer electronics stores; more than 90 percent of Americans lived or worked within five minutes of a Radio Shack store. If Hawkins could get Tandy to market his product, Radio Shack would inevitably sell it to the stores' millions of consumers.

Jeff contacted Howard Elias, the executive responsible for Tandy's advanced technology businesses. The two had gotten to know each other during Elias's visits with GRiD's management. By a stroke of luck for Jeff, Elias was also directly responsible for Radio Shack's computer business.

Tandy was always looking for new and unique products to put through its vast network of retail stores; Elias, cautiously interested, invited Jeff to a small brainstorming meeting. In that meeting, the project took further shape. The machine that Jeff had in mind would be small and come with built-in software to make it useful immediately.

Soon after, Elias called again. He wanted Hawkins to meet a wider circle of Tandy execs at Tandy's headquarters. "Fly out here to Fort Worth tomorrow," he said. "And get me a brief of the project before we meet."

Jeff had to work quickly. He wrote up a three-page overview about the project, which began like this:

> Palmtop computing devices will be as ubiquitous as calculators by the end of this decade. . . . To get an idea of the market size for these computers, consider the possibility

that most high school students, nearly all college students, and most professionals will own one. With prices starting at $200 (1995), it is entirely conceivable, and I believe likely, that 50% of those people will own or use a portable handheld computer at sometime in their life.

Jeff searched for a code name for the project. He wracked his brain. "Consumer, consumer, consumer—zoomer! Why not?" He typed *Project Zoomer* at the top of the document and sent it off to Texas, never dreaming that his arbitrary code name would remain attached to the project all the way through its development—and even on the finished product.

Hawkins's Zoomer project captivated the imagination of the Tandy managers—maybe too much. After a series of meetings, Tandy proposed to create a new subsidiary, led by Hawkins himself, to develop the product, with Jeff as its key employee.

This wasn't the kind of involvement he had imagined. The more Hawkins thought of it, the more it seemed impossible to build a great product within the confines of Tandy or a Tandy subsidiary. To pull off the Zoomer project, he knew that he'd need the very best engineers; but for Silicon Valley's best and brightest, a vast Texan company like Tandy scarcely seemed like a cutting-edge innovator. With the arrogance of elite programmers who work on leading-edge technology, GRiD's engineers, for example, considered Tandy a dowdy operation that trafficked in boring technology, even if it was GRiD's parent company. Furthermore, building the Zoomer as a Tandy subsidiary would mean that his decisions would always be beholden to corporate needs rather than those of the Zoomer business.

Fortunately, there were other options, particularly for a successful techie with a great idea. In Silicon Valley, men (and a very few women) with money were waiting for techies just like Jeff Hawkins.

From its modest beginnings in the early 1960s, the venture capital industry had blossomed into one that comprised several hundred firms. In just the first half of the 1990s—and even before the dot-com boom—the VCs of Silicon Valley had invested

$2 billion in a wide range of start-ups. (In 2000, the final year of the Internet bonanza, over 1,000 venture capital firms spent $87.5 billion on more than 4,000 start-up companies.)

Most of the venture capital firms that cluster in Palo Alto and Menlo Park, near Stanford University, are small partnerships of four or five partners, many of whom had been successful entrepreneurs or business executives in previous careers. The partners raise what one VC calls *OPM* (for *other people's money*), and invest the resulting fund in start-up companies, in exchange for shares of the new company.

The venture capital business could be extremely profitable; in 1991, venture capital firms averaged a return of 20 percent on their investors' money. (Later, during the dot-com boom, that number seemed laughably small. Elite firms like Kleiner Perkins, heavily invested in Internet companies, returned more than 70 percent in some years. When the boom turned to bust in 2000, investment profits declined accordingly.)

Successful VCs were bombarded with business plans and presentations daily, and had to separate the wheat from the chaff. In the space of a few hours, they had to make a decision that could make or cost the firm millions of dollars. If a start-up's leadership lacked the right business skills, even a good business idea could lose its value very quickly. That's why VCs are fond of saying that they like to meet good people even more than good ideas. "If it's a good person, the ideas will take care of themselves," they say.

In October of 1991, Hawkins had tagged along with a buddy who wanted to pitch an idea for a company to Sutter Hill Ventures, one of Silicon Valley's oldest venture capital firms. Jeff was there to act as an expert witness, a technical expert who could explain and vouch for the industrial-strength pen-based computer being pitched.

It was Jeff, however, who stole the show. An introvert by nature, Jeff didn't have the natural charisma of Apple founder Steve Jobs, or the all-powerful arrogance of Oracle's Larry Ellison. What he did have was a dispassionately logical mind and a fervent conviction that his technology vision was right.

When the venture capital partners asked Hawkins's opinion of the market for these machines, he described what he thought the future of computing looked like and painted a picture full of handheld computers. "It's inevitable that all computing will be mobile," Jeff told them. "There are so many colliding things that say, 'small, cheap, robust, on-your-person is better than big, slow, clunky, on-your-desk.' " The VCs liked his "technical abilities coupled with a natural effervescent personality," as one senior partner put it—so much so that, instead of investing in the friend's idea, they asked *Hawkins* to stick around after the meeting. They had detected his ability to project himself and sell an idea, key attributes of the "good people" VCs look for. Would he care to come back again, they asked, and expand on his notions on the future of computing?

As any budding entrepreneur looking for funding quickly learns, Silicon Valley venture capital offices aren't generally opulent or grand.

At Sutter Hill's headquarters there are no thick, soft carpets or oversized mahogany desks to put a visitor on notice. What makes the entrepreneurs nervous is the knowledge that their meeting will be their one and only shot to get heard by Sutter Hill. They will either pique the partners' interest or be back out on the street, peddling their business plans to any investor whose name they can dig up.

Jeff Hawkins wasn't nervous, and he didn't carry a presentation crammed full with charts and financial predictions. The way he saw it, he was there to tell the VCs about his ideas for mobile computing. Starting a company with venture capital money was just one of his options, and not his favorite one at that. "I was acting like a happy-go-lucky kid, totally uninterested, probably because I *was* uninterested," he says.

Once in the VC's conference room, Jeff discussed his brain studies as much as the Zoomer project. Clearly, the partners were more interested in Zoomer, so Jeff did his best to paint a picture of the product. It would be roughly the size of a paperback book and weigh about a pound. It would have all the functions of the popular paper-based organizers (i.e., an address book, a date book, a note pad, and a to-do list), but it could also include functions that paper-based organizers couldn't easily provide—travel information, a thesaurus, a language translator—the possibilities seemed endless. And, of course, it would use a pen, not a keyboard, as the primary means of data entry and interaction.

Like any computer, the Zoomer would consist of three different components: (1) the hardware, (2) the OS—the software that acted as the intermediary between the computer circuitry and the individual programs—and (3) the software programs that made the machine useful (e.g., the address book, date book, etc.). The VCs advised Jeff that his new company should avoid having to manufacture hardware—a difficult and expensive undertaking. Instead, they recommended that he join forces with a corporate partner already experienced in electronics manufacturing. Tandy, if it wanted to sell the Zoomer to its Radio Shack customers, might be able to assume that role.

As for the OS, Hawkins had already found one called GEOS from a company called GeoWorks. GEOS was perfect for the Zoomer project because, unlike the other operating systems on the market, it could run on inexpensive hardware. That left the task of writing the software programs for the little machine. The VCs immediately saw that the software posed an interesting business idea. In the desktop PC world, the real money was made in software, not in selling computer hardware. Surely, the same would be true for the avalanche of handheld computers that Hawkins expected to arrive. A start-up that made software for these machines would be a good investment.

At this second meeting, the partners were again impressed by the boyish technologist. Jeff struck them as both technically experienced and persuasive—a combination that's hard to find, but key to the success of a new company. After all, the founder of a start-up has to be able to recruit capable people, persuade the press to cover his or her products, and coax much larger companies to cooperate. In short, entrepreneurs must constantly sell themselves and their ideas. Jeff did it without even trying.

Just a few days later, yet another VC contacted Jeff: Bruce Dunlevie, a partner at Merrill, Pickard, Anderson & Eyre. At 35, only a year older than Hawkins, Dunlevie had already had a stellar career in the computer industry. He had founded the PC division at Everex, and nurtured it into a multi-hundred-million-dollar business unit in just four years. As a board member of GeoWorks, Dunlevie called Jeff Hawkins for an opinion of GEOS, the very OS that Hawkins was considering for use in the Zoomer.

Jeff agreed to meet Dunlevie at the Merrill Pickard offices. Dunlevie had been a VC for a little over two years, and had not yet had any "home runs," as he called deals that result in big payouts. Dunlevie, a former high school quarterback, still peppered his speech with sports metaphors. Jeff, who has never followed sports, had no idea what expressions like "swinging for the fences" might signify, but Dunlevie's unassuming demeanor immediately appealed to him.

At the end of the meeting, Dunlevie steered the conversation to Jeff's plans at GRiD.

"Well, actually, I might leave GRiD and start a company," Hawkins told him.

"Really? To do what?"

Jeff started his pitch about the small, handheld computer that he envisioned, and the millions of consumers who would buy it. He talked about his affiliation with Tandy, explaining that America's largest consumer electronics retailer was going to build and sell his computer. "This is going to be huge, there's no doubt about it," he finished.

As a member of GeoWorks' board of directors, Dunlevie was already convinced that handheld computers would be an interesting investment opportunity. Betting on a smart guy like Hawkins had paid off for VCs handsomely for decades.

An hour later, Jeff walked out of one of the Valley's leading venture capital firms with growing confidence that he'd have funding for his idea.

It was mid-November. Encouraged by the VCs, Jeff knew now for certain that he wanted to start a new company. If he could get the funding squared away in time, he might be able to start the new year as an independent entrepreneur.

Upon his return to GRiD, he told his bosses that he'd decided to leave; he'd stick around until the end of December, and then set up his new shop on January 2. His next step had to be to tell Tandy—gingerly, so as not to alienate Tandy's management—that he'd be setting up his own shop.

That's when his luck turned.

John Roach, Tandy's CEO, was very keen on Jeff's Zoomer. Howard Elias, who worked directly for Roach, had briefed him regularly on the project's progress. No wonder, then, that Roach was not pleased when he heard that Jeff was determined to set off on his own. He summoned Hawkins to Fort Worth.

Tandy's headquarters occupied twin towers in Fort Worth, 20 stories high. Going to Roach's office, on the top floor of the tower called Tandy One, was "like visiting the Wizard of Oz," Hawkins says. After a wait in a fifth-floor conference room, he was summoned to the reception desk on the 19th floor. From there, he took a ride up the one-way escalator to the 20th floor, where he was greeted by one of Roach's secretaries. The top floor was two stories high, lined with floor-to-ceiling windows. Now he was escorted around a corner, down a majestic corridor with walls of wood and granite. Light streamed in from the end of the corridor where it opened into Roach's office.

John Roach peered at Hawkins from behind his desk, the breathtaking view of the Dallas–Fort Worth skyline behind him.

"You should really do this project at Tandy. You can't pull something like that off on your own," Roach said in his Texas drawl.

"I need a bunch of really smart people on this," Hawkins told Roach, as delicately as he could. "I can't pull this off as part of Tandy. I won't have the flexibility and independence that I need to attract good people."

But Roach, who wanted his company to be a technology powerhouse, considered Jeff's machine the kind of flagship product that could draw attention to Tandy as a company on the leading edge of consumer technology. He laid out how Tandy would finance Jeff's project, how this would further Jeff's career, and how much Jeff stood to profit.

Hawkins agreed that staying at Tandy might be the easiest path, but maintained that the resulting product would suffer.

The best and brightest engineers in the Valley wanted to work for a cool start-up, not Radio Shack.

When Jeff explained that he had already lined up serious interest from VCs, Roach reacted strongly. "You don't know what you're getting involved with," Jeff remembers Roach saying. "Those venture capitalists, they're going to squash you like a gnat!" Roach rubbed out an imaginary bug on his desk with his thumb.

Roach ended the meeting on a positive note, saying, "Let's see if we can find a different way that gets us both what we think we want." Still, Hawkins worried that the VCs would withdraw their support if Tandy might not be on board. At the Dallas airport, Jeff called Bruce Dunlevie and the Sutter Hill partners. "I think Tandy is going to work with me, but I can't guarantee it," he told his prospective investors. On the plane ride home, Jeff started to think about concessions he could make to Tandy to keep the corporation on board.

Then, on December 9, during the Monday morning executive staff meeting, GRiD's president, Bruce Walter, turned to Jeff. He said that he'd been thinking about Jeff's departure over the weekend. Now that Hawkins was planning to develop his palmtop independently, rather than within the Tandy/GRiD family, Walter couldn't let Hawkins have PalmPrint.

This was a snag of show-stopping proportions. Technically, Jeff owned the recognition software and had simply licensed it to GRiD. Over the years, however, GRiD engineers had made many improvements to the software. Jeff didn't want to do without these enhancements—but now they belonged to GRiD. Having to re-create the improvements that had been made to his software would set the Zoomer project back by a year and cost hundreds of thousands of dollars.

Jeff broke into an impassioned plea in front of the assembled executives. "You have to hear this!" he said. "I've been talking about this for months now. I've said this a thousand times: I have no interest in competing with GRiD!"

Walter held firm. Jeff would not get the rights to use the improved recognition software.

Jeff went home that night, dejected. He had the vision, the concept, and was close to getting the financial backing—but now all his plans might fall apart.

The whole project appeared to be a Gordian knot. The VCs wanted Tandy involved, yet Tandy's John Roach didn't want Hawkins working with VCs; meanwhile, GRiD's Bruce Walter was refusing to give Hawkins the rights to a key technology. Without Tandy and PalmPrint, the VCs might not fund him. Worst of all, in Jeff's mind, was the fact that other people were counting on him; GeoWorks was expecting to work on the Zoomer, and Jeff had even lined up his first two employees. It was, as Hawkins says now, "the hardest month of my life."

Determined not to be stymied by the licensing issue, Jeff holed up in his office and immersed himself in the paperwork that governed the PalmPrint license. Deep in the contract, he found a key phrase: He had licensed his technology exclusively to GRiD, to run exclusively on *GRiD products.*

But that clause was long forgotten, In the months since, Hawkins had persuaded GRiD that it could get extra revenue and expand its market penetration by licensing its software— which operated the successful GRiDPad computers—to other computer hardware companies. The catch was that the licensed software included PalmPrint. Technically, Jeff had agreed to license PalmPrint *only* to GRiD.

Jeff had found the leverage he needed. GRiD was stuck. Unless he rewrote the contract, the company couldn't proceed with the licensing deals already in progress.

So Hawkins proposed a "horse trade," as he called it. He would permit GRiD to license PalmPrint, if GRiD would permit him to use the enhancements it had made to his technology. GRiD had no choice. They agreed to the trade of rights.

The only brush fire left to put out was getting Tandy back on board. Hawkins had concluded that Roach cared most about having first dibs on the Zoomer; keeping Jeff at Tandy was only a secondary goal. After discussing the dilemma with the two VCs, Jeff arrived at a plan: If they offered Tandy the chance to be an investor in the start-up, Roach might feel assured of his company's insider status.

John Roach agreed, investing $300,000 in the venture. With the half-million each VC had invested, Jeff now had $1.3 million with which to launch his new enterprise. On paper, his company was already worth $3 million. That was the good news. The bad news was that in return, Jeff had given up 40 percent of his new company.

All he needed was a name for his new venture. Over the Christmas holiday, Jeff spent days thinking of company names, brainstorming with his wife, friends, and two prospective employees. A name related to the hand was logical.

One of the engineers suggested Palm Software because Jeff's master plan was to write software for the Zoomer market.

Jeff, however, didn't necessarily want to stick to software for the rest of his life; he had a hunch that he should keep his options open.

"Let's just call it Palm Computing," he decided.

TWO
PALM COMPUTING

The doors Jeff Hawkins threw open on January 2, 1992, weren't actually Palm's. The 10-foot hardwood doors belonged to Merrill, Pickard, Anderson & Eyre, who'd offered the newborn company two starter offices.

Following him through the door were Palm's first two employees, both software engineers (that is, programmers). Art Lamb, a committed East Coaster with a thick Boston accent, had come to California from New York four years earlier with the goal of gaining enough Silicon Valley experience to one day join a start-up company. He was the first engineer Jeff recruited to work on his pen-based GRiD machines, and the two had worked together ever since. "It's gratifying to work with Jeff," he says. "You have a sense of accomplishing something. And there are no politics; it's pure meritocracy." At 36, he was a skilled software engineer with the reputation for being able to complete projects that eluded equally experienced programmers.

Jeff wanted to keep a good relationship with his previous employer, so he didn't dare poach any more of GRiD's engineers. Another executive might have picked up the phone and called contacts at other high-tech companies, but Jeff had never mastered the fine art of networking. Instead, he turned to Ain McKendrick, who worked as an intern at GRiD, to ask if he knew any engineering students looking for a job to fill the junior position. McKendrick convinced his parents to let him drop out of college to join the new start-up himself.

Palm's temporary offices were at the end of a hallway. Jeff chose the one room bordering a terrace, with the California winter light streaming in through a giant window. Lamb and McKendrick settled in the second room, which was windowless, chairless, and half-full of stored Merrill Pickard boxes and equipment.

On their second day at Palm, the engineers bought computers for the office. To preserve the company's cash, they picked up middle-of-the-line machines from a distributor who sold discontinued and reconditioned workstations. By the end of the day, Lamb and McKendrick had hooked up their new Sun workstations and printer. Palm Computing's software engineering department was now in business. For the next month, their routine would be to explore the inner workings of GEOS, taking occasional breaks for brainstorming sessions with Jeff.

Learning to program under a new OS is a considerable undertaking, even for the most experienced engineers. Operating systems are radically different from each other, and knowing one is only a slight advantage in working with a new one. It's like switching to a new car, and finding that it doesn't work anything like your last car. All you know is that you can use it for travel, but you need to figure out first that it uses joysticks for steering and dashboard buttons for braking, and sports an extra set of fog lights on the roof. Then when you start the engine, you find out that the car moves sideways.

For days, the Palm engineers worked to figure out how their new GEOS car worked. They pondered every line of the sample programs that GeoWorks had provided and wrote practice code. They knew that most of what they wrote at this early stage would be worthless in the long run, but it was the best way to learn the OS.

The Palm guys also found that GEOS was a complex OS— but it was the only one that would work on a low-cost consumer device.

Start-up companies need experienced business managers as well as inspired technologists. One person rarely fulfills that dual role. More often than not, though, a new entrepreneur doesn't want to give up control of his baby; it wasn't unusual for a start-up company's investors to have to force a management change on the founder. During their negotiations with Jeff, the VCs had broached the subject of hiring a CEO for Palm.

Jeff was neither interested in, nor cut out for, the CEO job, and he knew it. He had always been interested in product design—and distinctly uninterested in people issues. In fact, organizational issues of the type a CEO must handle drove him "nuts," as he puts it.

"I know I'm not the person to run this business," he told the VCs. "I've got to focus on other things. But I don't want to hire a CEO yet." Before handing over the reins, he wanted to learn something about the areas of business that he'd never experienced. "I wanted to know something about everything, so that later on, nobody could pull the wool over my eyes."

As unofficial CEO, Hawkins started shouldering such administrative duties as setting up his employees' benefits and running the payroll. For the first few months, Jeff wrote the engineers' paychecks by hand and delivered them with a disconcerting warning that they should check to make sure they were made out for the right amount.

Bruce Dunlevie proved a big help to Hawkins. The two engineers often found Dunlevie and Hawkins engrossed in conversations. "I just heard from Tandy. We have two options," Jeff would say. "What do you think?"

But the experience of running the day-to-day administrative tasks at Palm proved less valuable than Hawkins had hoped. During the company's infancy, the mundane tasks of setting up payroll and choosing an insurance plan had little in common with the systems required in a larger corporation.

On Bruce Dunlevie's advice, Jeff hired a part-time controller, Vicki Barklow, one day a week. At each visit, Barklow sat on the floor, made sense of the receipts in the shoebox Jeff used to collect them, wrote some checks, joked for a few minutes with the engineers, and left. Her favorite saying left a strong impression on the young Palm staff: "Cash is king."

In February, Howard Elias of Tandy held a kickoff meeting for the Zoomer project in Fort Worth. The meeting would include representatives from Tandy, GeoWorks, and a surprise partner: Casio.

Casio had been an original equipment manufacturer (OEM) supplier to Tandy for many years—that is, Casio had manufactured calculators, electronic music keyboards, and other products for Tandy, which stamped its own logo on the products and sold them under its own brand names. This arrangement opened the possibility that Casio would manufacture the Zoomer as well as sell it under its own name. Hawkins was ecstatic; coupled with Tandy's reach, Casio's brand power seemed to guarantee Zoomer's success.

On the day of the launch meeting, the Tandy conference room was packed. In addition to the Palm and GeoWorks teams, Tandy executives, curious about the project that John Roach had authorized, milled about, introducing themselves to the Japanese Casio managers. Even GRiD had sent a representative. The room presented a tableau of culture clashes: the California contingent in khakis or jeans, the Texans in button-down shirts, and the Japanese in dark business suits.

One by one, each attendee stepped to the front of the room and explained his company's involvement. The GeoWorks CEO committed his company to adapting his GEOS OS to work on this new machine. A Casio executive described his company's impressive manufacturing capacity for electronic devices. Hawkins, after dimming the lights in the room, projected a simple line drawing of the little computer on the white board. Roughly the size of a paperback book, most of the front of the machine was taken up by a screen. Buttons below the screen would switch the computer on and scroll through the software programs that would be built into the machine. Palm would write these programs: the calendar, phone book, note pad, and other programs.

The atmosphere in the room was electric. A few weeks earlier, Apple's CEO, John Sculley, had fanned the flames of pen-based computing in a speech about a handheld computer that he called a *personal digital assistant,* or PDA. A flurry of articles had instantly spread the news: Sculley had predicted a "$3.5 trillion" market for such gadgets. The Zoomer was just such a machine, and the people in Tandy's conference room were a dream team for making it happen. As Hawkins left Fort Worth, he was in high spirits.

It was the last time he'd feel that way about Project Zoomer.

"Things started to go bad with Zoomer almost immediately," says Palm engineer Art Lamb. In February 1992, soon after the Fort Worth meeting, Tandy forwarded Casio's manufacturing schedule to Palm and GeoWorks. It contained an almost devastating bombshell: Casio wanted the software and hardware completed by early 1993. "They gave us eleven months to develop the product from scratch. We were a company of only three people!" says Lamb. But without the leverage to negotiate, the small Palm team agreed to the task.

Further complicating things was the project's biggest question mark: the GEOS operating system. GEOS was a perfectly good OS, but it hadn't been designed with pen computers in mind; it didn't have electronic-ink features, Hawkins's PalmPrint handwriting recognition, the ability to detect taps on a touch screen, and so on. The engineers at GeoWorks had a lot of work to do before GEOS was ready to run the Zoomer.

Unfortunately, Palm couldn't wait. You can't write programs without an OS to run them on, but Palm couldn't afford to wait until GeoWorks had finished the GEOS overhaul before beginning work on the Zoomer's application software.

In the end, GeoWorks and Palm staff grimly agreed that they had only one hope: They would have to work simultaneously, rewriting the Zoomer programs over and over again as GeoWorks delivered new versions. They all knew they had a long, frustrating, and unpredictable process ahead.

Casio also demanded that Zoomer be useable for 100 hours without running out of battery power. "Acceptable battery life means you don't remember the last time you changed your batteries," the Casio managers said. This requirement came as something of a shock to the Palm and GeoWorks staff, whose experience was in the computer industry, where three hours of life on a laptop battery was considered extraordinary.

Throughout the evolution of computers, customers had been willing to endure the limitations of their machines. Casio, knew little about the computer industry, but the company had sold electronic gadgets for over 40 years. The Casio managers knew that their customers would never tolerate laptop-like battery life in a true consumer product. Each fax from Japan reiterated the demand: "One hundred hours of battery life!"

The consumer electronics and computer worlds collided. Hawkins faced a catch-22: The amount of battery power required by a computer's processor chip is directly proportional to the chip's speed. For the Zoomer to achieve Casio's best-case battery life, the team would have to build it around an extremely weak microprocessor; the computer would perform with the speed of a snail. Through clever coding, engineers could improve the Zoomer's speed a little—but not enough to make the product's performance acceptable for the customer. The only really effective way to speed up the Zoomer would be to use a more powerful processor, which, in turn, would reduce the battery life. Hawkins and GeoWorks' CEO Brian Dougherty agreed: 100 hours was too extreme. They'd have to do battle with Casio.

The Casio executives informed the California team that a processor for the Zoomer had already been selected: a custom-made chip based on Intel technology that ran at a painfully slow 7 megahertz (MHz).

Palm and GeoWorks would have to write an OS and application software for a chip with limited power.

The responsibility for his small company and staff weighed heavily on Jeff. He was as convinced as ever that a huge market awaited a mobile consumer computer, yet every day posed new problems outside his control. A worrier by nature, he agonized not only over technical problems, but also over whether he'd be able to convince additional engineers to risk joining his company. He fretted, too, that his employees might be worried about Palm's future.

At the same time, he tried to project an image of confidence. He felt that it was his job "to let everybody know that it's going to be great, and don't worry about it." Only his wife knew how he really felt.

Back in December, when Hawkins had written a rough business plan for his company, he'd calculated that he'd need to hire one more engineer by March, and no more new employees until June. Now, it was obvious that he needed to bring on several more people, and fast.

Jeff found the first engineer easily—or rather, Chris Raff found him. Raff, an IQ prodigy and Harvard grad, had interviewed with almost every pen-based computer company and had all but given up on the industry by the time he called Hawkins. At 27, Raff was already a veteran of three failed startups; he'd learned the meaning of "Cash is king" the hard way. The opulent spending habits of the companies he'd visited scared him off.

At the job interview with Hawkins, Raff asked most of the questions. "Why do you think there is a market for this? Can you really make enough money on it? Does the handwriting technology really work? Why is this better than the Sharp organizers?"

Hawkins was rattled—"I'm begging people to come work at this place. I'm feeling like I was on tenterhooks"—but gave Raff the job.

Bruce Dunlevie suggested Jeff should also have at least one nontechnical employee to act as a Jack-of-all-trades. He recommended Joel Jewitt, a tall, self-described "big-picture kind of guy" and amateur drummer who'd once worked for him. Jewitt jumped at the opportunity to work at a company funded by Dunlevie—in fact, he wanted the job so badly that he offered to work for free. (He got both the job *and* a salary.)

Kate Purmal started at Palm only a few weeks later as Palm's technical liaison with the other companies on the Zoomer project. She was the only woman and, at five-foot-one, had to look up to Dunlevie, Hawkins, and Lamb (at six-four, six-four, and six-three, respectively); still, she fit right in.

Purmal and Jewitt had to share the second desk and the single phone in Jeff's office. "After 1 P.M., it smelled like a locker room in there," Purmal recalls.

Chris Raff moved into the room across the hall, joining Lamb and McKendrick. Space had become so tight that Raff had to ask McKendrick to move his chair each time he needed to get up from his desk.

But none of that mattered. Only six years later, when the Internet bubble minted 65 new millionaires a day, employees would leave established companies in droves and flock to Silicon Valley start-ups, with the certain expectation of entering the ranks of the nouveaux riches within the year. In 1992, however, joining a high-tech start-up did not evoke instant envy. Most Valley workers knew the statistics: Nine out of 10 start-ups failed. Of those start-ups that became large, well-known companies, only the handful of founders and earliest employees were thought to have gotten rich. Working for software giant Microsoft or chip maker Intel and hanging in there for four to five years in a midlevel job were surer ways to make a bundle in salaries and stock options; start-ups meant pay cuts and working hours that were even longer than the workaholic Valley's norm. However, start-ups offered the mystique of inventing something new, of changing the world, the way many thought Apple Computer had. For the less starry-eyed, they were a chance to get away from the paralyzing bureaucracy of large corporations, to work in a fun environment, or to be a bigger fish in a little pond. All were true for the group at Palm.

For a few hours every day, Kate Purmal, Jeff, and the three engineers took over the VC's conference room and reasoned their way through a few screenfuls of one of their software applications. They started with the calendar. Would it show a single day's appointments? A whole week? A month? Kate drew an empty screen on the white board.

"What elements will the user see when he looks at a single day in his schedule?"

The whole group chimed in with suggestions.

"We need to show the date on top of the screen."

"No, that takes up screen space—wouldn't the user know what date he tapped?" Space on the small Zoomer screen was precious.

"Of course we need to show the date! *And* we need to display the day of the week. If you tapped on a day and then got distracted by a phone call, would *you* still remember that you were looking at Tuesday the 16th?"

The discussions were often heated. Raff, the only engineer who hadn't worked on product design with Jeff before, soon noticed his ability to cut through myriad details to the essence of a problem. "He had the sort of common sense and logic that just can't be learned," Chris Raff says. "He would say, 'What's *important* is . . .' and it would be clear what decision we should make." At the end of a few hours, the engineers returned to their desks and started coding the new features.

The four companies who now thought of themselves as "Zoomer partners" (Casio, Tandy, GeoWorks, and Palm) met monthly to discuss the project. Each time, between 10 and 15 people sat around a conference table in Texas, California, or even Tokyo. Each company observed Japanese etiquette, which demands that the highest-ranking representative of the company sat in the center, with his employees spread out on both sides according to rank. Jeff Hawkins sat at the center of one side of the table, with Kate Purmal and Joel Jewitt flanking him.

The partners discussed every aspect of the gadget. Each company presented the decisions it had made concerning its part in the product, and the other companies gave their input or questioned the wisdom of the decision. It was slow going, and the meetings stretched over days.

Invariably, the Palm team left the table with a long list of items "to study"—a term the team had adopted from the Japanese managers. *To study* could mean one of two things: (1) Casio had asked a question about a specific feature that Palm couldn't yet answer, or (2) Casio requested a feature with which Palm didn't agree. (Casio's meeting notes, which followed a few days after each meeting, might say, for example, "Palm to study making the fonts larger," or "Casio asked Palm to study displaying items in 'x' increments according to date.")

Imperceptibly at first, then painfully obviously, Jeff Hawkins had lost control over the design of the Zoomer. He was now just a leading participant in a design committee, suggesting, cajoling, questioning—but not making every decision concerning the product that he had invented. The Zoomer was becoming a hodgepodge victim of design by committee.

In May, a new tremor rattled the Zoomer team. At an event staged at a nightclub in Chicago during the biannual Consumer Electronics Show, Apple's CEO John Sculley announced the Newton, an amazingly ambitious handheld computer that appeared to be light-years more dazzling than the utilitarian Zoomer. Michael Tchao, the product's marketing manager, demonstrated what appeared to be a working palmtop, with finished-looking software and hardware. After an initial glitch (the Newton wouldn't turn on), the demo went flawlessly; the gadget could even recognize cursive handwriting.

Sculley told the 600 assembled journalists that what they were seeing was "nothing less than a revolution"; the press was blown away. "I felt queasy," admits Palm's Kate Purmal. "We were very practical in our approach. And here was Apple—with so much hype behind it. I realized that we'd be evaluated as much by the splash we made as what kind of product we delivered." Unless the Zoomer alliance could muster similar attention from the press, the palmtop would be doomed to the ranks of also-rans. Not only did it look like Apple was running rings around Palm with marketing, the Newton appeared to be nearly ready for prime time, even as the Zoomer's features were still being negotiated in committee. The Zoomer alliance found itself in a race with Apple, a race it might already have lost.

When Jeff hired two more engineers in rapid succession, Palm needed a third office. At the same time, the Palm team felt it had overstayed its welcome. "Merrill Pickard kept a fully stocked kitchen with the best cold cuts, fresh bread, Pepperidge Farm cookies, and Dove Bars," Art Lamb says. "All of a sudden, there were eight new mouths to feed, and some of them had a pretty good appetite. The VC staff would go shopping on Monday, and by Tuesday, the kitchen was empty."

Just in time, Joel Jewitt found them new offices. It was a large, single-room space in a two-story office building in Los Altos, an upscale residential community with a charming café-dotted downtown but very little corporate presence. (When Palm reached 15 employees, the mayor would congratulate them for having become the largest company in Los Altos.) Several other small tenants shared the building, including the Asian *Wall Street Journal* and a rental-property pamphlet publisher.

Across the street a carwash was as busy as an anthill on sunny day—which, in Los Altos, was almost *every* day. As soon as Hawkins had signed the lease, the entire team of eight piled into two cars to check out the new location. Except for a few power strips on the floor, the room was empty. It smelled of fresh paint and footsteps would echo back from the bare walls, but it was easy to envision a conference room along one wall and how the cubicles would be laid out. The Palm crew was excited to move. They appreciated the relative luxuries of the Merrill Pickard office, but they were ready to emerge from the womb. Palm moved into its first real home the first week of June 1992.

Joel Jewitt provided one of the new suite's first decorations. He'd seen a *Wall Street Journal* article that compared a speech by John Sculley with a speech by Intel's Andy Grove. Sculley predicted that Apple's Newton would launch the "mother of all markets"; Grove called the devices "a pipedream driven by greed." Clearly, the truth was important for Palm to discover, but the future was impossible to predict.

Greatly amused, Jewitt constructed a cardboard contraption about the size of a dinner plate, which he'd labeled "Today's Palmtop Business Outlook." Hand-printed on the top and bottom of the circle were the choices "Mother of All Markets" and "Pipedream Driven by Greed"; a cardboard arrow could be turned to point at one option or the other. He hung the contraption, which he called the PDA Market Meter, on a little bulletin board where Hawkins posted articles and other tidbits—and turned the arrow so that it pointed squarely at "Mother of All Markets."

Since the move to new digs, an empty corner of their space had become Palm's official meeting area. A month after settling in, Jeff called a meeting. As the eight employees pulled in their office chairs to join the circle around him, they noticed a stranger in her mid-30s. But Hawkins didn't introduce her right away.

"Last year, when we were in the financing stage," Jeff began, "Bruce Dunlevie and Dave Anderson suggested that we hire a CEO to run the company. I agreed with them: I'm not the person to run this business in the long run. But I didn't want to hire a CEO yet—it was still too early. At the time, I could see their eyebrows go up." He imitated the VC's distressed faces.

The employees exchanged a few glances. Where was this going?

"But now Palm is at the point where we *need* a CEO."

Several brows in the room were furrowed: Jeff hadn't said anything to anyone about conducting a search for a CEO, let alone hiring one.

Springing momentous news on the unprepared team wasn't the best management technique, but then, Jeff had never claimed to be a good people manager. "I didn't see any benefit of telling them—and I saw a downside: that they would get nervous. The last thing I wanted to do was say, 'Guess what, I don't know how to run a business; we're going to hire someone.' Then they'd be all nervous about it. I figured, just wait until it was over. What if I told them I was hiring a CEO and then I couldn't hire one? Then they'd think we're doomed!"

Now he turned to the woman next to him. She was dressed casually in black pants and a long red sweater, with thick, chin-length dark blond hair.

"I'd like you to meet the CEO of Palm Computing, Donna Dubinsky."

THREE

DONNA

Hawkins had hired Donna Dubinsky at exactly the right time; he had learned as much about running a company as he could bear.

Hawkins's wife Janet was also waiting eagerly for a CEO. After weeks of day-to-day corporate administration, negotiations with Casio and Tandy, and hiring staff, Jeff had been returning home each evening full of worries.

Hawkins had held off on hiring a CEO for several reasons. The longer he waited, the more he would learn about the skills his CEO candidates would need. Furthermore, the more the company had progressed, the more qualified a person he felt he could attract; now, at the product development stage, Palm would appear less risky, and therefore appeal to a broader set of candidates. Finally, Jeff wanted to get the company well along the right track before bringing in a CEO who might have a different set of ideas.

He drew up a list of characteristics of the ideal candidate:

- Great people manager
- Balanced fiscal attitude (pays attention to cost details, strives to reduce cost)

- Experienced in software publishing
- Experienced in software development
- Start-up and large company experience
- Well-respected industry name
- Proven negotiation skills
- Technology literate
- Strong market sense
- Likes to travel
- Familiar with Pen/Game/GEOS-like products

It was a tall order.

Like all VCs, Palm's backers had thick Rolodexes, bulging with useful contacts in the business world; they went to work drumming up candidates. Bruce Dunlevie preinterviewed the candidates, presenting only the best to Hawkins for final interviews. Over the course of a few weeks, Jeff met 12 candidates, but returned from each meeting feeling he hadn't met the right partner.

Then one day, he heard about Donna Dubinsky. A graduate of Yale and the Harvard Business School, she had discovered her interest in business as a teenager. Though the family lived in a suburban middle-class enclave in Benton Harbor, Michigan, high school was a different world. Many of the students couldn't read, and in the wake of the Detroit riots, security guards were stationed in the school hallways.

The students there attended school in two different shifts, the administration's attempt to solve two problems—overcrowding and illiteracy—with one stroke. Donna, in the 7-A.M.-to-noon shift, had her afternoons free to work as a salesclerk in a tiny local embroidery store. There she found a microcosm of the business world: Delivery people arrived with an endless supply of goods to be embroidered—the company's "raw materials." Downstairs, a small army of women stitched names on shirts and engraved bowling trophies and plaques—the company's "manufacturing." Donna herself, of course, was the sales department. She was fascinated, and hooked on business for life.

Although no student from her school had ever gone to an Ivy League school, she applied to Yale and got in, reducing her grandfather, a Russian immigrant, to tears of pride.

Still, Benton Harbor proved anything but a training ground for the Ivy League. "Yale was a huge shock," she says. Her classmates played sports she had never even heard of, like lacrosse. Until she moved off campus in her senior year, she felt like an outcast. To make matters worse, Dubinsky had no clue how to write an academic essay; her first-term report card was full of Cs and Ds. She was despondent. At home, she had excelled at her classes, but Yale shook her self-confidence to the bone.

Finally, a professor, taking her under his wing, taught her to write by circling the flaws in her papers without explaining them. He challenged her to figure out what was wrong on her own and rewrite the paper. "You could have to write the same essay over ten times," she says. The method worked.

By the time Dubinsky left Yale with a BA in history, she had acquired a great deal of the inner strength and fearlessness that would characterize her business career in the years to follow.

A two-year stint in commercial banking, handing out loans to cable-industry start-ups, opened Donna's eyes to the world of entrepreneurs. "I recognized that that's what I wanted to do: I wanted to build a business," she says. Harvard Business School was next.

One day, a computer programmer named Dan Bricklin came to business school class to demonstrate his invention: VisiCalc, the first computer spreadsheet, running on an Apple II computer. Today, VisiCalc is considered the "killer app"—a software program that's so attractive, people buy the gadget just to use that program—that turned PCs from an expensive hobbyist toy into a mass-market business tool.

The demo changed Dubinsky's life. As a loan officer, she had painstakingly calculated the bank's risk and interest income on potential loans by hand. Every time the loan committee wanted to analyze the impact of a change in percentage points, she'd have to redo all her calculations. She had an epiphany. She was certain that this unfamiliar contraption with an Apple logo, recalculating lengthy rows and columns of numbers on the fly, was the future.

She was determined to get a job at Apple, but it would take all her drive to secure one. When Apple's recruiters came to Harvard, they wouldn't grant Dubinsky a slot on the interview list—Apple wanted Harvard engineers, not MBAs. So Donna showed up at the interview location early, hoping to plead for even a 10-minute conversation with the recruiter, then sat in the anteroom for hours as candidate after candidate passed through the magic door—to no avail. The interviewers didn't want to see her.

Only a job-hunting pilgrimage to California after graduation finally opened Apple's doors. She landed offers from each of the three companies she'd visited, including Apple. Though Apple offered the lowest salary, she took the job, which entailed working in customer service. Even a low-paying job in a quickly growing company, she figured, would be the best way to advance and pick up new skills.

In six years at Apple, Dubinsky rocketed upward through the ranks. As a human resources manager put it, "Donna projects a lot of confidence and conviction in her beliefs. She's not a political animal at all." By April 1985, she was running a long list of Apple departments, including customer relations, product distribution, warehousing, developer relations, and forecasting.

In 1987, she followed her charismatic mentor Bill Campbell to Claris, the software subsidiary that Campbell founded to spin out from Apple.

After four exhausting years of running international sales at Claris, however, Donna found herself working for Apple again: Just months before the intended spinout, Apple changed its mind about selling off Claris as an independent company. Instead, it bought back Claris's stock and seized control. Dubinsky had had enough of working at a company whose strings were pulled by a larger corporate parent. Armed with a bank account fattened by the sale of her Claris founders' stock, she moved to France to spend some time decompressing, leaving behind a mourning staff.

In Paris, she spent a lot of time thinking about what she wanted to do next. After a year, ready to return, she knew what she wanted: to run a company herself.

Back in Silicon Valley, she jump-started her job search through her large network of business executive friends. Donna told them that the right company for her had three components: The first was a technologist who had a good sense for the product's market—expertise she felt she lacked herself. Second, she wanted to work in a product category to which she could relate—not semiconductor test equipment or networking gear, for example. Third, she wanted to work for a young business that had the potential to become large.

Soon Dubinsky found herself in interviews with a number of technologists. After she'd attended a series of meetings with potential employers in what she considered uninspiring businesses, her former boss Bill Campbell called his contacts in the VC world—among them, Bruce Dunlevie.

For decades, Silicon Valley's movers and shakers have gone to Buck's Restaurant in the town center of wealthy Woodside, California, to start a deal, or seal a deal, over a plate of Buck's house burger and fries. The restaurant's décor is hung with an eclectic mixture of truck-stop chic and Wild West memorabilia. A row of children's cowboy boots, an eight-foot anaconda snakeskin, and a framed display of old harmonicas fight for attention on walls that overflow with framed knickknacks. Three-foot airplane models, an even larger plastic fish, and a chandelier that would have done an Old West whorehouse credit hang from the ceiling.

Hawkins wasn't much of a socialite or networker; he had never been to Buck's. However, in June 1992, he agreed with Donna Dubinsky's suggestion to meet there for an interview.

He didn't have high hopes. Dunlevie had warned him that Dubinsky had never been the general manager of any business. "I liked her enormously," Dunlevie had said. "I thought that she was very intelligent. She doesn't want to be a CEO for the wrong reasons—a lot of people want to do it because they want to have power. She just wants to fully use her skills. But she's the least qualified of all the people we talked to."

When Donna arrived, she and Jeff clicked instantly. "It felt great from the start," Hawkins says.

To give her an idea of Palm's direction, Hawkins pulled out his Sony palmtop—a handheld computer that was only sold in Japan. About the size of a Walkman, it had a pen and a graphic interface; even in Japanese, it was easier to navigate than any current U.S. electronic organizers. It gave her the same tingle of excitement that she'd felt 12 years earlier at Dan Bricklin's demo of VisiCalc. "That's it!" she told Hawkins. "That's the next generation of computing. I'm sure of it!"

In Jeff, Donna recognized the product inventor she was looking for. For his part, Jeff sensed that she could be the CEO who could understand and respect him as the product guy, but take the tasks of running the business off his shoulders. It was a match made in Heaven.

Dubinsky left the meeting on a high. When she returned home, she sat down at her Macintosh and wrote Jeff a letter. In it, she told him how much she wanted the job. She typed up a list of references two pages long: people for whom she had worked, people with whom she had worked, people who had worked for her. "I am well known in Silicon Valley; please feel free to check me out with anybody," the letter said.

She also did something that none of the other candidates had done—she asked *Jeff* for references. If he was going to be her partner, she wanted to check him out, too.

She spent the week after the interview checking out Jeff's references. "They said that he was brilliant, and that he was a normal person, too, in spite of being brilliant," she says. Invariably, his references also brought up his sense of integrity, caring about people, and wish to build a good company culture—all values high on her own list of priorities. She stayed close to her phone and waited for a call.

Hawkins, for his part, got busy, too. He shared her list of references with his investors, who promised to check them out. Then he got on the phone himself. One of Dubinsky's old bosses called her "a real star," and another said she was "a one-in-a-million kind of person."

Hawkins also got "a few 'glass-ceiling' responses," he says. "Some people said, 'I think she's great, I'm sure she'd do a great job, but you want to think pretty seriously before you hire a woman. You're going to have to deal a lot with people who will not understand how to handle a woman executive.' "

He listened to their concerns politely, and then ignored them. He called Dubinsky and told her she had the job if she wanted it.

She was elated; from her perspective, she had it made. She had landed the hottest job in the Valley. She would run a company that could be a leader in a large new market. The company already had venture backing from two of the most respected VCs in Silicon Valley, and deals with Casio and Tandy, two giants of the consumer electronics world. In addition, her partner in this venture was a brilliant inventor. This, she figured, would be the perfect opportunity.

A few days later, she moved into her cubicle among Palm's tiny group of engineers. Her loud voice and louder laughter soon rang through the room, stirring amusement and curiosity among the engineers.

Chris Raff, in the cubicle next to her ("Every conversation she had, I had it too"), discovered her sweet tooth when he offered her cookies he kept in a file drawer. After polishing them off, Dubinsky replaced them. In the following days, Raff often looked up from his keyboard to find his new CEO feeding on cookies from his filing cabinet—always taking care to replace them. Eventually, Raff concluded that she was playing a dieter's trick on herself. That system, however ineffective, was fine by him.

Within days on the job, Dubinsky had found that Palm had no guidelines for stock options and salary levels. "We have to put together a human resources packet," she told Jeff.

"Why? We have ten employees!"

"Well, it's important, because it can get out of hand very quickly. If we don't put this system in place now, when we have ten employees, it's going to be really hard to put in place when we have a hundred employees. So let's do it now."

Using compensation plans she'd borrowed from friends at other companies as a model, she designed a pay structure for Palm. Looking it over, Jeff was both pleased and enlightened. "She taught me that you should never be in situations where you can be embarrassed by one employee finding out how much stock another employee has, or someone makes," Hawkins says. It was a lesson he would never forget. For the next board meeting with the VCs, Donna compiled a written agenda. Next, she hired a PR consultant, and made sure the company had letterhead and fax cover sheets with the Palm logo. The engineers marveled. "It made us look like a professional outfit," Raff says.

One aspect of life at Palm didn't change, however: Dubinsky was as frugal with Palm's money as Hawkins had been—a trait that would later save the company.

It quickly became evident that she and Jeff had an excellent rapport. He was comfortable letting go of the day-to-day decisions he'd been making, and was delighted by her interest in Palm's technology, such as the PalmPrint handwriting recognition software. "She really wanted to know how it worked," Hawkins says. "No one had ever asked me that—ever! For many years, I don't think anybody else in the company knew more about it than she did."

"My job is to make you successful," Jeff told Donna. "Because if the CEO can't be successful in the job, the company's going to fail." Donna was startled. She'd already come to think of her role in the same way: Her job was to create an environment where *he* could thrive and create products.

Dubinsky's job wasn't going to be easy, however. For starters, the agreements with Tandy and Casio were nothing more than handshake agreements. Palm hadn't yet finished a single one of the software programs it was supposed to create for the Zoomer.

Worse, the Zoomer's one-year development schedule seemed hopeless. A few months earlier, GeoWorks had sent Palm the first prototype of the reworked GEOS OS. After a lengthy installation process, the Palm engineers found that GeoWorks' new software broke their programs. Weeks of work had been wasted.

For the next couple of days, the engineers scrambled to figure out how to fix their software. They found no remedy for the problem. Worse, they were paralyzed until they received the next build, or version, of the GEOS from GeoWorks; they couldn't write more code, test their code for bugs, or even get their code installed properly.

To relieve the tension, somebody brought in Nerf-ball guns; the Palm team members started chasing each other around the cubicles in the afternoons. Hawkins and his wife tried to lift the group's spirits, too; one morning, the engineers arrived at work to find, on each desk, a basket filled with healthy snacks like pistachios and fruit roll-ups—hardly the junk food the engineers craved, but a nice gesture, nevertheless.

Every couple of weeks, GeoWorks sent down a new batch of code; every time, the Palm engineers installed it and prayed. More often than not, the new GEOS build broke everything the Palm team had done. Each time, it took the Palm engineers several days of scrambling, trying to figure out how to make it work again. Each time, they fell further behind schedule.

Not surprising, the relationship with GeoWorks became strained. In frustration, the Palm engineers nicknamed their GeoWorks counterparts "Hacks 'R' Us"—unfairly, as both teams were equally pressed for time.

At lunch time, Dubinsky often joined the engineers on their trips to the nearby deli, in an effort to learn about their work. She might ask Lamb, "What can we do to make up for the processor speed?" Or she'd ask him, "Explain why we're having such a hard time with GEOS," then fixing him with a piercing stare of deep concentration. "We loved her for that interest," Raff says. "And it gave her a good pulse on engineering, which is after all vital for the company."

The Zoomer's Alpha release date had been set for early fall 1992. *Alpha* is the stage of a software product's creation when all of its functions are working in some rudimentary, if very buggy, form. In general, software companies permit no new features to be introduced into the software after that; the engineers' job now, so the theory goes, is to spend their time fixing the bugs.

As the deadline approached, the partner meetings grew increasingly tense. By this time, Intuit (which makes the popular Quicken personal finance program) and America Online (AOL) had also joined the project; versions of Quicken and AOL's software were to be included on the Zoomer. Now, when the partners met, representatives from *six* companies had to negotiate every aspect of the project. The meetings dragged on for days as the group reviewed each feature, point by point. Hawkins, heretofore a tea drinker, started drinking coffee, available in the back of the room. "It was the only distraction available during these painful meetings," he says.

Monty Boyer, who had come to Palm from GRiD to manage the engineering group, watched his first partner meetings with astonishment. "They were an early example of somebody on the far end of featuritis," he contends. A quiet, composed engineering director, he becomes emphatic over the memory. "They had the longest, longest, *longest* list of features they wanted to put into the device. And it would not make any difference to them at all whether these things made sense or not. Our point of view was: 'Gee, we don't need all these things. Let's make this other stuff work really well,' " Boyer says.

"Everything and the kitchen sink had to be in the product," agrees Bruce Mendel, Casio's North American sales director at the time. "Every fax driver, every printer driver, every application—every everything." He couldn't help but notice Palm's frustration. "[Jeff and Donna] just couldn't believe some of the requests they were getting. You could see that they were trying to be patient, but were frustrated that we didn't seem to get it. Some of the things we were asking for, whether it was engineering stuff or features in the product, were just like, 'Why are we wasting our time on this?' "

Ironically, Mendel frequently found himself siding with Palm and GeoWorks instead of his Casio colleagues, perhaps because, having worked in the PC industry (unlike most other Casio managers), he could better appreciate the trade-offs involved in, for example, the speed and battery life issue. The relationship between the Zoomer partners, he says, was like "parents and kids." Tandy and Casio were the parents, and Palm and GeoWorks were the kids. "The kids were very enthusiastic and headstrong, and the parents would look disapprovingly and say, 'No, you can't do this.' But it was a twisted adult-child relationship, in the sense that the children knew what they were doing and the adults didn't."

Hawkins didn't know it at the time, but his struggle to prevent the Zoomer from sinking beneath the weight of unnecessary feature bloat was a crucial phase of Palm's development. The tiny team was learning to pledge allegiance to a strange new notion, one that seemed heretical at the time: *Simpler is better.*

While Hawkins and his engineers struggled to create the Zoomer software, Dubinsky set about getting signed contracts with Tandy and Casio, a task that proved harder than she had ever imagined. She had to negotiate separate contracts with Tandy, Casio, and GeoWorks—but the terms of each contract depended heavily on the two *other* contracts.

It was an extraordinarily complex arrangement: Tandy was Casio's customer for the Zoomer, GeoWorks was Casio's provider of the OS, and Palm was Casio's provider of the applications.

To make matters more complicated, once the Zoomer was for sale, Casio and Tandy would compete with each other for customers; similarly, Palm and GeoWorks would ultimately become competitors, as each planned to write add-on application software for the Zoomer once it went on sale.

Though potentially pitted against each other, the two software companies faced a common problem in their negotiations with Casio. The consumer electronics company was not used to licensing what is considered valuable intellectual property by the computing world. "Casio viewed Palm and GeoWorks as just software subcontractors for hire," says Casio's Mendel.

Fortunately for the project, Tandy's Howard Elias emerged as a capable broker between Casio and Tandy on one side and Palm and GeoWorks on the other. Having worked for Tandy, a company that sold consumer electronics as well as PC products, he understood the concerns of the various companies best.

Months passed. Each change in one of the simultaneous contract drafts caused multiple ripple changes in the others. Casio wanted the contract to specify financial penalties if the final software didn't meet all of Casio's specifications; Dubinsky refused even to consider signing such a contract, because in the software business, last-minute design changes are the rule, not the exception. As the date for the Alpha release came and went without an agreement, the problem seemed intractable.

Nor was the engineering proceeding smoothly. The unrealistic schedule had concerned Palm and GeoWorks since the beginning, but they found themselves unable to convince Casio about the need for more time. With no experience in creating brand-new OSs, Casio had little understanding for the challenges Palm and GeoWorks faced.

As each milestone approached, Casio was right on time meeting its hardware obligations. From its perspective, the software partners were the ones who were forcing the schedule to slip. The problem was stressful for Casio's project managers, too, because, as Kate Purmal notes, "They were constantly having to report yet another slip to their own management."

Dubinsky's second priority seemed easier than her first (snagging the elusive Casio and Tandy contracts). It was time for Palm to get more cash; it was her job to secure a second round of funding.

Venture capitalists Bruce Dunlevie and Dave Anderson of Sutter Hill indicated that they would again invest in Palm during this next round of financing. As a general rule, however, an outside investor must lead each successive round of investment, on the premise that the insiders no longer have the objectivity and distance from the company to set a price. Therefore, Dubinsky had to find at least one other investor to join the second-round financing party. This additional backer would have to calculate Palm's overall worth. Once the new valuation was set, Merrill Pickard and Sutter Hill would buy more Palm shares at the new, higher price.

Dunlevie and Anderson called their contacts in other venture capital firms and gave them a quick description of Palm. A few companies showed interest in investing, and Donna set up meetings to give them the big pitch.

The first firm that agreed to a meeting was Newtek Ventures; software companies were one of its specialties. In an effort to assess the young company, its two general partners visited the Palm offices.

Newtek was impressed, not so much by Palm's cramped, one-room office space, but by Dubinsky's pitch and by Jeff Hawkins's reputation. In fact, Barry Weinman, one of the Newtek partners, had seen Jeff speak at an industry conference. "We kept him in mind," says Weinman. "He was in our inventory of visionaries—it's a small inventory."

In December 1992, Weinman wrote Palm a check for $1.5 million in exchange for about one-tenth of the company. Another tenth went to Merrill Pickard and Sutter Hill, each of whom added another $750,000.

"Cash is king," said Vicki Barklow, Palm's part-time controller as she deposited the funds.

"Cash is queen," Dubinsky corrected her.

FOUR

ZOOMER

The year 1993 opened with a bang for Project Zoomer. A year after John Sculley had set the computer world on fire with his prediction that PDAs such as the Apple Newton would soon constitute a trillion-dollar market, and nearly eight months after Apple's Newton demo had excited the press in Chicago, the Zoomer partners were ready to announce that they, too, were readying a handheld.

The Consumer Electronics Show (CES) was held in January in Las Vegas. Nearly 200,000 people attended CES; journalists, company CEOs and sales execs, the buyers for retail stores, and thousands of consumers alike pushed their way through the crowds, viewing the latest electronic gadgets. The enormous tradeshow was an important buzz-generating event for consumer electronics companies, many of whom unveiled new products at the show.

The Zoomer would not be among the new products launched at CES; the gadget wasn't quite ready yet. Instead, the Zoomer partners had agreed to give journalists a preview of the device at CES.

The partner companies had high hopes. Tandy, the country's largest seller of consumer PCs, wanted to strengthen its position against rivals Apple and IBM, and Casio saw the Zoomer as a strategic addition to its vast line of handheld electronics. Despite all the delays and the engineers' daily struggles, the team was sure that their product could match the Newton. "We felt we absolutely had a far better consumer-oriented technology, which we could deliver less expensively and more robustly, and that jazzed everybody at the time," says Tandy's Howard Elias.

But Donna Dubinsky was worried. She had participated in many of Apple's famous product launch extravaganzas, and had worked at marketing-focused companies enough to know the ingredients of a successful product launch. In meeting after meeting with Casio and Tandy, it became clear to her that Palm's two large partners were planning a press event that would pale next to Apple's glitz.

Apple also planned to update the press on its Newton handheld at CES. In true Apple fashion, the Newton team put on a stage spectacle, just as Dubinsky had feared. As the journalists entered a vast theater, pulsing rock music greeted them; oversize Apple and Sharp logos formed the backdrop of a spectacular stage set. (Sharp, Casio's strongest competitor, had an agreement with Apple to sell Newton under its own brand name.) Gaston Bastiaens, the general manager of the 100-person Newton team, kicked off a choreographed pageant, which included sending a fax live from the Newton to an on-stage fax machine. After the demo, journalists mobbed the stage to get a close-up look at the slew of Newtons the product managers held up.

A few hours later, it was the Zoomer's turn. Casio and Tandy had rented a small conference room for the press briefing—no music, no lights, no showbiz. Each arriving journalist was handed a mud-gray folder and a golf cap with the words *Project Zoomer* printed on its beak. Senior managers from Casio and Tandy each rose to give a speech about the technologies that were necessary in a small handheld computer: pen-based input, hardware miniaturization, and low-power design. Then the briefing was over.

Casio had also rented a suite in the same hotel so that Bruce Mendel could give sneak previews to his most important customers: the chain-store product buyers, who make decisions about which products to stock. Mendel was thrilled. "Casio never spent any marketing money," he says. "To be able to have a suite where I could show the product to retail buyers—I thought that was the greatest!" To Dubinsky, on the other hand, a sales suite to brief the retailers was so essential, the possibility of not having one would have never occurred to her.

For Dubinsky, and the Palm team, the contrast in corporate presentations held an important lesson. Her partner companies were relying on the methods that had made them successful in their areas of business for decades. Casio had flourished by manufacturing and blanketing store shelves with electronic gadgets. Tandy, with its network of 7,000 Radio Shack stores, gained customers through monthly flyers and newspaper ads. However, the strategies that had served these companies so well had little relevance in a battle for public attention against a high-profile marketer like Apple—and, Palm felt, they fell short when it came to launching an entirely new product category that needed market development and marketing.

By the time Donna returned from Las Vegas, she was deeply concerned. If Zoomer flopped, the other partners would go on with the rest of their businesses. Palm didn't yet *have* any other business.

A few weeks later, it was becoming clear that the Newton wouldn't even be Zoomer's only competition. Rumor had it that Microsoft was getting into the pen computing game with a product called WinPad. In addition, a high-profile, well-funded startup called General Magic announced alliances with some impressive partners: AT&T, Sony, Motorola, Philips, Matsushita, even Apple. General Magic said it was working on an OS for *personal communicators* to be used by its partners. The competitive landscape had suddenly gotten crowded.

There was only one thing to do: Palm needed to influence Tandy and Casio's launch plans. If Palm couldn't persuade the two companies to approach Apple's marketing flair, Zoomer might simply be drowned out by the hype around its rival. Donna placed two calls. One was to an executive recruiter, whom she asked to start a search for a vice president of marketing. The second phone call was to me, Andrea Butter.

I had worked for Donna at Apple and Claris, where I had flourished in the fast-paced, no-nonsense environment she had created. Without doing a lick of research on Palm, its product, or its financial stability, I jumped at the chance to become Palm's marketing director.

I joined because of Donna, but stayed for the entire company. Since moving into its Los Altos office, Palm had grown to 16 people. At lunchtime, the conversations around the small kitchen table turned personal. Vitaly Kruglikov, a young engineer fresh out of college, told the group about emigrating from the Soviet Union at the age of 13. Another engineer, Roger Flores, passed a diamond ring around the table. He'd been carrying it in his pockets for weeks while he worked out how to ask his girlfriend to marry him. In the afternoons, Art Lamb and Chris Raff took off on their bicycles for an hour, racing each other through the tree-lined streets. Upon their return, they rode a sweaty victory lap around their colleagues' cubicles.

The engineers were exhausted from months of nearly constant coding; only frequent Nerf-ball or toy-missile wars broke the tension. At night, Lamb and Raff cranked up the stereo system under Lamb's desk and played a lot of blues music.

Every Friday afternoon, the employees rolled their chairs into the empty space at one corner of the room, gathering around Donna for an all-company announcement session that came to be called the communications meeting. Jeff and Donna reported on the rumors they'd heard, the new technology they'd seen, the VCs who were funding new handheld computing companies, and every shred of good news for the company.

The employees joined in, updating the team on their own progress. One thing everyone was sure of: Handheld computing was going to be the next wave of computing, and Palm was at the center of the action. It was exhilarating.

The Zoomer partners had agreed to launch the product at the next Consumer Electronics Show, slated for June in Chicago. Everyone fervently believed that the Zoomer was a better product than the Newton, and the January showing of Apple's PDA had offered hope that Zoomer could beat its rival to market. Reviewing the offerings at CES in Las Vegas, industry analyst Kimball Brown had told *PC Week,* "Now that Newton is not quite as far along as many had hoped, the Casio [machine] seems closer to becoming reality."

Much had to be done to pull off a persuasive launch, but Palm was by far the smallest of the six partner companies, with little money to spend on the Zoomer launch. All Palm could do was cajole the other partners and suggest marketing tactics.

Instead of planning a flashy introduction event or lengthy press tour featuring demos for reporters, they settled on a more modest plan: Casio and Tandy would demo the Zoomer in a joint booth at CES; John Roach, the CEO of Tandy, and John McDonald, president of Casio US, would speak at a press conference. Kate Purmal would give a demo of the product on stage.

In March of 1993, the first prototypes of the Zoomer arrived in Los Altos.

Donna, Jeff, and Art Lamb ripped open the packaging like kids at Christmas. After a year of seeing their software come alive only on their PC screens, holding the first Zoomers was an undeniable thrill.

But their initial joy quickly turned to disappointment; the Zoomer was sluggish well beyond their worst fears. Of course, the engineers knew that the finished Zoomer wouldn't be as fast as their PC simulators—but they had never imagined that it would be *this* slow.

One of the engineers quit, having lost hope for the project. The remaining seven closed ranks. "Making products is like an Everest expedition," says Art Lamb, the most experienced of the engineers. "Once you mount this campaign, you don't want to give up. Even if some of the evidence says it's doomed." The team had a few months left before the CES launch in which to speed up the Zoomer—and fix bugs, day and night.

The stress was taking its toll. Chris Raff, whose daily commute to San Francisco was the longest of any Palm employee, took to sleeping in the $28-a-night motel across the street from Palm instead of driving home well after midnight each night. Art Lamb, who carried the most responsibility for the software, became grumpy from the strain. All of the team members drove themselves to exhaustion.

On the first day of April, Jeff and Donna gathered their employees for an impromptu meeting. Their faces were grim. Dubinsky spoke in somber tones: There was very little money left.

Jeff Hawkins took over. "GeoWorks has made us an offer to buy Palm." The team was silent with astonishment. "Donna and I have considered the offer, and we've decided that it's the best thing for the company."

The others stared at Jeff in horror. Had Palm sold out to Hacks 'R Us, the company that had caused them so much anguish with its ever-changing software code?

Suddenly, Art Lamb laughed. "This is an April Fool's joke, right?"

Hawkins's poker face and deadpan intonation had given him away; when he wasn't acting, he never spoke with so little animation. The employees burst out laughing. Palm may have been on wobbly legs, but it wasn't time to sell yet.

The June CES took place in Chicago's McCormick Center, the largest exhibition facility in North America. In over 2 million square feet of floor space and about 100 meeting rooms, the world's biggest names in consumer electronics competed for the attention of consumers and retailers. This time, the Zoomer alliance was among them.

The CES was a gaudy carnival of competing sights and sounds. To attract attention, almost every booth employed temporary staff dressed as Las Vegas showgirls, or Michael Jackson moon-dancing, or Captain Kirk and Mr. Spock. Elvis look-alikes beckoned the passing show visitor, models handed out leaflets, and raffles for sports cars and trips to Hawaii lured passersby to check out the newest gadgets on display.

Upon arrival the day before the show opened, the Palm team went to the show floor to make sure that the press releases and Zoomer prototypes had arrived (models that looked real enough, but ran on unfinished software that could freeze at any moment).

Tandy's marketing team had secured a prime location for the Zoomer booth, close to the center of one of the exhibit halls. Compared with the dramatic booths of companies like Sony and

Panasonic, it looked tired and worn. Tandy had been using the same booth for tradeshow appearances for years. Its once shiny black surfaces were scuffed and dulled.

Joe Sipher, who had recently joined Palm as its new product manager, would conduct some of the demos in the booth's little theater. A rare mixture of marketer and closet techie, Sipher had been bitten by the computer bug at 16 after taking a computer science class. Fresh out of business school, he had moved to Silicon Valley from his native Michigan in search of a job in the hot handheld computing industry.

Now he was learning about Dubinsky's motto, "Cash is Queen." It even ruled the choice of accommodations: they stayed in a third-class hotel. At dinner, Sipher entertained the Palm team with the little item he had discovered underneath his bed: a pair of handcuffs.

Thursday, June 3, 1993, started out well. The *Chicago Tribune* featured the Zoomer on the front page of its business section. Having been briefed by the Tandy marketing manager in advance, tech writer James Coates quoted a Dataquest analyst as saying, "This product will sell well in the marketplace to a large family of users who are moving up from things like the Casio Boss and Sharp Wizard."

The Zoomer alliance had managed to scoop the Newton, which was mentioned only briefly near the end of the article. Palm hoped that the article would ensure that the invited journalists would show up at the Zoomer press conference—which, by sheer luck, had been scheduled to precede Apple's press conference by a few hours. The journalists, the Palm team hoped, would be able to gauge the Zoomer's merits before being inundated by Apple glitz.

From the reporters' point of view, of course, it wasn't glitz that counted so much as newsworthiness—and quality. The world's tech writers had, in their own way, been just as burned by the overhyped failures of earlier palmtops as the VCs; they approached each product announcement with equal parts of skepticism of the tech industry's glowing promises and hope that they might be true.

Once again, the Zoomer press conference featured speeches by Casio and Tandy executives, followed by Kate Purmal's live Zoomer demonstration.

Any product demo is designed to show off the product's best features—and hide its worst. In the Zoomer's case, Purmal would have to demonstrate entering an appointment, looking up a phone number, checking a to-do item, and reviewing a memo—all without permitting the audience to notice how unbearably slow it was. She also had to be careful in printing the letters on the Zoomer screen, in order for the PalmPrint software to recognize the writing correctly. She had rehearsed for weeks, using only simple words that the Zoomer recognized well, even if her hands were shaking.

The demo went flawlessly. Purmal simulated complete composure as she put the Zoomer through its paces, covering up the pauses with talk whenever the Zoomer's wait cursor was on the screen.

Watching the press conference with particular interest was Palm's new VP of Marketing, Ed Colligan, the product of a successful headhunter search. At 32, he was several years younger than Hawkins (36) and Dubinsky (38); he struck the team as an energetic and gregarious manager. Colligan, too, came from an Apple-influenced background, having worked most of his career at Radius, a company founded by ex-Apple managers that sold monitors primarily for Macintosh computers.

He was in a daze as he left the press conference. As he came to the Zoomer booth, he worried whether he'd made the right decision in joining Palm. "At Radius, we had put on pretty lavish press conferences, with great signage and demo stations," he says. "I sat there and asked myself—what have I gotten myself into?"

Later in the day, Casio's Bruce Mendel, who had sneaked into the Newton press conference, gave the Zoomer partners a report. "It was high drama and theater. They must have spent an unbelievable amount of money. It was like a Broadway production. The handwriting recognition worked, they nailed their demo."

Even so, the press was less overwhelmed by the Newton event than Apple's previous showings. "They're not rushing the stage anymore," one of the Apple managers said as he watched the crowd leave before the Q & A session was over. After a year of hype about the Newton, the journalists had expected Apple to release it, not just give a status report.

The Palm team left Chicago with great relief. The world seemed to perceive the Zoomer on par with the Newton. Of course, they firmly believed that Zoomer was by far the more usable product. For example, it had relatively dependable handwriting recognition software. The Newton's handwriting recognition, on the other hand, barely worked.

Ed Colligan showed up at Palm a few days later in his red BMW convertible. Deaf in one ear from a childhood disease, the outgoing Colligan spoke with a loud voice that easily matched Donna's. Within days of his arrival, he installed a small-scale basketball hoop with backboard on a seven-foot-high stand, which he set up in an empty corner of the room. From that moment on, basketball games joined the Nerf-ball wars when the engineers needed a break from the grind.

Ed brought important experience to the tiny company. Not only did he prove to be an inspired marketer, he'd also been one of Radius's first employees, and knew the challenges a start-up company faces once it becomes successful and grows quickly.

More important in the short term was the new level of fun that he brought to the next company communications meeting, wildly gesticulating and acting out the meetings with Casio and Tandy executives at CES.

The tales of the Zoomer's positive reception in Chicago had encouraged the engineers. They had "made Alpha" in early November of 1992, and had spent their time since then feverishly improving the software code. To no one's surprise but Casio's, the schedule had continued to slip throughout the spring. Now, however, everyone agreed that the engineers could finish the software by early August 1993, just barely in time to ship the Zoomer to stores for the fall—the all-important Christmas shopping season.

Meanwhile, tensions among the partners continued to mount. Casio's project leaders had become increasingly alarmed about what they perceived as the software companies' blasé attitude toward bugs. The software would be permanently burned into the Zoomer's read-only memory (ROM). If a bug were found after the ROM chips were manufactured with the software embedded, new chips would have to be manufactured with the improved software, wasting hundreds of thousands of dollars.

The mutual frustration arose from the partners' very different collective corporate experiences. Casio had years of experience programming watches or calculators, in which bugs are easy to find. There are only so many steps a customer might take: Punch number keys, punch the + button, and so on. In software of pocket calculator simplicity, it's reasonable to insist that every bug be found and fixed.

Full-fledged computer software, however, is far more complex. When writing applications like those in the Zoomer, engineers have no choice but to test the software by using the product in every imaginable way, logging and fixing whatever glitches arise. At some point, the testing department, engineers, and product marketing people declare the software good enough to ship. Everyone realizes that there may still be minor bugs—they may even know about them. However, some bugs are generally not worth fixing, because it's so unlikely that an average customer would ever encounter them.

Bruce Mendel, who had worked in the computer industry before joining Casio, often took Palm's side in debates. "Casio had bizarre quality requirements. They just came from a hardware engineering point of view," he says.

One morning, a phone call from Japan awoke Mendel at 4:00 A.M. "They were very alarmed, saying, 'Bruce-san, wake up. We've found a bug and we are getting ready to go to ROM!' "

This was a serious crisis. Mendel got out of bed and started up his computer, which ran a simulation of the Zoomer software.

The product testers in Tokyo described the bug: "If you write a four-line memo and then backspace all the way over it, then write another line, then close the memo, and then repeat these steps several times, the memo won't be there."

Mendel convinced his colleagues that this was not a bug worth worrying about, and ended the call. But before going back to sleep, he took the phone off the hook—just in case.

In Cupertino, only 15 minutes from Palm, the engineers at Apple Computer were enduring a parallel kind of torture. The Newton software was still riddled with serious bugs. In particular, the handwriting recognition software, advertised as being able to recognize cursive handwriting, was hopelessly flawed.

But Apple announced that it would ship the Newton on August 2, 1993. Apple had a lot riding on the timely release of the product; its hype machine had been touting the Newton and its "Newton Intelligence" for over a year. The engineers couldn't take any longer to finish the product—they *had* to ship it at the Macworld tradeshow in Boston. The Newton engineers came up with an apropos nickname for the sleepless final month of software writing in a desperate attempt to fix the device's problems: "The Death March."

When eager Macintosh computer fans arrived in Boston for the Expo, they saw, mounted on taxi rooftops all over the city, Newton photos bearing the caption "Now taking orders." The early adopters—the 40,000 gadget groupies who try out almost any new gizmo as soon as it's released quickly gobbled up the available Newton inventory in stores.

For Apple, however, that was the end of the good news. In a matter of weeks, the Newton turned into a PR nightmare. Apple's marketing machine should have tried to manage the press and customers' expectations of the Newton as a first-generation product, one that showed glimpses of fantastic new technologies. Instead, the public had started to believe that Newton could not only read handwriting, but practically its user's mind.

Scathing reviews rained on Apple like bombs. In the *New York Times:* "The bottom line on the Newton Message Pad is that Apple promised too much and failed to deliver a useful device." In *PC Week:* "The Newton is almost worthless . . . basically, shelfware. After three weeks, it still couldn't consistently differentiate my 1's from my t's." In the *Los Angeles Times:* "One user I spoke with had spent many hours with Newton during the last seven days, and it still recognizes only 80% of his words. I watched as it took him six minutes to add my name and address to his Newton phone directory. This is progress?"

By late August, cartoonist Garry Trudeau had dedicated a whole week of *Doonesbury* strips to ridiculing the Newton's goofy handwriting recognition. In it, Mike Doonesbury proudly owned a Newton, though day after day, the computer mangled everything he wrote. "Catching on?" Doonesbury wrote on the screen. "Egg freckles?" the Newton replied. Most people now believed that PDAs didn't work.

Palm watched the unfolding Newton drama intently. Apple's mistake was right out of the marketing textbook. As Colligan summed it up to his colleagues, "They over-promised and under-delivered."

The Newton no longer seemed a competitor to be feared. On the other hand, if the world believed that PDAs in general weren't ready for prime time, then Apple's missteps would drag down the Zoomer right with it.

Dubinsky had given each of Palm's 19 employees a Zoomer; all of them used it daily. For the most part, it was convenient. For some, it capably replaced the paper *DayTimer* booklet that they'd been carrying around.

The proof, however, was in the daily-use test. A typical Zoomer moment went like this:

(Phone rings.) Caller: "Are you free next Tuesday?"

Zoomer owner: "Let's see." *(Pause while waiting for the Zoomer to start up.)* "So . . . how is your wife's new job going?" *(Pause while switching to the date book program.)* "So . . . is she enjoying it?" *(Pause while tapping through to next Tuesday.)* "Ah, yes, I'm free on Tuesday."

Much later, when their honeymoon with Zoomer was over and the Palm team could see the gadget's limitations more clearly, they would use the phone test as a standard benchmark in evaluating other handhelds. If you had to stall a conversation while you waited for the computer to catch up, then the palm-top wasn't good enough for daily use.

Only Jeff Hawkins saw the flaws of the product he'd helped design. A few weeks after CES, at a talk at a swank computer industry conference, he demonstrated the Zoomer onstage. After his presentation, the moderator turned to the audience and asked, "Would you buy a Zoomer for yourself?" Three-quarters of the audience raised their hands.

"I sat there thinking, 'This is going to be a huge hit!' " Hawkins remembers. "On the other hand, when I personally used the product, I felt it was usable, but a lot lacking. I learned a lesson from that. You can't be swayed by public opinion about a product that people haven't had a chance to use."

The Zoomer arrived in stores in early October. Early adopters snapped up 20,000 units during the first two months. Then sales slowed to a trickle. The Palm executives believed that Apple had poisoned the market. In the aftermath of the Newton fiasco, how could anyone—in the press or in the computer store—keep an open mind about the Zoomer?

In reality, of course, the Zoomer's failure had only a little to do with Apple and a lot more to do with its design—its sluggishness, inconvenient size and weight, poor handwriting recognition software, and steep price ($700).

Palm desperately wanted and needed the Zoomer to succeed, but couldn't see the writing on the wall. Instead, the company turned to pressuring Tandy and Casio to step up their marketing efforts. Now it was Ed Colligan's turn to be frustrated by the fact that Palm was not in control. "All we could do was beg, 'Would you please do some point-of-sale [in-store advertising displays]? Would you please advertise? Gee, the ads aren't very good, could you change them?' From their perspective, we must have been a bunch of whiners."

But it was clear to the more pragmatic Tandy and Casio managers, that all the marketing in the world couldn't save the Zoomer. Spending money on an all-out market development effort might have sold a few thousand more machines, but wouldn't have turned the Zoomer into a success. Rather than throw good money after bad, the two larger companies decided to cut their losses and suspend Zoomer marketing altogether.

A flicker of hope and excitement arrived from an unexpected direction. At a meeting of the Zoomer partners shortly after

CES, Palm had picked up a new responsibility—and a critical component of what would one day become Palm's success.

The Zoomer needed two software enhancements. First, it needed a spreadsheet, which would appeal to the white-collar buyers the partners imagined the Zoomer's customers to be. And second, it needed a connectivity package—software and a cable that would let Zoomer owners transfer calendar and phone book data between their desktop computers and the handheld.

GeoWorks and Palm were the only Zoomer partners with the ability and interest to write such software. GeoWorks jumped on the chance to write a spreadsheet, believing that such a program might become the Zoomer's "killer app" as VisiCalc had been on the first personal computers. Palm, having written the Zoomer applications, was the natural choice to work on the connectivity kit, to be called PalmConnect.

The surprising twist came when Palm shipped PalmConnect in early November 1993. PalmConnect allowed Zoomer users to back up their data on the PC and move files between the Zoomer and the desktop computer. The Palm engineers thought the program primitive—they had programmed it very quickly—but the software worked reliably, and, as it turned out, was as good as or better than the connectivity kits available for Hewlett-Packard and Sharp organizers.

Dubinsky had grasped early on that, as a company that wrote software for other companies' products, it was crucial for Palm to have a good mailing list of those products' customers. She had therefore insisted in the contract negotiations not only that she'd have the right to use the list of Zoomer's registered users, but even that Palm was to receive the Zoomer's registration cards directly as they were returned by Zoomer buyers. The issue had been a contentious contract term with Casio to the very end.

Now, however, a package of registration cards arrived at Palm each week, revealing a startling fact to the Palm executives: Most Zoomer owners declared that they owned a PC.

When Palm began advertising PalmConnect directly to them, orders for PalmConnect began pouring in. Nearly half of the Zoomer owners bought the PC connection package.

Jeff Hawkins, and with him the rest of Palm, was learning firsthand a crucial lesson: People didn't necessarily want to own a second computer. They wanted an *accessory* to their PCs, some means of carrying around the data that were also on their hard drives. All the PC functions that Palm and GeoWorks had painstakingly built into the Zoomer did nothing but clutter the screen with options that the customer didn't need.

PalmConnect was important to Palm in another way, too: The income it generated was a great morale booster. As Palm's marketing director, I was also in charge of the company's meager sales. Each morning, I checked the fax machine for the detailed sales report for the previous day. If the total was at least $2,000 (i.e., 20 PalmConnect packages), I raced through Palm's offices performing what became known as the Cash Dance—a little jingle and wriggle to spread the excitement.

At Christmas time, Dubinsky arranged a small holiday party for the Palm employees and their spouses at the recreation room of her housing development. Everyone dressed up for the occasion; Art Lamb and Chris Raff even wore tuxedos. After dinner, Donna joined Jeff and Ed at the front of the room, where they sang Christmas carols whose lyrics she had slyly rewritten. To the tune of "O Tannenbaum," and to the particular delight of long-suffering testing manager Shawn Ford, they sang:

O Casio, O Casio, how splendid are thy Zoomers!
O Casio, O Casio, how splendid are thy Zoomers!
Tanaka drank his tears away,
Some bugs, it seems, are here to stay . . .

To the melody of "We Wish You a Merry Christmas," they somehow fit the words, "We're in Radio Shack's database." Finally, to the rowdy applause of the engineers, their executives sang, to the happy tune of "Jingle Bells":

GeoWorks, GeoWorks,
Working through the night,
Changing all the object code,
To give our team a fright, oh!

In the candlelight from the festive tables, Art Lamb and Chris Raff toasted Kate Purmal with their glasses of champagne. She'd held her own against the Casio, Tandy, and GeoWorks product managers all year, and sheltered the Palm engineers from most of the battles. Now that the deadline pressures were over, Lamb had regained his collegial composure, and Raff had abandoned the motel across the street; he once again slept in his own bed each night.

It had been a hell of a year, a roller-coaster-ride, a series of battles and short-lived triumphs. One day, there would be a tsunami wave of handheld computers, of that they were still sure. But they wouldn't be riding that wave with the Zoomer. Palm needed a new plan. Jeff, Donna, and Ed would figure out something.

FIVE

THE WRITING ON THE WALL

As 1994 dawned, a dark cloud hung over the pen computing market. The Newton's spectacular and public failure and the Zoomer's less noisy stumble were only the tip of the iceberg. A company called Momenta had flamboyantly failed trying to launch a pen computer. The heavily funded GO Corporation was sputtering; so was its hardware spin-off company EO. The software companies who'd written programs for the GO machines scrambled to find new markets that would keep them in business. All told, Dubinsky estimated that $200 million had already been spent and lost trying to launch pen-based computing devices.

As a result, the investment climate changed dramatically. As Bruce Dunlevie puts it, pen computing had gone "from star to dog," and no venture capital firm wanted to invest more money in a dog. By sheer luck, Donna had closed another round of financing in the fall, before the Zoomer's fate was apparent—or so she thought.

One of Palm's investors had introduced her to Innolion, the venture capital arm of the French bank Crédit Lyonnaise, which was interested in investing in a handheld computer company. She flew to Paris for a day. "I presented to them, they loved it, they gave me a commitment, and we agreed on a price," Dubinsky remembers. Crédit Lyonnaise valued Palm at $25 million, and committed to invest $1.5 million. Palm's VCs added another $1.5 million. The French bank managers sent Palm a signed letter of commitment in late December; the money, they said, would soon follow.

In February, however, the bank called Dubinsky to report that it had changed its investment philosophy. An investment in Palm, the French bankers said, was no longer interesting.

The very thought was frightening. If the Crédit Lyonnaise investment didn't come through, it was unlikely that Donna would be able to raise money from any other source when Palm needed it later. "It wasn't money we were running out of, it was time," she says. Dubinsky reminded the banker that Palm had a signed agreement.

A month later, the investment arrived. Palm now had cash in the bank to weather the storm for a while, but it needed a new strategy to stay alive in the long run.

Jeff Hawkins was painfully aware of the compromises he'd made to accommodate the conflicting agendas of the six corporate Zoomer partners. He judged the result to be usable, and his team had learned some valuable lessons—concerning the difficulty of designing a product by committee in particular—but the product was still lacking in many ways.

The Zoomer partners had long assumed that after the Zoomer, they'd begin work on a second-generation Zoomer, following standard tech-industry practice. Therefore, almost before the Zoomer was even out the door, Jeff began mulling over ways to fix the Zoomer's problems. In fact, he put his engineers to work on Zoomer II even before getting a firm participation commitment from Casio and Tandy. After all, Palm had no other projects to work on.

A key player on the Zoomer II project was Palm's latest hire: the witty, workaholic product manager Rob Haitani. A first-generation Japanese American, Rob had grown up in Buffalo ("the only Japanese kid in my high school"), but thanks to his six-year stint as a Sony product manager in Tokyo, his Japanese was flawless.

Job Number One on Zoomer II was speeding it up. Hawkins and Dubinsky managed to sell Casio on the idea of using a faster microprocessor. Haitani, meanwhile, set to work on software improvements—both speed boosts and a facelift of the various clunky Zoomer user interface (software screen) designs. The Palm team members had believed themselves to be experts on good user interface design for palmtops; but now, having actually used the Zoomer daily, Haitani determined that the Zoomer screens could become more minimalist and easier to use. For example, the thin line that framed each screen looked good— but it was completely unnecessary, using up several valuable pixels of screen space. With this revelation, another stone was laid in the foundation of what would one day become the Palm design philosophy.

Ed Colligan commissioned in-depth surveys of Zoomer buyers and, with the other Palm executives, pored over the data. The good news: Only 10 percent of customers had returned their Zoomers, a surprisingly low number for an expensive gadget. Nearly 75 percent were satisfied with their purchase, which boded well for a much-improved Zoomer II.

In his original product concept, Jeff had assumed that adding many small applications (e.g., the language translator, games, a dictionary, America Online, etc.) would enhance the customer's enjoyment of the machine. Even as they labored over these features, the engineers had known that nobody would use them all—"but everybody will find three or four things they love," they had said. However, Ed's survey showed that, in fact, Zoomer owners almost never touched those other programs. Instead, they used the $700 computer almost exclusively as an organizer: the date book, address book, and memo pad. Buyers couldn't have cared less about the other nifty features that Palm had painstakingly built.

Another finding: Almost no one printed from the Zoomer. So much for the premise that a handheld should be, at its core, a scaled-down PC.

The survey results also contained some scathing criticism of the handwriting recognition. More than half of the customers found it inaccurate and too slow. One user summed it up concisely: "Pen and paper are easier and more reliable."

The harsh critique came as no surprise to Hawkins. "I knew

PalmPrint wasn't very good, and that it probably never would be," he says.

Everyone—Donna, Ed, the Zoomer partners, and his colleagues in the pen computing world—pressured Jeff to improve PalmPrint. He was convinced, however, that this traditional recognition system was a dead end. "I was specifically not going to improve PalmPrint," he says. "That was a waste of time. Everyone kept encouraging me to work on it, and they thought I was sandbagging."

Industry analysts, press, and customers expected perfect handwriting recognition. However, from his two years of study at Berkeley, Hawkins had cultivated a deep-seated conviction that recognizing a person's handwriting took more than computer technology. It took the abilities of a human brain.

Handwriting recognition software like that built into the Apple Newton worked by comparing a written letter or word with a huge number of handwriting samples, looking for a close match. Even though Apple fed the software with expensive, high-powered microprocessors and a lot of memory, recognition was still slow and relatively inaccurate. A Newton owner often had to correct 1 or 2 out of every 10 words written on the screen.

Hawkins's PalmPrint, on the other hand, recognized individual printed letters by comparing each against a short set of master templates for each character. As a result, PalmPrint was much faster and more accurate than other handwriting recognition systems. Even so, the Zoomer's failure demonstrated that even PalmPrint wasn't good enough for daily use by everyday consumers.

Jeff wracked his brain for a more reliable method of entering data with a pen. After mulling over the problem for weeks, the solution one day came in an instant while he was typing an e-mail on his office PC. He remembered a message from a colleague about an article subtitled, "Typing with a stylus."

Hawkins leaned back in his office chair, staring blindly into the space ahead of him. "It got me thinking about touch-typing. And then it came to me in a flash. Touch-typing is a skill you *learn*."

At the next communications meeting, Jeff set up a projector, while the group of employees settled on the floor all around him.

He carefully placed a transparency on the projector, but covered it with a sheet of paper that contained a half-inch-square cutout. One handwritten word was visible through the hole.

"Can you read this word?" he asked the group.

"*due,*" read Joe Sipher.

"*clue,*" countered Joel Jewitt.

"*GEOS,*" cracked Shawn Ford.

Jeff was making a crucial point. The sample wasn't particularly bad handwriting, but even these highly educated brains couldn't be sure what they were looking at. If they couldn't, how could a computer?

"You need to know the *context* around this word to be sure which it is," Jeff declared, and he slid the paper a few inches further down. Now the entire phrase was revealed: *Your bills are due.* The original word was very obviously *due.*

But Hawkins's demonstration wasn't over yet. He slid the piece of paper down a bit further, now revealing a different phrase, incorporating the same central word written exactly the same way: *Get a clue.* Now the original word was very obviously *clue.*

Computer software would never be smart enough to make such contextual decisions, and yet handwriting recognition efforts so far continued to focus on training the computer to read. Jeff Hawkins took the opposite tack: He would train people how to write.

As he told his team, people don't mind learning new skills if there's a satisfying payoff. For years, people had told him that PalmPrint recognition worked better when they tried to mimic his writing style—forming the letter *E* like a backward *3*, for example.

Therefore, Jeff announced that Palm would develop a new software program, one that would produce 100 percent accurate recognition, as long as its customers wrote letter shapes a certain way. There would be one acceptable shape for each letter of the alphabet, and that was that.

Most of his employees thought it was the worst idea they'd ever heard.

Hawkins was well aware of the internal skepticism. "I knew they were wrong," he says. Besides, "There was nothing much else to do! It was worth a shot."

While developing PalmPrint, Hawkins had noticed that most letters could be written in a wide variety of ways. The capital *E,* for example, can be written using one, two, three, or even four separate pen strokes. "I had learned that the simpler versions of the letters always worked best," he says, describing what had become known as 'Jeff's way of writing' at GRiD and Palm. "If the simple versions of writing letters work best, well, just pick these, and forget about the other ones." Hawkins set about simplifying all letters of the alphabet, designing one-stroke shapes that were easy to learn and to remember.

When Hawkins invents something, he spends a lot of time pretending to use it in his everyday life, well before there's a real-world prototype. Practicing new technologies in "play mode," he says, helps him eliminate pipe dreams and verify good ideas.

That's why, for the next several days, his colleagues at Palm frequently observed him sitting in meetings, rapidly writing letters on a sheet of paper. Jeff wasn't writing from left to right across the page, like any normal person. Instead, he wrote one letter on top of another, over and over in the same spot, until there was nothing on the paper except a thick, inky square blotch.

Hawkins's new writing method solved another problem of handheld computers. Writing on small palmtop screens generally poses a problem to anyone who naturally writes from left to right: You run out of screen space after just a few words. That's a true annoyance, as Newton owners could attest. Hawkins's system, on the other hand, let someone rapidly write one letter on top of another in a designated writing area, leaving it up to the software to display them sequentially on the screen.

Ed Colligan appointed Joe Sipher as the P3 (code name for PowerPalmPrint) product manager, the marketing guy who would define every last detail of the software and work closely with the engineers.

He soon found that the specialized alphabet that Jeff had designed wasn't as bad as many at Palm had feared. Most of the letters, such as *B, C,* and *D,* were simple block capital letters. A few letters, those that normally require two strokes of the pen, looked slightly peculiar. For example, the *A* looked like an inverted *V* because it lacked its cross-stroke. The *T* looked like a 7.

Soon enough, the new product had a name, too. One day, over lunch, Kate Purmal told her comrades about a dream she'd had the night before. "I saw a brick wall, and the word *graffiti* written on it in the P3 letters." The name stuck.

Hawkins put a new engineer on the Graffiti project: Ron Marianetti. He'd worked with Rob Haitani and Ed Colligan at Radius, the Macintosh monitor company, and they had raved about his abilities. "Ron is absolutely brilliant. He's the best engineer we've ever worked with," they told Jeff. Much later, Art Lamb would assess Marianetti's engineering skills: "Probably 80 or 90 percent [of engineers], even given an unlimited amount of time, could never do what he does. The problems are just too complex for them to solve. Not only does he solve them much quicker, but he's capable of doing them, whereas a lot of [other engineers] aren't. That's why so many products are in development for years and years and years. They're beyond the ability of the people trying to do them."

There's a golden rule in Silicon Valley: When you have the chance to hire a truly brilliant engineer, do it, whether you need one or not. So Hawkins jumped at the opportunity to hire the quiet, unassuming engineer who'd become bored at his previous job.

Marianetti had reservations about the project, doubting that customers would actually use Graffiti. His friends at Radius had thought he was crazy. "They said, 'Here you can work on a Macintosh, doing cool stuff—and you're going to work on 15-year-old technology, working on Intel processors and dorky Windows PCs?' They thought it was a stupid move." Still, he took the job despite a 30 percent pay cut, because it offered the opportunity to learn something new.

Joe Sipher and Ron Marianetti spent much of their time bent over the list of glyphs, the simple shapes that would represent the letters of the alphabet and the numbers in Graffiti. Joe had to come up with easy penstrokes that would produce punctuation marks, accented characters, and the symbols found on computer keyboards. Frustrated with PalmPrint whenever he used his Zoomer, Sipher had slowly come around to believing that Jeff might be right: Learning the simple letter shapes would be a small price to pay if the result made the handheld computer a faster tool.

Ron Marianetti developed a method of printing Graffiti letters on his PC screen by writing on a tablet-size touchpad on his desk. Sipher was itching to try it out. He lifted the pen and drew an inverted *V,* the glyph for *A,* on the touchpad. As he drew, a dark line representing his stroke showed up on the PC screen. Then, the moment he lifted the pen, a printed *A* popped up on the PC. He wrote a *B,* a *C,* a *D*—each showed up on the screen in front of him, rapidly and flawlessly. His gut reaction: "This is going to kick ass! This is really going to work."

For a long time, however, he was the only believer.

In February 1994, Ed Colligan organized his marketing team for an off-site meeting to discuss the current state of the PDA market and future product ideas. The long-range plan was still for Palm to become the leading provider of software for the world's handheld computers—but Palm's prospects looked bleak. Thanks to the Zoomer's low sales rate, PalmConnect sales to Zoomer owners would not keep Palm financially afloat in the long run. Until the Zoomer II was finished and its sales took off, Palm needed another source of income.

The marketing team had become concerned that Jeff and Donna were focusing too much on making add-on products for the Zoomer. Apple had been the enemy, Zoomer's rival, for so long, that it had been easy to lose sight of Palm's original mission: to write software for whatever PDAs emerged victorious. Even though the press had hammered the Newton, nearly 80,000 Apple loyalists had bought the product. Colligan agreed with his staff: Palm should write Graffiti for the Zoomer *and* the Newton.

Colligan summed up the discussion in a memo to Jeff and Donna. "We concluded there were few compelling opportunities for revenue or profit," it said. "One product stood out as a winner—Graffiti. The only reason: we can sell Graffiti as an upgrade to Newton."

Dubinsky and Hawkins agreed.

While Ron Marianetti and Joe Sipher worked on Graffiti, Rob Haitani, Art Lamb, and the other engineers had made much progress on Zoomer II. They had dramatically improved both the speed and the design of the Zoomer software, and added useful features to the calendar and address book. By March 1994, the engineers were satisfied with the results.

Meanwhile, GeoWorks had continued to improve GEOS, which was now twice as fast. Prospects for the Zoomer II were promising, indeed: It could be a fast, well-designed handheld, and Palm's own survey showed that there was a market.

There was only one worry: Casio seemed to have lost interest in Zoomer II. Casio's Bruce Mendel supported the project, and had even traveled to Japan to present ideas for a much-improved Zoomer II; but after his 45-minute slide presentation, he sensed that his corporate managers, burned by stacks of unsold Zoomer packages in the warehouse, no longer believed in the project.

At the next partner meeting, Dubinsky tried to persuade the team to use the much-improved software for a quick fix to the first Zoomer's sales malaise, but the meeting fell apart quickly. The ranking member of the Casio delegation responded in the subtle Japanese business manner, "We are not so certain about this. Maybe we should wait."

"Our jaws dropped to the floor," Hawkins says. "In one instant, the death of Zoomer II." For the next week, Joel Jewitt's market meter was firmly stuck on "Pipedream driven by greed."

With Zoomer flailing and Zoomer II dead, Palm needed to shift its software development quickly to whichever new handhelds would sell in large numbers. By this time, Hawkins had become convinced that his original vision of a full-featured handheld was wrong—but other handheld companies seemed to be working on even more overstuffed devices.

The conventional wisdom was that a handheld computer wouldn't succeed unless it included, at the very least, fax and e-mail functions. Motorola and Sony were developing "communicators" that were variations on this theme, and IBM and BellSouth were working on a cellular phone/palmtop hybrid. Hawkins, however, had come to the conclusion that customers didn't want so many functions if it meant they'd have to compromise on the quality of any one of those components. People wanted a great cell phone, a great pager, *and* a great organizer.

In short, Jeff, Ed, and Donna needed a radically new strategy for Palm's survival. The only way for Palm to stay in business, they decided, was to give up on pen-based devices. Instead, Palm would make software for devices that *did* sell—palmtops with small keyboards, palmtops that *weren't* pen-operated. The most successful ones came from Hewlett-Packard and the British company Psion, who was leading the market in Europe. Until some company, somewhere, somehow, developed a successful handheld computer, Palm would focus on making connectivity kits—like PalmConnect for Zoomer—for these machines.

It took Hawkins, Dubinsky, and Jewitt several meetings to convince HP to work with the unknown Palm. As Joel Jewitt had observed in previous encounters with potential partner companies, Hawkins's presence in such meetings gave Palm instant credibility. "Jeff comes across so well," Jewitt says. "He's smart without being overbearing. He's direct and unfaltering, so you feel comfortable that he knows what he's doing."

In the end, the two companies agreed that Palm would write two versions of PalmConnect: one for HP's best-selling palmtop, the HP 200LX, and another for the OmniGo, a new palmtop that HP was developing with, of all companies, GeoWorks.

Palm now had a new lease on life. Hawkins and Monty Boyer put Chris Raff in charge of the HP software; Ed Colligan appointed Kate Purmal to work closely with HP and Raff in defining the two products. If they could also convince Psion to work with them, Palm could survive by writing connectivity software for the two best-selling keyboard palmtops on the market. A picture of a reinvented Palm was forming. They would modify the connectivity software to work on several different palmtop models, forming a tidy franchise in the connectivity area. This market niche wasn't quite the large business opportunity they had envisioned, but it might finally bring the volume of sales needed to stay afloat until the right kind of handheld computer took the market by storm.

At the next company communications meeting, Jeff and Donna brought the employees up to date on the new strategy. The plan sounded convincing to the team. The engineers were itching for new projects, and the marketing staff saw the hope for a profitable market niche. Despite the death of Zoomer II, Palm's leaders had kept their team confident in the company's future.

The arrow on the Market Meter turned to "Mother of all Markets" again.

The bad news came in a phone call several weeks later. Although Dubinsky's meetings at Psion's San Francisco office had gone well, Psion had ultimately decided to write its own connectivity software.

Early spring flowers may have been budding along the walkway leading up to the building's entry, but all over Silicon Valley, companies founded on the promise of handheld computing were dying. In the six months since Zoomer had shipped and faltered, Hawkins and Dubinsky had embraced two promising business strategies; both had turned into dead ends.

Thanks to the last-minute investment from Crédit Lyonnaise, Palm had about $3 million in the bank, but only a trickle of income. Graffiti would come out in the fall, and PalmConnect the following spring. If things went really well, Palm might be able to bring in $2 million a year—but despite Dubinsky's frugal money management, the company was spending about $2.5 million annually. Unless its executives could come up with a breakthrough idea soon, Palm Computing would slowly bleed to death.

SIX

THE ZEN OF PALM

nly hours after Psion closed the book on Palm's latest strategy, Jeff and Ed gathered in Donna's office to toss around ideas and seek a way out of their dilemma: How could they generate a profitable business in 18 months with nine engineers and $3 million?

Maybe, Colligan suggested, they could go into the fledgling Internet business. They could write a Web browser like the program called Mosaic that was making the rounds of the Silicon Valley rumor mill. Or maybe Palm should simply close down now instead of waiting until the last dollar was gone. Why waste the investors' money?

Despite the morbid topic, the meeting was casual and rambunctious as always, punctuated by Ed and Donna's loud laughter. The grim facts notwithstanding, they concluded that there was no reason to give up on Palm, or the handheld industry.

"I'm generally naturally optimistic," Hawkins says, "I absolutely believed in a market for handheld computing. I never felt, 'Oh, what a dumb business this is.' I felt sure that this was going to be a very successful business. OK, we hadn't gotten the formula right the first time—so now we've learned, let's get the formula right the next time."

Colligan felt the same way. Only a few years later, Silicon

Valley culture would change significantly. Leading employees in Internet companies would make vast riches practically overnight. Executives would jump ship at the slightest suggestion that there was more money to be made faster at another company. In 1994, however, enjoying his workplace and colleagues was enough to keep Colligan from looking for another job. "We were all driven by the fact that this was a great team. We were confident we would figure something out. We were all naïve," he says, laughing.

Nor did the Palm troops worry about the company's prospects. Confident in their executives, they disregarded the signs of ensuing poverty, which included a de facto hiring freeze and Dubinsky's sale of Palm's old UNIX workstations for about $1,000 each. Every penny counted.

Donna kept the weekly all-company communications meetings upbeat and lively. "You had the sense that Jeff, Ed, and Donna were in control," says Rob Haitani. "In the worst case, we were kind of lost in the woods, but they said, 'If we head east, we'll get to the coast.' So we all went east. Looking back, I'm surprised that nobody left Palm during that time; frankly, I attribute that to the leadership of Jeff, Donna, and Ed."

In the middle of April, Hawkins and Dubinsky drove to VC Bruce Dunlevie's office at the Merrill Pickard offices on Sand Hill Road. Dunlevie's wit and smarts always energized them, and they hoped that a conversation with him would help crystallize their thinking.

Dunlevie's office was rather modestly furnished for a man whose profession it was to hand out millions of dollars at a time. One of its few comforts was a gray, low-slung sofa that seemed more likely a hand-me-down from an apartment dweller than an intentional purchase by the office staff.

As the meeting began, Dubinsky launched into a litany of Palm's grievances with its partners. Casio had slammed the door, Sharp had pulled the plug on a tablet-style device codenamed Bullet (for which Palm had adapted its Zoomer application software), and Hewlett-Packard was only lukewarm in its partnership with Palm. As far as Hawkins was concerned, no other companies even wanted to talk to Palm anymore.

No one, said Hawkins, seemed capable of building the right sort of handheld computer. Worse, Hawkins knew that the future wouldn't bring any better news. He knew what was on the drawing boards at other companies, and was sure that every one of them was missing the boat.

"Bruce, what are we going to do?" he said.

Dunlevie tossed a football from hand to hand while he studied Hawkins. Then he leaned forward.

"Let me ask you something," he said. "Do you think *you* know what consumers would want in a handheld?"

Nobody had posed that question to Hawkins before. It had been years, and a technical eternity, since he had spec'd out the Zoomer. Since then, he hadn't really thought about what exactly such a product would be like. But even if he didn't know the answer on the spot, he was sure he could figure it out.

"Yes," he said without hesitation.

"Well, then why don't you stop complaining about partners and go do it yourselves?"

"Easy for you to say!" said Hawkins. "That would involve doing everything: the hardware, the operating system, the software—everything. We can't do that."

"Why can't we?" insisted Dunlevie.

Hawkins and Dubinsky argued with Dunlevie for a while. The proposal was preposterous for several important reasons. First of all, a hardware project would be almost hopelessly complex for a company of 27 people with very limited funds, and, more to the point, a company without a single hardware engineer.

Second, everyone knew that software was in, hardware was out, at least as far as VCs and start-up companies were concerned. A software company could put together a disk and a manual that cost $3 and then charge $100 for the package, whereas a hardware company had extremely high manufacturing costs and thin profit margins. Furthermore, if you found a mistake in your software, it was no big deal: You'd fix the bug and recopy the disks. If you made a mistake in a hardware component, however, you threw out hundreds of thousands of dollars of inventory and spent weeks or months building a revised version. In the technology industry, the real money was made in software, not hardware. Going the hardware route flew in the face of all conventional wisdom.

Yet, as Dunlevie pointed out, there was nothing else that Palm *could* do; the company had reached Plan Z.

Hawkins played devil's advocate by throwing out all of the rational arguments against such a plan; but secretly, he was thrilled. He had been handed a clean slate—the opportunity to design a product from scratch, without constraints, without the compromises imposed by partner companies.

That night, at home, he sat down with a notepad and wrote down the premise of what he envisioned the right product to be. As it turns out, the guidelines that he scribbled out during that hour of intense creativity proved prophetic; they define the success of Palm-based handhelds even today. At the end of the evening, Jeff had written down four essential goals for the product:

1. *Price: $299.*   The right handheld would have to be affordable. Anything over $300 would move it out of impulse-buy range.
2. *Size.*   It would have to be small enough to fit comfortably into a man's shirt pocket.
3. *Simplicity.*   It had to be easy to use for the average consumer, not a product for techno geeks, but as easy and fast to use as the millions of Day-Timer and Filofax paper organizers that were sold each year.
4. *Synchronization with the PC.*   In his biggest leap from established industry wisdom, Hawkins imagined a gadget that was an *accessory* to the PC rather than a junior version of it. Most previous attempts at creating a handheld were focused on duplicating the functions of desktop computers: printing, faxing, sending e-mail, and so on. However, Hawkins believed that the vast majority of customers didn't need and want those features. Instead, the handheld should be designed to synchronize calendar and phone book information with the PC, at the press of a single button, thus saving the consumer the trouble of reentering all of his or her information on a second machine. He had living proof: the Zoomer, whose customers bought PalmConnect and transferred the data to their computers.

Three of Hawkins's design goals were hardly revolutionary, yet they were utterly contrary to how the companies in the handheld industry defined their products. Even though their $700 price tags had been anchors around the Newton and Zoomer's necks, the products that other companies were readying would all cost that much or more. A low price tag sounded good on paper, but was hard to achieve; after all, there are component costs involved in building a computer. Stuffing a palmtop with costly features inevitably resulted in a costly product.

In retrospect, the size point would seem a no-brainer, too. Because they were too big for a shirt pocket, failures like the Newton and Zoomer couldn't be carried around at all times, limiting their usefulness. True consumer electronics companies, such as Casio and Sharp, understood that point; their small, lightweight organizers were more likely to be carried by their owners at all times. The real trick for Jeff was to choose components that were small enough so that the resulting gadget could indeed fit into a shirt pocket.

Several handheld companies, especially Apple and General Magic, had built user-friendly machines, but the results were frustratingly slow. Hawkins's idea wasn't to entertain customers with bunnies hopping slowly across the screen while the software switched from the calendar to the address book, as the General Magic–based machine did. He wanted a handheld that was so fast and simple to use that it would rival the convenience of pen and paper.

However, Hawkins's true breakthrough was in envisioning a handheld computer that was connected to a desktop PC. Today, of course, a synchronization cradle is standard equipment for any kind of pocket computer, from PocketPCs to Blackberry pagers and Motorola text pagers. But the idea was born that night in Jeff Hawkins's home office.

The first thing Hawkins had to do was to calculate whether, once all of the device's components were factored in, the small pocket size was even attainable.

That evening and the next day, he worked on a *stack-up* (a precise, cross-sectional drawing). First, he listed all of the components he would need. Then, using a mechanical pencil, he made three drawings of the various components: side, top, and bottom views. By adding together the dimensions of the components he'd need, he could calculate the dimensions of the result with great precision. Clearly, the most space-hungry components in a handheld computer would be the batteries, the screen, and a keyboard.

When it came to batteries, he faced the same catch-22 that had bedeviled the Zoomer: A tiny computer that offered good battery life would have to use a weak microprocessor with the speed of a snail. A faster processor would work if it were accompanied by longer-life, larger batteries; but nothing larger than a pair of AAA batteries would work if Hawkins stood a prayer of preserving shirt-pocket dimensions. He decided to rely on the skills of his team, especially Ron Marianetti, to design an OS that was smart and efficient in the use of battery power. Two AAA batteries would be it.

Choosing the screen size represented another catch-22. Of course, the larger the screen, the more it can show, and the easier it is to read. At the same time, the larger the screen, the larger the palmtop. Jeff chose a screen size of 160×160 pixels (dots) and about 2¼ inches square. If the software screens were laid out carefully, he figured that would be enough to show the machine's owner a full day's schedule.

The third space-hungry component would be the keyboard, and Hawkins envisioned his new machine without one. Graffiti was still months away from being ready. That night, however, convinced that he was right, and customers would indeed adopt a new way of writing, Jeff gambled on Graffiti as a means to eliminate the keyboard altogether.

By the end of the evening, he had completed the stack-up; he could now predict the dimensions of his handheld computer to within a millimeter. In theory, at least, the palmtop design he imagined could, in fact, fit nicely into a standard shirt pocket.

The night after his visit to Dunlevie's office, Hawkins headed out to the small workshop in his garage. Over the years, he had assembled a few tools, among them a table saw, perhaps 50 years old, that his family had used to build a house and several boats.

He used it now to cut a piece of balsa wood to the dimensions he had worked out for his new product, a rectangle no larger than a deck of cards. Next he drilled a hole the diameter of a rose stem three inches into one side of the wooden block. It would become the pocket for the stylus, the inkless plastic pen used for tapping buttons on the screen.

Jeff went back into his small home office and fired up his PC. Using a drawing program, he drew what he expected the surface of the little computer to look like, complete with a screen showing a day's appointments and several buttons beneath it. He printed out his graphic and pasted it on top of the wooden block.

"Do we have a spare chopstick?" he called out to his wife. Janet found a pair of chopsticks left over from an evening of take-out Chinese food. He cut one of them and sanded it down to fit the hole he had made in the wooden block; the first prototype stylus was born.

The final missing component of his model was the cradle that he expected to synchronize the handheld computer's data with the PC. From a piece of white cardboard, he cobbled together what looked like a small reclining chair that could hold the wooden block.

Within a matter of hours, Hawkins had roughed out the size, shape, and even the look of a machine that would change the world.

The task that remained, however, could be challenging: He had to convince Dubinsky and Colligan, his employees, and his investors that Palm should jettison its plans, embark on a multi-year journey, and remake itself as a hardware company. Moreover, he had to persuade them that his handheld computer would succeed where so many had failed. They knew as well as anyone that if they bet the company on this gamble and lost, Palm was dead.

The first thing the following morning, he stepped into Donna's office in a dark and uninspiring corner of Palm's office space. The window above her desk looked out onto the dingy landing of an outside stairway that blocked most of the bright sunlight that should have poured into her office. As in the other two formal offices, occupied by Jeff and Ed, a wall of glass separated Donna's office from the cubicle space of the other Palm employees. The glass wall made it easy to tell if Dubinsky was in her office, if she was free, or if she was in a meeting.

Hawkins laid the product model in front of her and launched into an explanation of his concept. She liked it immediately.

"It became quickly clear that this was a good idea," she says. "I was very worried how we would sell this thing, but from a product perspective, I liked it immediately."

Donna suggested a code name for the project: Touchdown. Normally, her staff voted down her code-name suggestions, but this one stuck.

Next, Hawkins prepared to tell Palm's board of directors of his complete change of course. The meetings of the board, composed of the three VCs, Jeff, and Donna, were usually informal. For this crucial meeting, though, Jeff prepared a PowerPoint presentation.

The crux of the presentation, of course, came as no surprise to Bruce Dunlevie. His colleagues, however, were taken aback.

"Their jaws just dropped," says Hawkins. Their objections ran along perfectly rational lines: "It was nuts to go into hardware, we were nuts to go it alone, it was nuts to do this without a big company as a partner," as Dubinsky puts it.

But his board's skepticism didn't change Hawkins's conviction one bit; he had gone into the meeting with his mind made up to change Palm's course. The VCs could only urge that Palm not try to pull this project off alone. "You've got to get somebody like Compaq or Motorola to go in on this with you," they said. The meeting adjourned with the Palm executives' promise to seek out potential partners.

With the board meeting behind them, Hawkins and Dubinsky decided that it was time to announce the new company direction to the employees. They both knew that they needed the employees to believe in this risky change of strategy.

By this time, in May 1994, the all-company weekly communications meetings were held in the center of the back room usually occupied by the six-member marketing team. The meetings always began the same way: A few minutes before 3:30 P.M., a few of the engineers entered the room, tossed the basketball a few times, and then settled down on the floor, in the empty center or leaning against the cubicle walls that framed the room. Jeff and Donna soon followed, pulling their office chairs behind them. Until the rest of the employees had come in one by one,

Donna entertained the staff with anecdotes from her meetings with industry people, her mother's experiences with her Zoomer, and her prospects to find a date for a dinner party on the weekend.

Unlike other communications meetings, this one started out with the whiff of formality: Donna had brought an overhead projector into the room, and Jeff carried a folder of transparencies.

As Donna stood up and switched on the projector, the room quieted. She started with an overview of Palm's current situation: Combined, the people in the room knew more about handheld computing than almost any other company, yet couldn't make a business out of selling software.

Then Jeff took the floor. The first slide showed Palm's mission statement:

Mission: To become the leading software provider for handheld computing and communications devices.

Dubinsky pointed out a subtle change. Palm's mission statement used to say "the leading *applications* software provider."

Hawkins went on: "Donna, Ed, and I have looked around and talked with nearly everyone in the industry. We know the products that are planned. I've seen some of them, and it seems to me that the industry itself is unable to produce the right kind of product."

All around him, faces turned apprehensive.

"I've thought about what the right kind of product would be. Last week, I presented my ideas to the board." Using the slides from his board presentation, he gave an overview of the Touchdown product he envisioned.

When he finished the presentation, the engineering team was doubtful.

"Doesn't that mean we'll be a hardware company?" asked Ron Marianetti, who seldom spoke up in company meetings.

Until now, they had had their hands full just writing a few software programs. Now the same tiny team would be writing all new software programs *and* an OS to run them *and* software that could synchronize the data with a PC, *plus* it would have to engineer and design the organizer itself (which Jeff called the "viewer") and its synchronization cradle.

Art Lamb had even stronger doubts. From his days at GRiD, he knew how devastating hardware design failures and manufacturing problems could be for a small company. He approached Donna after the meeting.

"I don't think we should do this," he told her. "This could put us out of business." However, he promised to work on the project if Palm was truly committed to this risky scheme.

"We're going to do it," she told him. "I'm not interested in running a little software company. We're either going to make this place successful and big, or we'll all go some place else to work."

"OK," said Lamb, and that was that for him.

The most critical employee to the project, though, was Ron Marianetti. Jeff needed an engineer of Marianetti's caliber to write the OS. Ron, however, had cold feet—very cold feet.

He had come to Palm from Radius, where for two years, he had worked on creating a Macintosh clone code-named Skylab; eventually, the project, and very nearly the company, completely collapsed. "I thought this might bury Palm, that it was too much to bite off," he remembers. "We would start this big effort, we would do hardware that we had never done before, do completely new software from scratch, and sell the product—I thought it would be Skylab all over again."

He voiced his concern the next day. Ed Colligan, Joe Sipher, and Rob Haitani pulled him into a conference room and set about trying to convince him that this time would be different. "He was essentially saying, 'Are we betting the company?'" Sipher remembers. "Ron doesn't usually say much. He doesn't usually raise his hand and say, 'I don't feel good about this.' So when he does, you really take it seriously."

In the end, Marianetti decided to give Touchdown a shot. "I was having fun. I figured it would be good experience, I was enjoying what I was doing, and if Palm failed, I'd get another job."

The other engineers agreed. "I thought Touchdown would be a failure as a product," says Chris Raff. "But it was a fun project. Financial success didn't matter as much as the chance to do something groundbreaking. Starting from scratch, creating, inventing—that's exciting stuff to an engineer."

Within a few days, all hands were on deck, unfazed by the fact that they had 27 people, 18 months, and $3 million to create a new machine—when it had taken Apple hundreds of engineers, over five years, and roughly $200 million to launch the ill-fated Newton.

In the following weeks, it became a common sight to see Jeff Hawkins in the hallway, interacting earnestly with his block of balsa wood. He began to carry the wooden Touchdown model to Palm meetings, experimenting with it as though it were a working handheld computer. When everyone else pulled out their Zoomers to set a date for another meeting, Jeff pulled out the model and its chopstick and pretended to check his calendar.

Rob Haitani and Joe Sipher were to serve as Touchdown's product managers; because the project was so large, Sipher would oversee the creation of Touchdown's PC software, and Haitani would shepherd the device itself into existence. At this early stage of the project, a large part of their job was to translate Hawkins's vision for the device into actual specifications that the engineers could turn into reality.

Only a month later, the Palm team had in its hands a confidential document that described, in detail, its new project and new direction:

> Palm desires to build and market the world's best handheld organization and communication tool . . . Most competition believes the reason these devices are not selling is lack of appropriate features. Palm believes the reason they aren't selling is the devices aren't simple enough . . .
>
> Most of the press coverage of the handheld market is coming from computer journals. These people believe more is better. More processing power, more RAM, more applications, more communication functionality. All the more's add up to a very high price . . .
>
> Palm envisions a product that is smaller than today's PDAs or even most of today's electronic organizers. The device target design would be shirt pocket–sized . . .

Code name for the product is Touchdown. It is a direct extension, it could even be called an accessory, to your desktop PC . . . The product will download unread e-mails for on the road review. It will have an all-inclusive desktop software solution and cradle for docking at the desk . . . The product will have an updated schedule, all address files and contacts, your to do list, a desktop application file viewer, and the e-mail creator and reader. . . .

Since this is a nascent market, we believe an enormous amount of education on the functionality of these type products is still necessary. Our plan is to launch each version of the product direct for three months through the development and production of 30-minute infomercials. These programs will run on television to a broad audience.

Although some of the original planned features were ultimately postponed or dropped, the document was uncannily accurate at describing the product that emerged over the coming months.

Through the late spring, summer, and fall, the design of the new machine began in earnest. Hawkins, who presided over these meetings, was unyielding when it came to keeping what he saw as nonessential features out of the product. If the new machine were to fail, he vowed that it *wouldn't* be because it had been junked up with unnecessary functions, like its predecessors.

Soon, the team became experts at killing features.

"Is this feature going to sell one more unit?" Ed Colligan would ask. Ninety percent of the time, the team said no, and that was the end of it.

Sometimes Jeff's $299 price ceiling was the rationale for dropping a feature. For example, the design team quickly established that Touchdown would not contain expansion-card (PCMCIA) slots, which would both force it to exceed the $299 limit and to outgrow Hawkins's deck-of-cards case size.

Backlighting was another compromise. Ed campaigned hard for a backlight on the little screen, so that its users could check their calendars or address books in the dark. But Jeff overruled him, concerned, as always, with the schedule, cost, battery drain, and above all, the threat of "feature creep" (i.e., the tendency for dozens of features, individually with merit, to sink a product into a swamp of mediocrity when combined).

Eventually, Ed came around to Jeff's point of view. "You know what? Compared with the Apple Newton, you're going to say: Breakthrough form factor, one-touch synchronization, $299," he said. "No one is going to say, 'No backlight? Forget it!' "

The machine's shape came under close scrutiny, too. By flipping open the Palo Alto Yellow Pages, Colligan had found a company called Palo Alto Design Group (PADG) whose managers were willing to design the machine for a reduced fee in exchange for Palm stock.

In each round of design proposals, PADG submitted a set of painted Styrofoam models for Palm's consideration. The first models that arrived at Palm's offices were boxy-looking, with straight edges all around. PADG's designers reassured Palm that they'd add some curves to the next generation of foam models, making the case more attractive.

But Hawkins stopped them in their tracks, "Curves never subtract space—they always add space," he said. Curved edges would have to protrude beyond the boxy basic shape, making the handheld computer larger overall—to Hawkins, an unacceptable trade-off. And so the decision was made: Palm would release a very boxy, but very small, handheld computer. Even so, keeping the device slim enough to fit into a shirt pocket was a never-ending struggle.

As Marianetti, Lamb, and the other programmers worked on the OS and software, Hawkins insisted that they live by several design guidelines. He banished the hourglass or wristwatch wait cursor that appears in Windows, the Mac OS, or almost any other OS. If an operation was slow enough to merit the appearance of the hourglass, the engineers reworked their code. Similarly, there should be no need for error messages to startle the consumer; to the extent that it is technically possible, this tiny OS should be able to recover from its own problems.

Part of Rob Haitani's task was designing the user interface— the actual screens, buttons, and menus for the five built-in primary programs: calendar, address book, to-do list, memo pad, and a database program (which was eventually dropped)—so that it fit into a space 160 pixels square.

"Do you think you can do that?" said Jeff. "Oh, yeah, absolutely

I can do that," replied Rob, without any idea how difficult it would be. The Palm engineers had struggled to fit all the necessary screen controls onto the Zoomer screen, whose dimensions were 320 by 240 pixels. How would he fit entire calendars or address books onto a screen half that size?

That evening, he went home, intrigued by the challenge. He considered his task the software version of the hardware miniaturization for which Sony, his former employer, had become famous.

Sitting at his kitchen table, Ed Colligan's Macintosh laptop before him, he began by designing the date book screen, using Apple's HyperCard program as his sketchpad. (Even today, the light dotted lines upon which text sits in HyperCard text areas show up in many Palm programs, including the date book and memo pad.)

His goal was to display an entire workday's worth of appointments, from 8:00 A.M. to 5:00 P.M., on a single screen without requiring scrolling. For days, Haitani struggled; even the calendar program on the relatively enormous Apple Newton screen, at 320 by 240 pixels, could show only the hours from 8:00 A.M. to 3:00 P.M. on a single screen.

Ed Colligan came up with a mantra that guided Haitani, and soon the entire team, in his design decisions: "Delight the customer." Delighting the customer meant minimizing the number of steps required to perform some function, putting the options the customer wanted right under his or her nose, doing the right thing.

Along these lines, Haitani developed a religion of *counting taps*. The idea was to reduce the number of steps to achieve any function to the absolute minimum, even avoiding the use of the stylus, when possible (making a button big enough to tap with your finger, for example).

"We would be trying to decide if some function should be a button on the screen or a command in the menu," says Haitani. "And the engineers would say, 'Why does it have to be on the screen? It's only one more step if it's in the menu.' And I said, 'OK, wait, how is your own desk organized? You have things on the top of your desk and you have things in the drawers. Why is that? Things on the top of your desk you need all the time. Take your mouse and stick it in a drawer. Then anytime you need to use it, take it out of the drawer. It's only one step, but I guarantee it'll drive you absolutely crazy.' "

The discussions could get heated, even emotional. "I use a date book like this," someone would say. "Well, you're not a typical user," would come the reply. And then, inevitably, "Well, neither are you."

Even today, however, Palm employees and executives speak of the Zen of Palm, a term that Haitani coined, tongue in cheek, to describe the design philosophy of simplicity and immediacy that ultimately made Touchdown a runaway success.

Opinions about Graffiti were divided; some still wondered if a tiny keyboard might be a superior solution. However, Hawkins insisted that offering both a touch screen and a keyboard would flop. "We've got to go one way or the other. If we try to do both, it's going to be the worst of both worlds," he would say. Still, Colligan and Haitani were careful to consider all avenues.

At a focus group, Palm showed its subjects a mock-up of this clamshell design, its screen represented by a glued-on piece of paper. If the focus group members were wild about the tiny keyboard, there was still time for Palm to change its direction.

One man in particular had a strong reaction. "Well, I'm a one-hundred-percent keyboard guy," he began. Rob Haitani could see where this was going—this customer would prefer the clamshell design. "So I vote for the model *without* the keyboard. I wouldn't be able to type on those little keys," he concluded, to Haitani's surprise.

He was only the first of many test subjects to dislike the keyboarded design. In general, Haitani says, the focus groups "just puked on it."

Even so, the team couldn't be sure that consumers would be any fonder of Graffiti. To the very day in 1996 when Touchdown finally reached the marketplace, Palm considered Graffiti the biggest risk to its success.

Turning Hawkins's vision into hardware, however, would require manpower and skills that Palm's 27 people simply didn't have. Donna Dubinsky, reluctant to hire additional staff and deplete Palm's precious cash, agreed to hiring only one new employee, Bill MacKenzie, as Palm's new director of product programs. Part of his job was to choose suppliers for each of the 350 component parts of the palmtop—with precious little time or money.

For the hardware expertise that Palm needed, Jeff and Donna decided to assemble a "virtual team" of outside contractors; because Dubinsky couldn't offer much money, she sweetened her offers with Palm stock options and the hope of future contracts. This team included a pair of hardware engineers; a software company hired to write the PC software, later called Palm Desktop, that would serve as the desktop-PC home for the Touchdown's data; design firm PADG; and Flextronics, a contract manufacturing company, which would build the machines in a plant in Singapore. All of them squeezed into Palm's largest conference room for weekly cross-functional review meetings over which Bill MacKenzie presided.

MacKenzie's job was made both harder and easier by the fact that Jeff wanted to use off-the-shelf parts. Such everyday components were time-tested, reliable, and far less expensive than custom-designed parts. Palm had already incorporated a question mark into the product's design: the new Motorola Dragonball chip, which was still under development. Hawkins didn't want to risk introducing other unknown elements.

For some components, however, MacKenzie's procurement efforts were challenged by the fact that the high-tech world had already moved on to new technologies.

For example, after the screen and the Dragonball processor, the most expensive element of the device would be its memory. In fact, the steep price of state-of-the-art memory chips threatened to put the $299 price goal out of reach.

An older, less sophisticated kind of memory called PS-RAM would cost only about a third as much. Unfortunately, by 1995, almost every memory manufacturer had stopped selling PS-RAM. Toshiba, the last remaining manufacturer, was already in the process of shutting down the assembly line forever.

The situation was critical. Bill MacKenzie flew to Singapore, where he paid a visit to the man who ran Toshiba's memory board plant. MacKenzie pulled out all stops, showing off his Touchdown dummy model and describing Touchdown's bright future in the marketplace (which also implied that Palm would be buying a lot of PS-RAM chips).

The plant director said no. It made no sense for Toshiba to keep open an obsolete product line whose only customers would be the unknown Palm, which, as far as anybody could tell, could fold at any minute.

Upon his return to California, Bill MacKenzie gave Hawkins the bad news. But Jeff was adamant: Bill would have to return to Singapore. He would have to find a way.

MacKenzie flew to Singapore for the second time, returned to the Toshiba plant, and begged the plant manager to keep the line running at least temporarily. "Keep it in production at least until we've introduced the product," MacKenzie pleaded.

The plant director relented; Palm would get its memory.

"**S**omewhere along the line, somebody has to be the bad guy. Somebody has to say no," Hawkins says about his role as Touchdown's stubborn taskmaster. Week after week, one team member or another suggested that, thanks to some technical snafu, the device would have to be thicker, or slower, or less elegant; over and over again, Jeff simply refused, insisting that some other solution be found.

"He was really anal about a lot of stuff, and I think a lot of people got frustrated with him in these meetings," remembers Karl Townsend, the consultant Palm hired to design the electronics. "He said, 'Look, it's really important how thin it is, it's really important how the buttons feel. When you push the button, it's got to *jump* to the application—it does matter!' All the other products I had worked on, people didn't have the same passion that Jeff had, and the product then becomes a huge gigantic compromise."

Hawkins's resolve would be tested to the very end. Just as the assembly line was about to swing into production of the organizer's plastic shell, a seemingly insurmountable challenge arose. The liquid crystal display (LCD) screen was interfering with another electronic component; the only solution was to rearrange the components. "I have bad news," said Bill MacKenzie. "We're going to have to increase the thickness by one millimeter."

Hawkins considered any increase in the Touchdown's thickness completely unacceptable. "I'll pay whatever it takes—$50,000—for a millimeter," he announced at the next cross-functional review meeting.

The mechanical engineers scrambled, only to find themselves stumped.

Hawkins urgently paged Dubinsky, who was out of state for a meeting. When she called him back, he described their dilemma: "I have five ideas on how we can get the height back. But the problem is, the plastics have to go today to make our schedule," Hawkins explained. "Here's the risk. We can leave the plastics at the current thickness. But I may not be right; it may not work in the end, and we'll have to scrap it all. Or we can make it bigger. I want to take the risk. What do you think?"

Dubinsky decided on the spot.

"Pull the trigger on the plastics," she said, thereby giving the go-ahead to manufacture a case that, at the moment, was too small for its contents. "Necessity is the mother of invention. One of those five ways will work in the end."

Sure enough, the engineers eventually managed to solve the component interference by reshuffling their positions inside the machine. Dubinsky's faith had been well placed.

As the summer of 1995 turned into fall, Jeff Hawkins's team had achieved virtually all of his original design goals, despite the bumps and detours along the way. The new machine was small enough to fit into a shirt pocket; Bill MacKenzie had succeeded in keeping down the component and manufacturing costs to meet the $299 price goal; and Rob Haitani's late nights designing each screen, pixel by pixel, resulted in a user interface that would withstand the test of time.

Finally, Haitani was ready for one last, crucial test. He fired up the breadboard, an 8½-by-11-inch circuit board that contained all the electronics of the device, and called Ed Colligan's extension. "Ed, what are you doing next Tuesday? How about

12:00 noon? And do you want Ron's phone number?" Haitani tapped away on the prototype screen that was hooked up to the simulator, producing the answers so fast that no small talk was required.

It was a small milestone, and yet an important one: Touchdown passed the phone test.

SEVEN

CROSSING THE DESERT

In the summer of 1994, a few months after Jeff Hawkins had turned his attention to creating the right handheld computer, Donna Dubinsky took stock of Palm's finances. She estimated that Palm's bank account, together with the expected sales of Graffiti and PalmConnect for HP palmtops, would keep the company afloat just long enough to complete the hardware design and software work on Touchdown.

But it wouldn't be enough to pay for manufacturing or promoting the product once it was ready. Building hardware was expensive. Tooling costs to make the molds for Touchdown's plastic components alone—the casing and buttons, for example—could cost half a million dollars. Dubinsky turned once again to the challenge of raising money.

She calculated that $5 million would cover manufacturing and marketing for the first couple of months in the new machine's life. Once Touchdown shipped, its sales could bring the company closer to an even financial keel and, at least in theory, make it easier to raise more money.

When the topic came up at the board meeting, Sutter Hill's Dave Anderson advised Palm to seek an investment from an established corporation. Such a deal could lend Touchdown the marketing and sales muscle that Palm's own meager budgets couldn't afford.

Donna, Jeff, and the VCs pulled out their Rolodexes and started looking for contacts in potential partner companies, as well as other venture capital firms and offshore investors. As potential investors, Dubinsky ruled out rivals like HP and Apple. She also eliminated companies who'd already failed on a grand scale in the pen computing business, notably AT&T, who was still smarting from its expensive losses with GO. However, plenty of telecommunications companies and computer manufacturers remained on Palm's list of prospects.

Joel Jewitt hit the phone and the fax machine. For the lack of contacts at the executive level, he pitched midlevel managers. Most had little interest in pursuing the idea for a handheld computer, well-known to be a failed product category, by an unknown start-up.

For introductions to overseas investors, Dubinsky contracted with a consultant firm who specialized in Korean and Japanese companies looking for a lucrative investment opportunity in the United States. Often called *dumb money* by hopeful but unkind entrepreneurs, off-shore companies sometimes invested in high-tech start-ups without having much say in the companies' direction. Though Hawkins and Dubinsky made their pitches to a number of investor groups, their presentations were for naught. Even overseas, investors weren't interested in handheld computing.

Dubinsky expected that landing an investment from venture capital firms would also pose a challenge. The climate for funding handheld computing companies had turned disastrous. Those VCs who had funded pen computing companies had watched their investments crumble. Those VCs who hadn't invested in the erstwhile hot trend were relieved that they hadn't—and were certainly not going to do so now. Their incoming mail each day was full of proposals for new businesses and technologies that hadn't yet failed.

Still, Donna and Jeff held out the hope that the strength of the Touchdown idea would be enough to turn some VCs' heads. To bring the idea alive during his pitches, Hawkins commissioned a plastic model of a Touchdown and its synchronization cradle. Surely, at least a handful of VCs would be able to recognize the Touchdown's promise of success, rather than be held ransom by the conventional wisdom on PDAs.

Five VC firms gave the presentation a lukewarm reception.

"Time after time, they asked, 'Does it have a spreadsheet, does it have a card slot?' " Dubinsky remembers. These were precisely the same features that, in Hawkins's mind, had dragged down the previous doomed products. One VC told him, "You can't do a device like this without wireless communications in it. You have to add e-mail."

The answer, of course, was that everyday consumers didn't *want* e-mail, let alone the wireless kind. In Palm's research, consumers had categorically rejected the built-in e-mail feature Jeff had planned for Touchdown. "I get three e-mails a day, and I check them in the morning," one tester had said. "Why would I need this?"

Even Ed Colligan and Rob Haitani, watching from behind one-way mirrors at focus groups in San Diego, Denver, and Portland, had been surprised at how little everyday Americans outside Silicon Valley cared about e-mail.

(E-mail and wireless communications, of course, were precisely the selling point of the new Magic Cap personal communicators. When the Motorola and Sony models launched a few months later, neither found a following. Wireless mobile computing would, however, remain a hot button in the industry for years to come. Even in late 2001, only two wireless handhelds, the Palm VII and the RIM Blackberry, achieved even moderate success.)

All five VCs politely turned Palm down. The sixth firm didn't quite slam the door, but may as well have. It offered to invest $1 million in Palm—in exchange for one-ninth of the company stock.

It was a slap in the face. At the last round of financing, Palm had been valued at $25 million, and the company had made much progress since then. Graffiti had just started shipping, and PalmConnect's future looked bright. At least in theory, the company should be more valuable now than it had been at the last round of investment. "A $9 million valuation was lower than liquidation value," says Dubinsky. "Our patents, Graffiti, and the

Graffiti technology were worth more than that, let alone Touch-down."

A valuation of $9 million also meant that Jeff and Donna would have to sell one-third of the company in order to get a $3 million investment, the minimum Palm needed, which would leave very little control in their hands.

Dubinsky declined the offer and gave up on pitching VCs. If those whose insights were most respected by their peers didn't "get" Touchdown, then pitching any more would just prove a waste of time.

"In some ways, I blame myself," says Hawkins. "Maybe if I had been more of a salesperson . . . ? We were very cautious. We felt that we couldn't say, 'This is going to be the best seller ever created,' which it turned out to be and which we were hoping it to be. Instead, we acknowledged all the failures that had come before us. And when they asked us how big this would be, we'd say, 'It's either going to be really big, or it's going to be really small. Our forecast is 100,000 units in the first year, but we know that's wrong. It's either going to be 20,000 units and the product is a dog, or it will be a fantastic success.' We thought it would be big, everything indicated it would be, but we were just too honest."

Hawkins's unwavering conviction in his Zoomer ideas had garnered him nearly effortless investments earlier. However, the two Palm executives were no longer the wide-eyed entrepreneurs who hadn't yet failed. Seeing the Zoomer die and the Newton limp along had given them too much of a dose of reality.

Having exhausted her leads among VCs and offshore funds, Dubinsky doubled her efforts to convince a corporation to invest in Palm. An elaborate chain of contingencies had emerged among Palm's VCs, which made an investment from a corporation mandatory. Bruce Dunlevie was willing to back Palm even without a corporate partner, but his partners at Merrill Pickard insisted that he invest only if Sutter Hill invested. Sutter Hill, however, would commit to another round of financing only if Dubinsky could drum up a major corporate partner.

Fortunately, not every effort in gaining a corporation's fancy had fizzled. During the following year of corporate courtship, Palm found a handful of companies that seemed willing to pursue a relationship—among them, Motorola, Ericsson, and Compaq.

Motorola seemed like a natural partner; after all, it had been successful selling small electronic products like pagers and cell phones. As luck would have it, Joel Jewitt, Palm's director of business development, had heard that Motorola was looking into developing a "smart pager," a gadget that would be able to both send and receive messages using a tiny keyboard. Armed with the phone number of Motorola's Florida facilities in Boyington Beach, he set to work.

"We'd like to come and talk about what we are doing. There may be a match," he said. If Motorola was working on a new pager, he reckoned, the company might need an OS designed for a small microprocessor and small screen, exactly what Palm's Ron Marianetti was coding in the late summer of 1994.

At Motorola's Florida campus, Jewitt showed 15 Motorola managers a PowerPoint presentation that illustrated Palm's view on the future of paging. (Actually, he says, "We *had* no view of the paging market, but I put some pretty decent slides together of what a pager could be.") Motorola was interested enough to set up a second meeting, so that Jeff Hawkins could meet Doug Kraul.

Kraul was a Motorola product executive with a deeply felt, uncannily Palm-like philosophy of simplicity and design elegance. In May 1994, he'd had a sudden inspiration: What the world needed, he felt, was a simple, small, two-way text communicator. "I wanted to create what people might call today *instant messaging in your pocket*," he says. "It was then (and now) a compelling product concept—easy to articulate, but very difficult to pull off."

He wasn't particularly looking forward to the meeting with Hawkins. Kraul knew exactly what he wanted in his product; he found it implausible that a complete outsider could come in and "help" with this vision. Still, Motorola needed an OS for its future device—Kraul had dismissed the Newton OS, MagicCap, and Microsoft's WinPad as too slow and memory-hungry.

It soon became evident, however, that Palm and Kraul were

made for each other, acolytes in the religion of "just a few features implemented extremely well." More important for Palm, Kraul was interested in using Palm's operating system (later called the Palm OS) for his communicator.

Jewitt and Colligan posted Motorola magazine ads on the central bulletin board next to the Market Meter. "Boy, these guys really know how to make good products," Jewitt said as they stepped away from the display. Motorola could be Palm's salvation, not only a collaborator with complementary strengths, but also the corporate investor Sutter Hill insisted on.

Jeff and Donna developed a plan. Palm could license Palm OS to Motorola, earning a royalty for each communicator sold. Meanwhile, Dubinsky, unwilling to put all of Palm's eggs in one basket, identified groups in several other Motorola divisions who were natural targets for her pitch.

One was the semiconductor group, which was responsible for producing Motorola's chips, including the Dragonball chip at the heart of the Touchdown. It stood to reason that this group would be interested in an investment in Palm. She also pursued Motorola's business development and cell-phone groups. But slowly, painfully, over many months, each thread she followed through Motorola's maze turned to dust.

In the meantime, Palm's original and best remaining hope for an investment, the group led by Kraul, began to fall apart—ironically, precisely because Hawkins and Kraul were so similar. Kraul wanted to create the best possible communicator; organizer features were secondary. Hawkins had his eye on creating the ultimate organizer and didn't want to dilute its effectiveness with communications features. Both men feared that compromise might diffuse the focus of their products, repeating the mistake of so many failed handheld makers.

The contractual problems were equally intractable. Kraul worried that Motorola's future options would be limited if Palm retained control of the OS. He didn't want to simply license the Palm OS; he wanted Motorola to own it.

Kraul proposed buying the operating system and licensing it back to Palm for use in Touchdown. Hawkins and Dubinsky, of course, wanted exactly the opposite arrangement. Ownership of the Palm OS was the basis for Palm's very future.

"Each side tried to apply pressure on the other," Jewitt says. "We'd say, 'Listen, this intellectual property issue is a really sticky one. We can't give this up—that's our whole company!' And Doug would say, 'I hear you. Let's keep working on it.' Both sides were trying to get the project to a point where there was so much pressure on the other side that this concession didn't mean so much any more."

In the end, Kraul even proposed buying Palm outright, although even he wasn't especially comfortable with this proposal. "I had witnessed first-hand how a larger organization can coddle a smaller one to the point of suffocating. It's done out of 'love,' the desire to 'help' the smaller organization survive in the challenges ahead," he says.

Still, he called Dubinsky to offer her the buyout.

She said no. If Motorola acquired Palm, it would be in order to own and develop the Palm OS to its needs. Touchdown would not see the light of day. "That's not what we're here for," Dubinsky told Kraul. "That's not what we're about."

As 1994 drew to an end, with $2 million in the bank, Dubinsky had to accept that Motorola wouldn't be an investor.

Fortunately, Palm had recently put another iron in the fire. In October 1994, Jeff Hawkins got a call from Ted Clark, an old friend from GRiD. Clark now worked at Compaq's headquarters in Houston, heading a group that was trying to bring a handheld computer to market. Clark's group had been testing a palmtop based on WinPad; in his market research, when everyday consumers tried to use the machine, it was a flop. Clark knew that Jeff's company was heavily involved in the handheld industry, such as it was, and he wanted to compare notes with him.

Rob Haitani joined Colligan and Hawkins at the meeting in Palm's small conference room. Clark's presentation of his group's mobile computing strategy fell on fertile ground. "I remember thinking, this is a guy from a big company, but he understands why the Microsoft products suck," Haitani says. "He struck me as a very competent guy, the kind of manager who would be the backbone of Compaq."

"What they were looking for was exactly what we were

building," adds Dubinsky. "They talked about connectivity with the PC—they had the same vision. It was amazing."

A month later, Ed Colligan flew to Houston to sell Compaq on Palm as a collaborator for a new palmtop. His pitch was simple: Compaq's own plans for a handheld computer had been severely set back by the shortcomings of the Microsoft OS. If Compaq worked with Palm, it could bring a device to market much sooner than if it started from scratch.

He returned to Palm, elated. The Compaq managers soon got in touch again. "We had high synergy, high affinity, everybody saw it exactly the same way and—boom! We were off and running on a deal," remembers Dubinsky.

An exciting plan rapidly evolved: Compaq would invest the required $1 million in Palm in exchange for the right to sell a version of Touchdown under Compaq's label.

The timing of the deal was exquisite. With Motorola out of the picture for good, Compaq's money would be just the corporate investment Dubinsky needed. Within weeks, Compaq and Palm had signed a letter of intent.

To flesh out further product details, Hawkins, Colligan, and Haitani regularly met with Ted Clark and Annie Bacon, a spirited Compaq product manager who had been assigned to the project.

At first, much of the discussion concerned how Compaq could differentiate its Touchdown version from the one Palm would sell. As Hawkins had come to expect, Compaq's specifications for a handheld device included what he perceived to be unnecessary, bulky, expense-adding features.

In meeting after meeting, the two teams chipped away at the list of specifications. The most persuasive argument against added features was that it would delay Compaq's version of Touchdown. It helped when, in March, a focus-group test commissioned by Bacon suggested that if it were sold under the trusted Compaq label, Touchdown would be a home run. Slowly, Compaq's team was persuaded that the Palm and Compaq versions of the device should be essentially similar, differing only in the amount of memory, perhaps, or the included software applications.

At one of the meetings, however, the Compaq team made a surprising request that proved very important in the long run.

Touchdown absolutely had to synchronize with Lotus Organizer, with Outlook, and some other personal information management software. "I said, 'Yes, *eventually* it'll do that,'" says Hawkins. "But they said it was a requirement. 'We won't even talk further unless you commit to this.'"

Unwilling to see the project lose momentum, he agreed. "We have to figure this out," he told his staff the next day. The engineers sat down to puzzle out the technical hurdles of permitting a single handheld to exchange its data with a wide range of desktop software programs. (What they came up with would later be granted the 6 millionth patent by the U.S. Patent Office; Palm was even invited to Washington for a Patent Office celebration.)

Their solution was the invention of *conduits*—individual software translators that exchanged Touchdown data with desktop software programs. What began as acquiescence to a Compaq design demand became a core feature of the Palm OS, one that, a year later, would help the Palm device become a megahit.

But even as the technical collaboration proceeded smoothly, the Palm/Compaq ship was sailing slowly but surely toward another dangerous reef. Once again, the snag was the contract.

One of Compaq's chief concerns was competition from Palm. Because the first-generation Palm and Compaq organizers would have only minor differences, for example, Compaq didn't want its version to be sold side by side with Palm's on store shelves. Dubinsky offered to sell Palm's Touchdown models only by mail order, leaving retail stores to Compaq, but there was a long list of concerns left to address.

Microsoft was also on the Compaq managers' minds. "Compaq always had a very close relationship with Microsoft, and here was a product that's not a Microsoft product," says J Tempesta, Compaq's negotiator on the deal. "How do you deal with Microsoft? Do you merge them [Touchdown and Microsoft-based models] down the road, do you maintain two different product lines? We were trying to work through this in our own heads."

As the negotiations proceeded, Dubinsky found herself having to make a growing list of concessions. "In the beginning, it seemed like a partnership," Dubinsky says. "We would both sell Touchdown under our respective labels. But as it progressed, they kept trying to get a more favorable deal. It evolved into a relationship where Compaq had all the control, and we were relegated to a supplier role with very little ability to build and control our company."

But for Palm, time was running out. Donna needed Compaq's investment so VCs would contribute more money—and, if possible, another $1 million from another company. She needed $5 million to manufacture Touchdown, and to pay for the marketing and sales expenses.

Backed into a corner, Dubinsky gave in to an ever-increasing number of Compaq's requests.

While the Compaq negotiations dragged on, Palm's financial situation took a turn for the worse in the spring of 1995. Palm engineer Chris Raff, working with an outside contractor and a junior engineer, had finished their work on PalmConnect for the HP's 200 LX palmtop, a project that Palm had code-named Vogon. Palm had hoped that by keeping PalmConnect alive, it would be able to generate at least some cash and help keep the company afloat. Vogon was also a useful decoy; Palm's employees could freely tell their colleagues in the palmtop industry, "We have a few projects with HP," without tipping their hand about the secret palmtop in the works.

Yet, when Ed Colligan's team marketed the package to HP's customers, orders came in at a disappointing pace.

Looking back at their former plan of making a living as a connectivity software company, the Palm executives were nearly grateful to Psion for having left them at the altar. There was, however, one very useful aspect to having worked on PalmConnect: Chris Raff had written the first incarnation of what would later become Touchdown's HotSync function.

Throughout the spring of 1995, Joel Jewitt continued doing what he did best: contacting people who were in some way interested in handheld computers. One chance meeting with a manager from Swedish electronics giant Ericsson had led to another, and his efforts resulted in an invitation to visit Ericsson's headquarters outside of Stockholm, Sweden.

Jeff Hawkins was the obvious choice of Palm ambassador, but he needed a second representative to take care of the business details. "It's always better if I go with somebody else, because I can't remember things," admits Hawkins. Ed Colligan was the natural choice for this important mission; his enthusiastic presentations in selling Touchdown were so infectious, one reporter later noted that he could sell "ice to Eskimos."

But the day before their trip to Scandinavia, disaster struck. Ed's wife had found his passport, and it had expired. A few frantic phone calls later, it was clear that the passport could not be renewed overnight. Ed would have to sit out the meeting.

So Jeff left for Stockholm alone. "I was buried in the bowels of Ericsson, someplace in a corporate meeting room. They had twelve people in the room, and it's just me!"

About 15 minutes into the meeting, the door flew open; in burst Joel Jewitt, looking disheveled and completely exhausted. Donna had managed to get him onto a subsequent flight, the better to represent the company.

Hawkins presented his views on how a mobile phone could evolve into a "smart phone," and showed the assembled Swedes the Touchdown model.

The Ericcson managers were intrigued. If they could come to an agreement with Palm, its executives might license Palm's software to build smart phones. Despite its hectic beginnings, the trip to Scandinavia appeared to have borne promising fruit.

Jewitt flew back to Sweden in the early summer to hammer out an agreement. A lot was riding on his performance.

His tactic was to pressure Ericsson into moving quickly. He stressed Touchdown's tight development schedule, and implied interest from an unnamed other corporate partner.

A few days later, Ericsson's letter arrived at the Los Altos fax machine, confirming the company's intention to invest $1 million in Palm. More important, as it would later turn out, the Swedish company put Palm's value at $30 million—more than triple the valuation of the last VC Dubinsky had approached.

"That letter was really good for us," Jewitt recalls. "Finally somebody had written down a price [for Palm], and it was from a reputable company."

However, in her heart, Donna knew well that a letter of

intent didn't mean that Palm was out of the woods. After all, she had also had a letter of intent from Compaq, but it hadn't yet led to an agreement with which Palm could live.

Over and over again, she ran the math in her head. If she could come to agreements with both Compaq and Ericsson, persuading each to commit $1 million, and then talk all three of Palm's VCs into investing another $1 million apiece, she would have the $5 million she needed.

But that was a best-case scenario. What if only one company invested and only two VCs hung in there with Palm? Or what if no companies invested, and no VCs joined the party? Touchdown would never ship, and Palm would never know if its handheld would indeed be successful with consumers.

With time running out, Dubinsky took the red-eye flight to Texas in early July 1995, determined to seal the deal. Touchdown would be finished in another four months. Unless she could gain Compaq's commitment and VC funds soon, Touchdown would not go into production. Maybe, she figured, if she was actually in the room with all the decision makers at Compaq, she could cut through the red tape and finish the deal.

As the flight touched down at 7:00 A.M., Annie Bacon met her and took her to Compaq's Houston campus. Bleary from the overnight flight, Donna stared out the window at the fragments of elevated highways that seemed everywhere around her. "All these highways that go nowhere," she remembers. "Beside you, above you, and below you. I couldn't tell if they were old and abandoned or semi-built. It was like a graveyard of highways." She couldn't help feeling that she was looking at symbols of her own efforts to build connections with America's corporate giants.

The meeting lasted all day. A flock of Compaq managers attended, but frequently dipped out of the windowless conference room to attend to other business or take breaks. Dubinsky and J Tempesta, however, remained focused all day long, determined to pound through every issue and conclude the negotiations once and for all.

After nearly seven hours, they had finally agreed on every single detail; Compaq's lawyers would draw up a final draft of the contract and send it to Palm for signatures.

It was by no means a good deal for Palm—just the best that Dubinsky could negotiate with so little leverage. For an investment of $1 million and a small royalty payment on each organizer sold, Compaq would gain the exclusive rights to sell a Compaq-labeled Touchdown model in computer stores worldwide. Palm, for its part, would be allowed to sell only a Palm-labeled version of Touchdown that synchronized with Macintosh computers—at that time less than 10 percent of the computer market.

Still, Donna was willing to sign the contract, and Jeff agreed. "We had no alternative," Hawkins says.

The months of rejections by VCs and investors, futile pursuits of corporate partners, and demoralizing negotiations had taken their toll on Donna. Usually a rock of strength, her morale was propped up now only by support from Jeff and Ed.

"It was wearing on her," Hawkins says. "I was the corporate cheerleader through all of this, and I tried to never, ever, be down about it." He refused to believe that Palm, after all it had been through, would close its doors because it ran out of money. "We had this product we were working on, and it seemed like a great product! The further along we got, the better the product looked; I just figured the closer we got, the more interest we'd get."

It would take all of Hawkins's rational arguments and all of Colligan's wisecracks to prop up Dubinsky's spirit—and then, when the Compaq contract showed up in the mail, she discovered that Compaq had added new conditions.

"Why had I even bothered getting on a plane and going there?" Dubinsky says.

Another round of deliberations began.

EIGHT

U.S. ROBOTICS

"You can't row with one oar in the water. You just keep going around in circles." With Compaq's latest contract in front of her, Dubinsky smiled as she recalled the words of a friend whose company excelled at juggling corporate partnerships.

Without interest from another party, Palm had little leverage against Compaq's demands. Meanwhile, the dwindling Palm bank account simply wasn't big enough to pay for launching and marketing Touchdown when it was ready to fly; the money had to come from somewhere. Her mistake, she thought, had been in her single-minded pursuit of Motorola's various divisions, which had left her little time to raise serious interest by another suitor. Since a deal with Motorola had fallen through, no other company had emerged as an alternative to Compaq.

But she refused to give up. Somewhere, somehow she had to find a company that might have an interest in partnering with Palm.

Donna stumbled onto the choicest candidate by sheer luck. Palm wanted to approach U.S. Robotics (USR), manufacturer of the world's best-selling modems, about building a snap-on modem for Touchdown. Founded in the late 1970s by an economics grad school dropout named Casey Cowell (who was now the company's CEO), USR was now a company with over 2,500 employees and valued at $3.2 billion.

Maybe, Dubinsky thought, Palm could combine its quest to get a modem for Touchdown with its quest for $1 million. (These days, the Palm executive trio maintained this hope at *every* corporate meeting they attended.)

An investment-banker friend of Dubinsky's offered to introduce her to Jon Zakin, the executive VP of strategy and business development at USR. Zakin's job was to evaluate companies for their strategic value to USR.

One of Zakin's largest and most recent acquisitions had been Megahertz Corporation in Salt Lake City, which made modems for laptops. Zakin offered to meet with the Palm executives during a visit to Salt Lake City, at the facilities of the new Megahertz division. If Palm and USR were to collaborate, he reasoned, Megahertz would be the division to design a Touchdown modem.

So it was that at 6:30 A.M. in the early heat of an exceptionally hot July day, Jeff Hawkins and Ed Colligan boarded a plane to Utah.

Megahertz manufactured its products in a building right on-site; because it was only 10 minutes away from the Salt Lake City airport, the company could distribute its products fast and efficiently. Despite the merger with USR, the buildings displayed the old name Megahertz, a testament to the pride the managers felt for their identity even after the merger.

When Hawkins and Colligan arrived at the brand-new building that housed Megahertz's executive offices, they found a lobby, like those of many Silicon Valley companies, that exuded high-tech chic.

Spencer Kirk, the general manager of the Megahertz division, welcomed them to Utah and led them to an upstairs conference room, where Jon Zakin and a few other Megahertz executives were already waiting.

Zakin, a thin, fit man with sharp features and a taste for stylish and expensive clothing, stood out among the Utah managers. He moved faster, and with more determination, than anyone else in the room. He and several other senior managers were there to evaluate both the Touchdown palmtop and the work required to produce a modem for it.

Once again, Hawkins and Colligan pitched their hearts out. As always, they used a tag-team approach, with Jeff in the lead role and Ed as a supporting actor. It was a presentation they both knew by heart, which Hawkins always opened with a short history of Palm. Then he moved into more controversial territory: handheld computing. It was critical that he establish Palm's credibility. If his audience didn't completely believe that he, and by extension Palm, had finally figured out how to make a successful handheld, the meeting was as good as over.

Hawkins started out by explaining why the previous handheld products had failed, touching on their disappointing size, speed, weight, user interface, and price. Everybody in the meeting nodded; after the fact, it was easy to see that these products had been dogs.

Then Hawkins painted a picture of the opportunity that awaited the company that came up with the right product. There was a huge market out there, he implied—if only there were the right kind of mobile, electronic product!

Next came the hard part of the presentation: convincing the USR executives that Palm could design that elusive product. One by one, Hawkins ticked off the bullet points on the next slide, the key features that would make Touchdown successful where everyone else had failed. The product Palm is working on, he told the group, is small enough to fit into a man's shirt pocket, shows data instantly when turned on, connects to the PC effortlessly, and will be priced at only $299.

Only then did he reach into his pocket, pull out the plastic, still nonfunctional, Touchdown model and cradle, and place them on the middle of the table. This was the big moment; the model had to make believers out of the Megahertz group.

One by one, the Megahertz managers picked up the model and weighed it in their hands, touching the pasted-on screen with its little stylus and pretending to enter some data.

Jon Zakin clearly liked what he saw. "It was wild," Colligan told Dubinsky the next day. "He got it immediately."

In fact, upon his return to the USR headquarters, Zakin walked right into the office of Casey Cowell, USR's CEO, to tell him about Palm and its product.

Cowell was immediately interested. He and Zakin believed what few other companies and investors had believed: that

Touchdown was a breakthrough product. "We thought Jeff had done a spectacular job at designing this product," Jon Zakin said later. "We really liked this product. I wasn't really interested in making modems for the device, because we thought the volumes would be too low. But I kicked around the idea of acquiring the company."

Cowell and Zakin had long discussed a strategy that would make USR a leader in the anticipated home networking market, a market that to date did not exist, simply because there were no good reasons for consumers to network their homes.

U.S. Robotics saw the acquisition of the Touchdown palmtop as a long-term strategy that would help the company sell home networking equipment. "The idea was to sell an individual a [Touchdown]; he could go around his house or his office and stick it into various specialized cradles. If he put it into one cradle, it would be a phone; when his wife stuck it in there, it would be *her* phone; and then they could put it next to his bed and turn it into the Touchdown alarm clock. Another cradle would be able to download from the Internet. We thought that by networking these cradles, we would have the ideal product for home networking."

After his meeting with Cowell, Zakin called Palm to suggest another meeting. Only a few days later, Hawkins and Dubinsky met him at the Fishmarket, a casual, often noisy restaurant just upscale enough to attract middle managers for business lunches or dinner. There he presented a radical idea: Suppose U.S. Robotics were to make an offer—not to invest in Palm, but to buy it?

He pointed out to Dubinsky that Palm would be able to grow much faster with USR's financial backing than without it. In addition, USR was a powerhouse in the all-important retail channel. Computer stores carried its modems from coast to coast and in many countries overseas; the USR name would ensure that these retailers carried Touchdown. Without the backing of USR, by contrast, it was far from certain that retailers would risk giving precious shelf space to a handheld product, a category everyone knew couldn't make money, from Palm, a tiny company few had ever heard of.

Better yet, Zakin made clear that a merger with USR would put an end to Dubinsky's fund-raising trauma for good. A mere investment from Compaq, or any other company, would be only a short-term solution. "We would have to turn right around and get more money after that because we would need to scale the company," she says. "I had been raising money full-time for three straight years, almost from the day I had joined Palm in '92. The thought of not having to raise money, and to focus on the business, was very appealing."

Hawkins, too, left the restaurant wondering if an acquisition from U.S. Robotics might be Palm's best option if the terms Compaq offered didn't improve. "I was thinking, what's the best thing for the product? How would we get this product to market?"

The next day—a Saturday—Hawkins packed his two daughters, ages 5 and 7, into the car and drove the few miles to Dubinsky's house, nestled in a planned Portola Valley community of matching redwood-clad houses.

Donna and her 4-year-old daughter waited for the Hawkins tribe at the community's private pool. While the three girls splashed around in the water to cool off, she brought him up to date. "What do you think?" she asked.

Their plans had never included selling the company. At the same time, they had spent 18 disheartening months knocking on doors that remained firmly closed. Donna in particular was exhausted from the months of travel, meetings, and negotiations; she'd carried the brunt of the business meetings while Jeff remained behind to work with the engineers. The Compaq negotiations, while still dragging on, weren't looking promising. If they were to put Touchdown into production by the end of the year, then they were close to running out of time.

It had been an easy choice to reject Motorola's offer to buy Palm. Motorola's primary interest was in using Palm's technology for its own goals, not bringing Touchdown to market. Zakin, on the other hand, had made it clear that he thought Touchdown would be a winner. In short, to the exhausted Palm executives, USR's attention began to look like a lifeline.

"We should at least look into it," Jeff said. "Let's find out what they have to offer."

On Monday, Dubinsky called Zakin. "You should know that we have a letter of intent from Ericsson for an investment that would value Palm in the low $30 million range. We would only consider selling the whole company for a good premium over that valuation. Otherwise, we're not interested."

Without missing a beat, Zakin agreed in principle, and offered to fly out to California right away to start the negotiations. After a year of working with large companies who seemed to drag their feet at every step, Dubinsky was delighted by the speed of Zakin's response.

Jeff, Donna, and Ed huddled. Together, they drew up a list of the most important issues that they'd need to cover at this critical meeting. On top of the list was USR's business outlook. Was this a sound company that would be a stable and potentially lucrative corporate parent? If not, there was no point to further discussions.

The next important point was one that they believed key for Palm's chances at success: How would the company be organized within USR if it were bought? Could Palm continue to operate independently? Would Palm have autonomy in its product plans, its marketing activities, its sales force? Would Palm be expected to relocate to Chicago? Control over Palm was key. Without an assurance of independence, the deal was off.

Only days later, Dubinsky and Hawkins flew to Chicago to meet Casey Cowell, USR's CEO and founder.

Cowell's persona surprised the Palm execs. "Casey was an ex-hippy kind of guy," says Hawkins of the stocky, mustachioed CEO. "He had this big office, plush, with wood paneling all around, sort of the old-world, corporate type. But then he had decorated it with his things—his guitar in a corner, his motorbike in the parking lot."

In turn, Cowell was intrigued by Hawkins. He had already heard the lore of the balsa-wood model Hawkins had carved in his garage, and had seen Palm's plastic Touchdown prototype. In his day, Cowell himself had built mahogany models of his products and walked them around to get funding; he felt an instantaneous affinity for Palm and the process its team was going through. He was pleased with the working relationship he saw between Dubinsky and Hawkins, too. "They had skills that were quite complementary," he remembers. "Jeff was comfortable focusing on the product, and letting go of the day-to-day business and operational management."

For once, Hawkins and Dubinsky could bask in a decidedly positive reaction to the product they had worked on for so long. "It's just a beautiful concept," Cowell told them. "It's miles ahead of anything out there."

Hawkins and Dubinsky left Chicago on a high. They liked USR, and they liked being liked. The effect wasn't lost on Zakin: "At that time, Jeff and Donna wanted someone who loved them—there was not a lot of love coming from the VCs, as I understood it." Hawkins and Dubinsky had finally met a company that understood Touchdown's potential for success.

What they didn't know was that Cowell and Zakin were the only senior executives at USR who loved Touchdown. Most of the others were unenthusiastic.

They had good arguments against an acquisition. The Megahertz managers feared that it would take resources away from their business. Many managers worried about getting tangled up with a handheld computer when so many palmtops had already died. Did USR really want to risk its reputation by attaching its name to it? U.S. Robotics owed much of its sales success to its strong ties with computer stores; if they persuaded its retail partners to carry Touchdown and then sales didn't take off, USR's position would be hurt.

"This wasn't a product that was just a little bit different, it was quite a bit different," Cowell says. "The risk was that it could be very distracting. Not only did we have to divide our own management focus and attention to the project, but it would require a lot of coordination with the rest of the company." Even so, he worked hard to convince the rest of USR and its board of directors that the Palm acquisition was a good idea.

Over time, he persuaded most of his people to agree, if only reluctantly. "To some extent, our people just said: 'Cowell and Zakin have been right on a lot of things in the past, so we'll go this round with them. But they better be right.' "

Back in Los Altos, Dubinsky had received yet another iteration of a Compaq contract, containing, as always, new clauses that would require concessions from Palm. She called J Tempesta, Compaq's unwavering negotiator, and dropped hints that Compaq was no longer the only game in town. Interest from a third party like U.S. Robotics might apply some pressure to Compaq. "I said, 'We may not be able to do this deal with you unless you move quickly—no, I can't tell you why.' "

Even so, she felt that she was running out of time. Zakin had been moving quickly. If there was to be an agreement with Compaq, it would have to come together promptly. She hopped on yet another plane to meet with the head of Compaq's mobile computing division, in hopes that a personal meeting would speed the deal along. "You've got to make this happen," she told him. "Otherwise, this deal is going away."

At the same time, all indications were that the USR deal was squarely on track, and at breakneck speed. Following their meeting with Casey Cowell, Dubinsky told Jon Zakin that Palm was indeed open to being purchased. He immediately proposed making the four-hour flight to California, hammering out the terms, and flying back to Chicago, all on the same day.

Again, Hawkins, Dubinsky, and Colligan huddled. Selling the company was still a last-resort option, and the executives were plagued with doubt. "We would have preferred an investment from U.S. Robotics," Hawkins says, "but the way negotiations go, you can't always put things back on the table. We couldn't say no to an acquisition now—not knowing if they *would* make an investment. It was better to take the bird in hand, which was the acquisition."

For the meeting with Zakin, Dubinsky had reserved one of the upstairs conference rooms at the posh Pacific Athletics Club for the day. They couldn't meet Zakin at Palm; secrecy was important to both U.S. Robotics, whose stock price could easily be rocked by rumor, and to Palm, whose employees might panic if they heard about an impending deal prematurely. Ed Colligan had itemized the topics for discussion.

The Palm executives ran down the list one item at a time, seeking clarity on the terms that USR was willing to offer: Palm's independent status after the acquisition, Palm's control over the Touchdown development, the employee benefits, permission to maintain its own separate sales force, and the Palm employees' unvested stock options.

Zakin's stance on all their concerns impressed them, especially on the most crucial point: "He absolutely committed to us that we would be independent. We would run the show," Dubinsky says.

Zakin also promised Palm enough money to launch Touchdown well. "That was my personal turning point, when he said, 'We're going to put what it takes behind this, even if it takes $15 million in marketing," says Dubinsky. "To me, someone who'd been looking for a million, a million, a million—oh my God, that was huge!"

Finally, they came to the sticky issue: How much, exactly, was U.S. Robotics willing to pay for Palm?

In typical corporate acquisitions, the price is a multiple of the acquired company's yearly revenue. Clearly, that statistic was of no use here; Palm's $2 million revenue for the current year had nothing to do with the real value of the company, because Touchdown hadn't yet gone on sale (and USR certainly wasn't buying Palm for its Graffiti and connectivity software business).

A better indication of Palm's value would be its projected revenue once Touchdown was launched—but that calculation, too, was a problem. Touchdown would be either a complete boom or a total bust. The executive trio was sure that there would be no such thing as a halfway success with this product.

At an apparent standstill, Zakin left the room, giving the Palm executives a chance to confer privately. They all agreed that $50 million would be a sensational price for the company; that price would make Palm, as Colligan put it, "pretty darn happy." Zakin, however, had begun the negotiations with an opening bid of $35 million. Proposals and counterproposals had been exchanged, always cordially and with rational arguments on both sides. "Well, this is where we're coming from, and this is why we think this is valuable," one side would say. "Yes, but the market for handhelds is lousy," the other would reply.

The math was delicate; Tandy and Palm's VCs already owned 60 percent of the company. The remaining shares of Palm stock were in the hands of Palm employees (the largest portion in Hawkins's); the executives felt responsible for bringing back a per-share price that would please its investors and employees.

Colligan suggested a price. "I can't imagine going back to my folks with anything less than five bucks," he said. "It just doesn't sound right less than that."

Five dollars per share would put the value of Palm Computing at $44 million. When Zakin returned to the room, Dubinsky told him that $44 million was Palm's final offer.

Zakin accepted on the spot.

By the standards of the deals that would follow during the dot-com mania of the late 1990s, of course, $44 million was a drop in the bucket. Even so, in September of 1995, $44 million was a rich deal indeed, especially in the context of what was perceived as a dying market.

The deal was structured like a merger. In the process of being absorbed into U.S. Robotics, Palm's own stock would cease to exist; in exchange, Palm's stockholders (the investors and employees) would receive USR stock. In addition, Zakin offered the three Palm executives a large number of USR stock options as an incentive to remain at Palm and see Touchdown through to a successful launch.

Before he departed, Zakin promised that USR would send Palm a letter of intent containing the negotiated terms. Even then, the deal wasn't a sure thing; Cowell would still have to get the consent of the USR board of directors, and Palm's VCs would also have to agree to the sale. Furthermore, although the important points had been hammered out, many details were still to be determined. Finally, Palm could still back out of the sale—if Dubinsky were to wring a satisfactory agreement out of Compaq, for example. The negotiations with USR precluded Palm from seeking another corporate owner, but not from pursuing its few investment options.

When the three Palm executives stepped out of the air-conditioned sports club into the July heat of the parking lot, Donna and Ed were elated and relieved. "I was excited that we had a future for Touchdown," Dubinsky says.

Jeff, too, felt relieved. "We wouldn't be sitting around, not knowing if we can launch the product. We could work on getting the product out." He only had one key concern left. "Would we have control over it?"

Independence for Palm was crucial to keep the team together and the product on track, as Donna knew only too well from her days at Apple. In four years of running the international operations of Claris, Apple's "independent" software subsidiary, she had learned the hard way that managing a business under the auspices of a corporate parent could be challenging, especially when the goals of the small and large companies were at odds. In the end, when Apple folded Claris back into the parent corporation, Dubinsky correctly predicted the end of the company's ability to make decisions for itself. Both she and Claris CEO Bill Campbell left the company six months later. Within a year, most of Claris's other VPs followed suit.

The day after the negotiations with Zakin, Dubinsky called Spencer Kirk, the founder of Megahertz. U.S. Robotics had acquired Megahertz about six months earlier. Who would be in a better position to describe what it was like for an independent company to become a division of USR?

"What do you think about these guys?" she asked him.

She reported his reassuring answer to Hawkins and Colligan: "He said, 'Well, I don't agree with everything they do, but I tell you one thing—they are men of their words. If they give you their word, your can believe them.' "

Kirk's encouragement sealed it. "We really felt they would leave us alone," says Hawkins. "We were physically remote, and in a different business. We'd basically continue exactly as before."

Despite Dubinsky's eleventh-hour flight to Houston, and despite the new leverage that the USR deal should have given Palm, negotiations with Compaq continued to deteriorate. When the latest version of the contract arrived on Dubinsky's desk, she found a new clause that prevented Palm from launching its own versions of Touchdown before Compaq chose to launch its own. In effect, Compaq could block Palm from starting to sell the product or its future versions when they became ready.

"We would effectively lose the ability to control our destiny," she said to Hawkins, pushing the thick document in front of him. After he'd read the new clause, Hawkins was emphatic. "I won't do it. We can't do a deal if we lose control of the product. We've gone through this with Casio!"

Zakin flew out to California one more time, this time to meet with the Palm VCs, who would receive U.S. Robotics stock after the acquisition. "Our goal was to convince them that our stock was going to be good," Zakin says.

He had good arguments; USRX, as the stock symbol was known, had experienced a fabulous run-up throughout the year, starting in January in the high-$40 range, and going in a nearly straight line to the $130 range at this point in August 1995. And there were few signs it would lose steam; the analysts on Wall Street were giving the stock two thumbs up.

All but one of Palm's investors supported the acquisition. "They were very much in favor of it, because they had written us off," Dubinsky remembers. "The fact that they were getting something out of us after all delighted them. In fact, they were going to get an above-average return on their investment."

However, Palm's most ardent VC believer, Bruce Dunlevie, took a different stance. He drove to Palm to make his position clear in person.

"Look, this is your company, it's not mine. You guys work here 80 hours a week; I just help out when I can. So this is your decision," he told Jeff and Donna. "That said, I would like to see Palm stay independent. I think you guys are terrific, and I'm excited about Touchdown—I think there's a big potential future for it. You have my support if you decide to stay independent—and I'd rather do that."

Though grateful for his support, Dubinsky saw no alternatives to U.S. Robotics. "I'd really like not to sell the company, too," she replied, the memories of 18 months of failed negotiations fresh in her mind. "I just don't see how to get around it. Just who is going to invest in Palm?"

U.S. Robotics intended to close the acquisition by the end of August, 30 days after the company had sent Palm its letter of commitment. By then, the two companies would have to iron out hundreds of details. For his part, Jeff Hawkins wanted to arrange part-time work at Palm once his employment contract with USR began; once Touchdown was launched, the time had finally come to spend more time on brain research.

Dubinsky still spoke daily with the Compaq managers. As long as there was a glimmer of hope for a Compaq deal, selling Palm didn't appear to be a certainty. In fact, the negotiations had recently picked up speed. However, the day before she was to sign Palm's acquisition agreement with USR, she saw that Compaq still hadn't changed the terms that were most onerous to Palm. "In the end, the option for us was that we would be a captive supplier for Compaq, and they would invest one million dollars," Dubinsky says. "It didn't seem like a good deal. The irony was, an acquisition by U.S. Robotics looked more like it would grant us independence than the Compaq deal."

An hour later, the fax machine spit out a new draft of the USR contract. It contained a new clause: Palm was to abandon Flextronics, the manufacturing company in Singapore with whom Palm had been working for months on the construction of the actual Touchdown palmtops.

Dubinsky was alarmed. This topic had never come up in the negotiations. Why did USR feel the need to prevent her from contracting Flextronics now? Was this a warning sign of Palm's relationship with its future parent?

She called Zakin. "What happened to this 'running independent' thing?" she asked. "I thought that was something you had committed to us?"

With factories in Illinois and Utah, U.S. Robotics prided itself on its own production capacity. In Zakin's mind, producing Touchdown at the USR plant in Salt Lake City could be an advantage to Palm.

Dubinsky and Zakin had a lengthy argument. "It was an exercise in control," Zakin says now. "Who was going to run the company: the corporate parent or Donna?" Zakin wanted to keep open the option to manufacture in-house; Dubinsky insisted that, at this point in Touchdown's development, Flextronics was the only choice. Finally, they agreed to disagree, at least for the moment, and leave the issue out of the contract altogether.

But in the months to come, Dubinsky would come to view the disagreement as a bad omen.

The next day, she signed the contract with USR. For better or worse, Palm's fate was sealed. On September 1, two weeks away, Palm would cease to be an independent company.

Dubinsky felt relief, exhilaration—and a nagging worry.

There was still one delicate task ahead of the Palm executive trio: telling their employees about the sale.

Even before the dot-com explosion of the late 1990s, going to work for a fledgling start-up technology company still meant believing, every hour of every workday, that your hard work was leading up to an initial public stock offering (IPO). In these pre-Internet bubble years, IPO hadn't yet come to mean "instant millionaires"; even so, every start-up dreamed of going public. For a start-up's employees, an IPO meant validation for the hard work in obscurity and public recognition of the company they had built. Three weeks earlier, on August 9, a relatively unknown company called Netscape had gone public; the people at Palm and everywhere else in Silicon Valley had watched in disbelief as the Netscape stock price tripled in a single day. As the Palm employees gathered at 3:00 P.M. on the last day of August, Donna and Jeff looked forward to telling them that their illiquid stock could now be turned into hard cash. The executives hoped that their employees would be pleased, but they couldn't be sure. What if their employees had pinned their hearts on a Netscape-like outcome for themselves? And how would the group take the news that they were no longer a completely autonomous company? Hawkins, Dubinsky, and Colligan anticipated that questions about Palm's independent status would dominate the meeting.

As the three executives surveyed the 25 faces around them, they wondered if any of these gifted young people would leave Palm once the USR era began. The last thing the company could afford at this point was an exodus of talented workers.

They could be sure that Art Lamb, at least, would still be on board. Hawkins had called him the night before at home and told him about the sale. Hawkins felt a special allegiance to Lamb, his long-time associate, the first Palm employee, and—because of his formidable engineering talent—one of the least replaceable members on the Touchdown team. Lamb's mercurial nature was hard to predict; Hawkins feared that without an opportunity to digest the news, Lamb might well "lose it" in the company meeting, influencing the mood of the entire team.

For the employees, the fact that this company communications meeting was called for a Thursday rather than a Friday was a signal that something out of the ordinary was going on. Instead of strolling in casually at the appointed time, hitting the Coke machine and tossing a basketball into its hoop as usual, the entire staff was assembled on the floor well before 3:00 P.M.

Donna, uncharacteristically serious, began by recounting the perils for Palm's future. She reiterated her many attempts at fund-raising, the need for millions of dollars to properly launch Touchdown, and the need for even more millions to manufacture it. What Palm desperately needed, she told her audience, was somebody who would back it with a large sum of money—and such an entity had been found.

At this point, Jeff took over the meeting. He cut to the chase: U.S. Robotics had offered to buy Palm Computing for five dollars per share, and he, Donna, and the board had accepted the offer.

The room erupted. What did this mean? Would Donna still run Palm? Would the company move to Chicago? Would USR want to make changes to Palm's product strategy?

Dubinsky reiterated USR's assurances that Palm would remain independent. No one would be moving to Illinois; in fact, USR executives liked the fact that now they would have a foothold in Silicon Valley. Furthermore, the days of scrimping were over. Even the employee benefits would be better—in fact, USR would adopt the best employee benefits of each company.

"It's not clear that this is the best thing for us personally," Donna said in closing. "What *is* clear is that this is the best thing for the product. This product deserves the best chance, and anything short of this would not give it the best chance. That's why we are doing this—even though I, personally, really don't want to sell the company."

Cocktails and hors d'oeuvres awaited the Palm team after the meeting in the private upstairs room at a nearby restaurant. Donna Dubinsky scanned the small groups of talking people; she was most concerned about the key people of the Touchdown project.

Ron Marianetti appeared calm. "I wasn't concerned. It was presented that we would stay in our building, and USR would stay in Skokie," he remembers. "We would be separated so far that there wouldn't be an issue. And I was happy that our stock now was worth something. On the way to the party I was multiplying how many shares I had times five," Marianetti laughs.

Joe Sipher, on the other hand, looked upset. "I wanted to work at a start-up, a small company—I've worked for big companies already," he told Donna. "This is not what I came here for." Furthermore, Sipher argued that there was no synergy between USR's business (the manufacturer of PC modems, one of which he owned himself) and Palm. "How is this supposed to work?" he asked Dubinsky. Without admitting it to her, he was wondering if it was time to leave Palm.

Chris Raff, the engineer who had first designed the HotSync software, was even more upset. He sought out Jeff, who stood fielding questions from a small group of people, and told him he thought that Palm had sold out cheap.

"Some of the dumber start-ups I'd been at," he says, "had had higher valuations than that before they went out of business!" Like Sipher, he didn't want to be part of a big corporation. "My attitude was, 'Let's make it on our own, or die trying.' "

In truth, Palm almost certainly would, in fact, have died trying. Whether its staff liked it or not, the die was cast: The next day, on September 1, 1995, Palm became a tiny part of the multibillion-dollar U.S. Robotics Corporation.

NINE

THE SHORTEST HONEYMOON

Few people took notice a few days later of the six-line column under the heading "Palmed off" in the *San Francisco Chronicle* that announced Palm's acquisition by U.S. Robotics (USR). Those who did, for the most part executives of struggling pen computing companies, called Jeff Hawkins.

"A lot of people called in disbelief that we had gotten so much money," Hawkins says. Because the Touchdown project was still secret, it seemed that Palm had somehow received $44 million, despite having had less than $2 million of revenue for the year. "How did you do that?" the callers asked Hawkins. Only a few guessed that Palm had something up its sleeve, but Dubinsky and Hawkins weren't telling.

As Palm's largest shareholder, Jeff had made close to $13 million in the transaction—not a lot by the standards of the Internet IPOs circus that would soon follow, but no small amount, either.

His only real indulgence was buying a used 33-foot sailboat for weekend outings with his family on the San Francisco Bay. Hawkins had held a lifelong passion for the sport since his early days on Long Island Sound, riding his dad's creations.

Life for the employees of Palm Computing didn't change

much, either. Other than the red USR logo now printed on the biweekly paychecks, there were few visible signs of Palm's new parent company.

The weekly company meetings centered around Touchdown: the progress that the engineers had made ("Roger's finished the address book"), Colligan's schedule for briefing analysts and journalists ("we'll need a working model by late October"), Dubinsky's plans to add more staff ("A couple salesguys in January. Nobody before then").

With only months to go before Touchdown's scheduled completion, most employees handled multiple job functions and went home in the evenings exhausted yet exhilarated by the product taking visible shape. Invariably, the last to leave were the engineers who coded late into the night. On Sundays, Art Lamb and Chris Raff turned the cheap TV-VCR combo outside their cubes to the 49ers' football games. They took occasional breaks by rolling their chairs back from their PCs to watch the game for a few minutes with the sound-off. The marketing team had taken to interspersing creative brainstorms with brief games of chairball—basketball played while seated in wheeled desk chairs—which Joe Sipher inevitably won. When testing manager Shawn Ford needed volunteers to help his team check the software for bugs, Ed Colligan made a contest out of it: Whoever found the most bugs would be honored as the winner of the Great Bug Hunt. Within days, half the company, including the marketing staff, tech-support rep, and even the office manager, spent extra time each day testing the software.

For Donna Dubinsky, however, life changed radically and immediately, but not because of sudden riches.

"**W**e didn't spend enough time in courtship," Dubinsky would later say. "We didn't really know each other." U.S. Robotics' company culture and management style came as a complete surprise.

USR had grown from humble beginnings above an Army-Navy camping and travel store, 19 years earlier, to become the worldwide leader in modems. In an impressive drive to success, which observers credited to Casey Cowell's leadership and a slaughter-the-competition culture, the company rose in a crowded field of modem makers to capture the No. 1 market position. In 1990, with annual sales of $56 million, Cowell set his executives an aggressive goal: to reach $500 million during the next five years. They succeeded, at the same time getting rich on USR's rising stock, and promptly reset the goal to $2 billion by 2002.

In the process, a corporate culture that thrived on conflict had arisen among the executives. Meetings could turn combative—yet teamwork rarely seemed to suffer. "At the end of the day, we made a decision, walked out of the room, and got to work," says Jon Zakin, who was now Dubinsky's boss.

Zakin himself enjoyed the battles of ideas, and saw their value in shaking out the best arguments. Donna, who had entered the acquisition expecting full autonomy over Palm, instead found herself having to defend her decisions to the USR executives.

It wasn't the situation that the Palm executives thought they'd signed up for. "We thought when he was saying, 'We want you to be independent,' that meant, 'We want you to *really* be independent,' " Colligan says. The U.S. Robotics executives, on the other hand, felt that they were already giving Palm, with its own marketing staff and product team, more independence than they gave their other divisions.

Only a few weeks after the acquisition, Dubinsky's trust in USR took a jolt. During the negotiations, she had brought a list of Palm's employees to a dinner meeting with Zakin and Cowell. She had explained the importance of each individual on the list, describing his or her job and arguing for a specific amount of new U.S. Robotics stock options. Now that Palm would no longer have its own stock, USR stock options—the right to buy USR stock at a set price—could help to bolster company loyalty, since employees aren't permitted to cash them in until after they've remained at the company for a specified number of years. The large option grants for Jeff, Ed, and Donna were specified in the acquisition terms, but not for the employees whose interests Dubinsky wanted to protect. By the end of the evening, Zakin and Cowell had consented to the option quantities she proposed.

But after the acquisition, a manager at U.S. Robotics' headquarters called Donna to tell her how many options USR would be giving Palm to distribute among the employees. The number was a fraction of what Zakin, Cowell, and Dubinsky had agreed upon.

There was a misunderstanding, Dubinsky explained. But the USR manager wouldn't budge, explaining that she had no instructions that Palm was to be exempt from the policies that governed USR's other divisions.

Dubinsky was upset. "This was a huge blow for me," she says, "because the last thing in the world I would do is protect myself and not other people."

Shortly thereafter, Casey Cowell arrived in his private plane to visit his new company. Donna met him at the airport and asked him to back up the promise she believed he'd made over dinner all those weeks before. He promised to look into the matter.

Dubinsky left it at that, but inside, she was seething. She shouldn't have to fight for these options now—she believed she'd had a commitment. If the USR executives weren't to stand by their word, she would resign. "If I couldn't get that basic level of trust and understanding, I couldn't stay," she says.

The next day, Cowell called to give her the news, she'd have the options she asked for. But her faith in the promises of Palm's new corporate parent had been badly shaken.

Meanwhile, the issue of whose plants would manufacture Touchdown had not gone away. Dubinsky's arguments with the USR executives soon turned into a full-fledged battle.

At first, Palm's Bill MacKenzie, who was responsible for getting Touchdown built, felt that moving some of the production to USR's former Megahertz factory in Salt Lake City might not be such a bad idea.

Once he looked over the factory and its engineering and test facilities, however, he changed his mind. Some of the procedures involved in building modems—the plant's traditional business—would be applicable to building the Touchdown, but many more would be new to Megahertz. For example, the plant had never before handled the delicate liquid-crystal display (LCD) screens that Palm would be using in its product—a screen with an electrostatic discharge that must be handled a certain way. "They were excellent at doing high-volume, low part-count assemblies for modems," MacKenzie concluded, "but they had never built a handheld computer before and had no experience in it." In his judgment, the U.S. Robotics plant could not come up to speed in time for the Touchdown launch.

The Flextronics factory that Palm had planned to use, on the other hand, had the specific equipment, skills, and experience that the USR factory lacked. A Flextronics engineer had even been part of the Touchdown team, advising at every stage of the project how to design the hardware to make sure his factory could flawlessly construct the product at the lowest cost.

On the return flight from Salt Lake City, MacKenzie wrote up his findings in a report for Dubinsky. "It's the biggest risk to date if we build in this plant," he wrote. "I strongly suggest that we start out with Flextronics, who's built this kind of devices, buys from the supplier base we have established, has the right supply chain."

MacKenzie's memo set a clash of two organizations in motion.

Even by 1995, outsourcing manufacturing was a common practice among American technology firms. Then, as now, many high-tech companies believed that using a contract manufacturer like Flextronics, rather than owning and running their own plants, could speed a product's time to market. Later, if a product falls from favor, a company can reduce the manufacturing volume without letting expensive factories of its own sit idle.

But U.S. Robotics didn't outsource, believing that it could get its products to market faster and less expensively than its competitors precisely because the company owned its own production plants. In fact, USR had doubled its manufacturing capacity in the year before Palm's acquisition.

Although it meant a confrontation with her new bosses only weeks after the acquisition, Dubinsky insisted that moving away from Flextronics would hurt Touchdown. "I don't mind taking advantage of [the USR plant] when the time is right, but right now we would hurt this product's introduction time if we don't use Flextronics," she explained. "They've been involved in the whole project; there is no way we can hit our schedule if you derail us."

Donna's intractable focus on Palm's interests surprised the

USR executives. Even if she were right in her argument that the Salt Lake City plant was not at the moment capable of building products like Touchdown—a notion the USR manufacturing executives disputed—it was to U.S. Robotics' benefit to fill unused capacity at its own plants.

The managers of USR's divisions were expected to work as a team, sacrificing the performance of their own product lines if necessary for the greater good of the company. If the company as a whole did well, everyone got a big bonus, even managers whose divisions were lagging. "Intelligent people with the same information and the same goals will always make the same decision," was a favorite saying among the USR executives.

But here was Dubinsky, insisting that her division's special needs were her priority.

Eventually, she and Rick Edson, the executive in charge of U.S. Robotics' manufacturing, reached a compromise: Flextronics would build Touchdown in Singapore, and then send the organizers to Salt Lake City, where Megahertz employees would package them—an arrangement that would prevent a risky eleventh-hour factory switch. Once the operation had been moving smoothly for several months, the Megahertz plant would phase in as a second manufacturer of the palmtops.

With the Touchdown launch only five months away, Ed Colligan needed somebody to manage developer relations, a new field for Palm. Touchdown was what the tech industry calls a *platform*—a technology that can act as the foundation for software and hardware products from other companies. If Palm could entice the world of amateur and professional programmers to write add-on programs for Touchdown, the device would become even more useful, fueling still more sales. A successful developer-relations effort could create the "network effect" that could turbo-charge a product's sales: The more customers bought a Touchdown, the more developers would create software for it, which in turn would lead even more customers to buy one, and so on.

The position required business sense as well as a great deal of technical knowledge. Ed asked Kate Purmal to take on the role.

In countless encounters with the Zoomer partners and later with Hewlett-Packard, she had proven herself a good negotiator and ambassador for Palm.

It wasn't just add-on programs Palm hoped would emerge. A key selling point of Touchdown was its ability to synchronize its data with calendar and address book software, such as Microsoft Outlook or ACT, running on the desktop PC. Millions of people kept their schedules and address books in the two bestselling personal-information management (PIM) programs, Microsoft Schedule+ and Lotus Organizer. Colligan calculated that these customers—or at least those who didn't sit at their computers all day—were the most likely customers for Touchdown.

But Touchdown couldn't communicate with a PIM program without the translator software Palm called a *conduit*. Even more important than evangelizing companies to make add-on software, therefore, was convincing software companies to write the conduits that would make the handhelds indispensable satellites for desktop computers.

Purmal and Colligan had hoped that the software companies that published such programs would take it upon themselves to write the corresponding conduits.

Purmal soon found, however, that it was an uphill battle. "They were very skeptical," she says. "The only reason we got in the door was Donna's reputation." Much later, having become known as the father of handheld computing, Jeff Hawkins's name opened many doors. "But in those days," Purmal says, "Jeff wasn't the father of anything."

Lotus turned them down flat. So did Symantec, whose ACT software was the primary contact management software used by traveling salespeople—a prime target for Palm's marketing. Skeptical about the failed category of handheld computers, these companies had far more important projects on their plates.

Only one software company filled the void: IntelliLink (later Intellisync), a company of about 15 employees in Nashua, New Hampshire, that was in the business of making specialized connectivity kits for organizers. The company promised to start work on conduits for six of the most important PIM programs, including the all-important Microsoft Schedule+ and Lotus

Organizer. A few other small software companies, including Now Software and Starfish, also succumbed to Purmal's pitch.

Writing conduit software, however, proved to be a massive undertaking, requiring specialized software tools. Engineer Chris Raff, who had finished writing his share of the Touchdown code, began working on these development tools. Once they existed, writing software for Touchdown would be relatively easy. Unfortunately, the software companies couldn't wait; they began work on their conduits using crude, half-completed versions that were accompanied by almost unintelligible instructions. Only two years earlier, of course, it was Palm who'd had to suffer with a half-completed development kit—the one provided by GeoWorks for the Zoomer project. Still, despite having an acute understanding of what Palm's software partners were going through, Raff simply couldn't crank out the kit any faster.

Nobody at Palm had any clue what sort of add-on programs developers might come up with, and that was fine with Hawkins. He believed that developers would create hundreds of applications, some useful and unexpected, some strange and limited in use, some brilliant and creative. "No matter how many smart people there are at Palm, there will always be more smart people outside of Palm, creating interesting stuff," he told his team. The main thing was to make the tools available to them, and then to step out of the way; the marketplace would find the worthwhile programs and bring them to the top.

There was only one program that Palm specifically wanted to see developed: a pocket version of Quicken, the popular personal finance software. Intuit, the creator of Quicken, had written a program called PocketQuicken that was built into the Zoomer. Unfortunately, Intuit had gotten badly burned in the Zoomer project; soon after, it had disbanded the small group that had worked on PocketQuicken. The company had no interest in investing time and manpower on yet another mobile version of Quicken.

It was also high time to set the wheels in motion for a successful product launch. Anticipating small budgets, Ed Colligan set about finding advertising and PR firms to represent Palm. The requirements were talent and a willingness to take a risk on an unknown start-up—the acquisition by USR was in the works, but hadn't yet been announced. For all the agencies knew, Palm was still a tiny, unimportant start-up of 28 people.

A&R Partners, a PR firm who had worked with Ed for many years at Radius, agreed to take the risk. Several advertising agencies were excited by his demonstration and the plastic Touchdown model; Ed, however, dismissed some of them after seeing their uninspiring sample ads. Two agencies proposed intriguing campaigns, but proposed charging several hundred thousand dollars more than Palm could possibly afford, even with USR's backing.

Finally, a colleague in the marketing world gave Colligan the name of Helen Lindberg, an accomplished advertising designer in the Bay Area. Her collaborator, Brad Londy, wrote the text of the ads in his New York City office. Their transcontinental partnership had given life to many memorable ads for technology companies.

Ed had found just what Palm was looking for: a highly creative, experienced advertising team who was willing to take a risk on working with Palm without the costly overhead of an advertising agency. With the addition of The DesignWorks, the small Los Angeles design agency that had been designing Palm's Graffiti and PalmConnect packages and brochures, the marketing team was now complete.

One key task that still remained: finding a name for the product. Touchdown was fine as a code name, but it carried more meaning for Palm internally than it would for consumers hoping to navigate their lives. Within the next few weeks, The DesignWorks would need to know what product name to put on packaging designs and brochures.

Everyone at Palm and its ad agency suggested names, which Lindberg and Londy compiled and categorized in a stack of paper. Some names were meant to sound like a trusted friend (e.g., Pal, Max, or Friday). Others evoked product benefits (e.g., Quickpad or Smartz). There was a whole list that contained the word *Palm,* including PalmPad, PalMate, and PalmPal. Some names, such as Taxi and Passport, suggested mobility and travel.

The last page showed a category Lindberg and Londy had

titled "off the wall." It contained such ideas as Whussup?, Way to Go, and Pilot.

Jeff liked Pilot. Donna liked her own entry—Comrade—but was soundly voted down by the marketing team; Communist overtones, they were sure, wouldn't play well in the United States. Everyone had an opinion, and no two of them were the same.

The next Monday, Ed emerged from a meeting with Donna and Jeff with a decision: Touchdown's name was to be Taxi. The name was short, catchy, and memorable. Better yet, it suggested a portable, mobile invention that would take you wherever you wanted to go.

Ed's staff tried out the new name in random marketing sentences just to see how it felt. "Taxi is a remarkably small, low-cost solution for organizing personal information." After 18 months of using the name Touchdown, Taxi felt odd.

Ron Marianetti got used to the new name in his own way: During one long night in the office, he built an Easter egg around it. Easter eggs are hidden surprises that engineers smuggle into their code, usually without their bosses' knowledge, that appear on the screen only in response to an unlikely sequence of keystrokes. An Easter egg is most often a secret list of programming credits; after all, programmers usually don't get any public recognition for their work. The counterculture of Easter eggs offers them a way to strike back.

However, Marianetti's Easter egg was just for fun. It was an animated taxicab, roughly the shape of a fat VW Beetle, which he programmed to race across the Touchdown screen. Unlike most software Easter eggs, no specific sequence of keystrokes or pen strokes was necessary to call this one up; instead, it was programmed to drive across the screen at random moments, providing a merry little surprise for the palmtop's user.

To make sure that his fellow programmers wouldn't discover the Easter egg, Marianetti also programmed the taxi not to appear until after February 1996, when Touchdown was scheduled to be shipping.

In the cube across from Marianetti, Chris Raff also worked on a few Easter Eggs of his own that night. In his spare time, he had written a Space Invaders–like game that he called Giraffe to help people learn how to write with the Graffiti alphabet.

Now Raff wanted to memorialize what he judged were three important characters in Palm's life. As a reward that would appear when the customer had played a perfect round of Giraffe, Raff planted an animation of a dancing Sheldon the Palm Tree (Palm's mascot). He also added to the game a scanned photo of Rob Haitani and himself at the previous year's formal Palm Christmas party. In the unlikely event that a Touchdown user were to hold down the stylus in the lower-right corner of the Giraffe game screen and then press a scroll button, the image of two grinning guys in tuxedos would inexplicably appear.

In late November, USR lawyers brought Palm some discouraging news: After performing a trademark search, they had discovered that a small technology company had already registered the product name Taxi.

There would have been no problem if the two products were in completely different product categories—one an electronic organizer and the other a TV, or a pen, or a financial service. Because both products were in similar categories, though, the lawyers explained that using the same name could confuse customers of the other company, who could sue Palm over trademark infringement. Whatever Palm wound up calling its revolutionary device, *Taxi* wouldn't be it.

The timing could not have been worse. The deadline for sending the final marketing materials, packaging, manuals, and other materials to the printing plants was only two weeks away; advertising was due at the nation's newspapers and magazines in order to make the deadline for their January issues. This time, there would be no time for company-wide democracy.

After reviewing the long lists of names that their ad team had compiled two months earlier, Donna, Jeff, and Ed sequestered themselves in an office to make an executive decision. The product would be called Pilot.

TEN

SELLING THE PILOT

Beginning in July 1995, Ed Colligan and his team had begun to devise a launch strategy for the new product. On a hot summer day, they left the office behind for a launch-planning off-site meeting, for once at an actual rented meeting room at a VC office, whose gigantic windows looked out over the range of low mountains that separate the Valley from the coast.

In working up a profile of the Pilot's target customer, the team came up with these qualities: a PC user, but not necessarily a PC expert, who also used an electronic or paper organizer ("PC users with a desire to be organized," as Ed put it), who was mobile, but not necessarily a constant traveler. Finally, the early Pilot target customer would be somebody who was not afraid of new technology.

In an effort to avoid the tainted term *personal digital assistant* (PDA), Jeff and Donna had suggested calling the Pilot a *pocket computer* or a *PC companion*. The marketing team strongly disagreed. "We need to call it an organizer. For the moment, that's what the product does, that's what people will use it for, that's what customers will look to buy," they argued.

In the end, the marketing team chose the term *connected organizer* to emphasize the feature that set the Pilot apart from its rivals: its connection to the PC. Instead of trying to create a new market category, which typically takes years and a lot of money, this strategy allowed Palm to enter a large, established market category—electronic organizers, which sold millions each year—with a product the team believed was head and shoulders above the rest.

With limited marketing funds, Colligan had to adopt a brains-not-brawn strategy. His plan was, first, to win over the industry influencers. At the outset, these critical opinion makers would include primarily industry analysts; journalists came next, because they often *call* the analysts before writing up their reports. If Palm hoped to make the Pilot a hit when it became available in stores in February 1996, the first step was to convince most of these analysts in the late fall of 1995 that Pilot (then still called Taxi) would be a winner.

This tactic, in itself, wasn't rocket science; every self-respecting marketer in the technology business knows to target these groups in a carefully orchestrated order. For Ed, the key to success was doing this well. Before attempting to reach these influencers, he would have to spend much time on getting the pitch right.

Technology analysts are an odd mix of people in a curious profession. They make their income selling opinions, publishing analyses, selling subscriptions to their research papers, hosting industry conferences, and providing consulting services to companies. They gain their inside knowledge from the technology CEOs and VPs of the very companies they cover; these executives may make the pilgrimage to the analysts whenever they come up with a new product or a new strategy they want to discuss at length, or the analyst may call the executives to discuss their companies. After compiling and filtering what they've learned, the analysts are ready to turn around and sell their views of the market and technology trends right back to the very companies who've given them the information in the first place.

Palm's mission of influencing the influencers began on the East Coast. Ed had lined up 24 show-and-tell presentations in a single week for analysts and those journalists whose magazine issues are prepared months in advance.

During the many meetings with hoped-for partners and investors, the Palm execs had honed their demo to an art; Jeff's down-to-earth, yet persuasive presence and Ed's infectious enthusiasm made a great combination. This time around, however, they had a stealth weapon: a Pilot prototype, a hand-built working model that Bill MacKenzie and Karl Townsend had completed only days before. It ran alpha software (i.e., extremely shaky, "first-draft" software) and it crashed occasionally—but for the most part, it worked.

Their first slide read: "Introducing Two Breakthrough Developments: Palm Connected Operating System and Taxi, The Connected Organizer." Hawkins and Colligan had debated the value of mentioning the newly dubbed Palm OS; they didn't want to be perceived as following in the footsteps of the Apple Newton, and other doomed palmtops that ran on OSs that their makers declared would be "a new standard."

Indeed, before Jeff had even changed his first slide, the very first analyst asked why Palm would want to introduce an OS. "The market is overloaded with competing operating systems," he said.

The answer, of course, was that Palm had *had* to produce a new OS. No existing OS would permit the design of a fast, easy-to-use, and inexpensive handheld computer. The Palm OS was small, fast, powerful, flexible, and designed for connectivity to the PC—all the things the other OS options were not.

Once he saw the Pilot in action, the analyst was convinced. Even though he was sure that the market was going to "go wireless" (in his mind, a clear drawback to the Pilot), he agreed that Pilot was "very clever." Hawkins and Colligan left the office building with a sense of huge relief.

The remaining meetings followed a similar path. One analyst wanted the Pilot to connect to his phone *and* the World Wide Web (a fantasy that was, technologically speaking, at least five years away). Another predicted that as soon as Pilot was on the market and successful, Japanese consumer companies like Sony, Sharp, and Seiko would improve on the idea and overtake Palm. Most analysts questioned the Pilot's lack of wireless capability and PCMCIA (expansion card) slot.

Overall, however, the analysts liked what they saw. "There was reasonable skepticism, but 90 percent of the press and analysts walked away saying, 'Wow, I think you've really got something here,' " Colligan remembers. Several analysts said that they'd use a Pilot themselves. One of them, a fan of Palm's handwriting recognition software for the Newton, had even said, "Praise Jesus, it runs Graffiti."

After their exhausting week in analysts' offices, Jeff and Ed returned to California. They entertained their team with anecdotes from their road trip, happily imitating analysts who didn't want to put down the Pilot once they held it in their hands. From the marketing point of view, things were looking encouraging.

Just-in-time manufacturing is a technique that involves buying components immediately before they're required at the factory, keeping the manufacturer's money in hand as long as possible and sparing the manufacturer the costs of storing parts. Donna Dubinsky, ever frugal, hoped to apply this technique to people, hiring new staff members only when their presence was immediately needed. Unfortunately, hiring people always took longer than she expected, which made her new hires not so much just in time as already late.

After a year of avoiding hiring anyone new at all, she finally hired a VP of sales—already late. In late November, a headhunter had contacted Pat McVeigh, a seasoned sales executive in his early 40s with many years' experience at Apple. McVeigh, a large man with huge hands and a low, booming voice, had been taken aback. "I said, 'A handheld? Do you hate me? I am not going with a handheld!' "

McVeigh knew Donna Dubinsky's reputation from his days at Apple; when he heard she was the CEO, he decided to check the company out. "I went there, pretty darn skeptical, because of course I had been involved in the Newton," he says. As Palm had come to predict, what won him over was the Pilot prototype. "Geez, this is very cool," he told the Palm team. "It's simple, but it looks like it actually might solve a problem. Maybe we can make this work."

In the late fall, Donna had had to make an agonizing decision: how many Pilots to manufacture. If Palm produced too many, it would waste money that could have been used for marketing the product; if it produced too few, however, shortages could easily squelch the Pilot's success.

After deliberating with the other executives, she had forecast that Palm might sell 10,000 units the first month, and then 8,000 units the second and third months. Given that it had taken Newton a whole year to sell 80,000 units despite millions of advertising dollars, a forecast of 26,000 units in the first three months seemed quite brazen. She found it much easier to make a prediction for Palm's long-term sales success, which she pegged at $500 million by the year 2000. (In the palmtops-are-dead atmosphere of late 1995, the prediction might have struck some as hopelessly optimistic; as it turned out, the estimate wasn't nearly optimistic enough. By 2000, Palm's sales would reach over $1 billion.)

Meanwhile, even without a sales VP, Dubinsky and Colligan had already made progress on preselling the first batch of 10,000 Pilots. Months earlier, for example, a Toshiba marketing manager had committed to buying them for resale under the Toshiba label.

Palm's new affiliation with USR would also be very helpful. USR's good relationship with the nation's computer stores would make it easier for Palm to get its product onto the shelves.

Even Palm's old connection to Tandy had come through: In exchange for a high discount from Palm, Tandy had promised to place a large order, which it would sell under the Palm label through its Radio Shack stores. "This smells of tonnage," Radio Shack's vice president of merchandising had told Colligan with glee. He, for one, expected to sell a *lot* of Pilots.

All told, Dubinsky believed she had ordering commitments for about two-thirds of the Pilots that would be manufactured in the first month. McVeigh, liking what he heard, accepted the job in late December.

His first orders of business would be securing the actual orders from Tandy and Toshiba, drumming up orders from other sources, and setting up an infrastructure at Palm where orders could be received and correctly processed—and shipped by late February.

Pat McVeigh started his tenure at Palm at the vast Consumer Electronics Show (CES) in Las Vegas, at a meeting with the USR sales execs. Within minutes, he realized that USR's strong relationships with computer stores would be less useful than he had hoped.

U.S. Robotics had invited McVeigh and Colligan to a meeting with their contacts at Best Buy. With over 200 stores across the country, it was at the time the fastest-growing mass merchant in America. The USR execs believed that Best Buy would be an ideal chain to carry the Pilot. McVeigh agreed.

As the introductions were made, however, Pat became aware that the gentleman from Best Buy was its buyer for *modems*. The Pilot, of course, was a very different product. It would be displayed in a different part of each store, and a different buyer would make the decision whether to carry it. U.S. Robotics' name would open doors, and its distribution system would get the Pilot packages to the stores, but when it came to drumming up orders from retailers, McVeigh was on his own. "Although it was definitely important to have USR's financial backing, it became very clear that this wasn't going to be any slam dunk," says McVeigh. "That was a little bit of a shock there."

He left the meeting knowing that he needed to develop a completely new set of contacts among the retailers, one that his new colleagues at USR wouldn't be able to help him with.

After his return from CES, he asked to see Toshiba's purchase agreement. As it turned out, there was no such contract; Toshiba had signed only a letter of intent.

Without a signed purchase contract, the Toshiba deal was all but worthless, so McVeigh decided to visit Toshiba in Southern California himself to finalize the deal. Right away, though, he ran into bad omens. "Week after week, we couldn't get a meeting," he remembers.

Eventually, the meeting was arranged. When Pat arrived at Toshiba's offices in Irvine, however, an embarrassed receptionist informed him that all of the people he was asking to see were at a meeting—away from the company offices. The receptionist called a number of people, looking for someone, anyone, who could meet with McVeigh.

After about an hour, a red-faced marketing staff member came down the stairs and shook McVeigh's hand. "I don't know how to tell you this," the staff member said, "but let me tell you what's going on." The bad news came quickly: Nobody had ever presented the Pilot deal to Toshiba's senior executives.

McVeigh returned to Palm empty-handed. When, later, the issue was finally taken to Toshiba's head of sales, his response was, in effect, "I need this like a hole in my head," McVeigh remembers. "There was no deal. End of story."

Worse, at just about the same time, Tandy called McVeigh to renegotiate its order. Instead of ordering over 6,000 Pilots, Tandy now wanted to buy only 500—but still at the large-quantity discount.

McVeigh said no. "That just isn't good for us," he told Tandy.

With less than eight weeks before the Pilot was scheduled to ship, Pat McVeigh had not a single confirmed customer.

Another leg of Ed Colligan's launch strategy involved unveiling the Pilot at a high-profile trade show. A high-profile event for the product announcement was Palm's best opportunity to generate the interest of the press and the computer industry opinion leaders.

U.S. Robotics favored launching the Pilot at CES, a show that drew hundreds of thousands of visitors, including both consumers and the retailers and industry execs who dominate many tradeshows.

Instead, Ed secured a slot at Demo '96, a small but prestigious conference attended by reporters, VCs, and computer industry executives. Getting selected to be one of the presenters at Demo was a coup. From hundreds of applicants, David Coursey, the industry pundit who organized and hosted the show, selected only about 30 new products for stage time.

The rules at Demo were simple: A company had exactly eight minutes on the stage to demonstrate its new technology. A good demo could make a long-lasting good impression on the industry's most influential. A bad demo could make the product and its presenter a laughingstock.

U.S. Robotics gave Colligan a lot of flack for his decision. Its executives believed strongly that Pilot should be launched at an event that could attract a large audience.

Ed conceded that Demo, with an audience of only 800, was

relatively small. But he pointed out that at CES, Pilot might get lost among the thousands of products on display. At Demo, Palm stood a good chance of standing out.

Coursey, who had made a name for himself as a colorful and often abrasive technology commentator, ran a tight ship. All year long, he auditioned hopeful technology companies for this showcase event. The lucky few were asked to return to Coursey's offices several weeks before the event, so that he could watch the presentation they intended to make. He insisted that most of the eight-minute time slot be filled with live product demonstrations rather than talking from slides, which Coursey forbade. "It's Demo, not Slido," he was fond of saying.

Hawkins and Colligan wrote and rehearsed a demo that covered all of the Pilot's major points in precisely the allotted time. Unfortunately, the Pilot software wasn't yet complete; their worst nightmare, and a distinct possibility, was that the device might crash onstage.

Demo was held at the swank Indian Wells resort in the Southern California desert. A turntable stage ensured that not a minute of time was lost between presentations. From the audience's point of view, Demo felt more like a game show than an event that could launch or crush a new start-up overnight. Clocks facing the stage displayed huge red numbers that counted down to a two-minute warning. When the allotted time was up, the stage rotated, sending the current speakers backstage, whether their spiel was finished or not.

In fact, if David Coursey felt that the presentation wasn't particularly compelling, the stage sometimes rotated *before* the time was up. "He would literally gong you if he didn't like you," says one entrepreneur who had gone through the ordeal. "He'd get up and say 'OK, we've seen enough of this, get out of here.' "

January 28, 1996: showtime.

"Oh God, we were so nervous," remembers Colligan.

Palm's slot was early on the first morning of the three-day event—a prime time slot, because it assured that most attendees were still watching attentively rather than catching up on their phone calls or chatting on the patio.

The Palm duo stood on the hidden side of the rotating stage. Their PC ran the Pilot's desktop software; the Pilot sat on a small platform beneath an overhead video camera called an Elmo, which would project the little palmtop's image onto a huge screen.

Peeking through the curtains that separated the backstage area from the auditorium, Ed saw a room that was packed to the gills. "We'd never been exposed to an audience of that size, of a lot of really influential people in the tech business. You're thinking not only about launching your product, but about the future of your career in the technology business," Colligan laughs.

The stage turned, moving Hawkins, Colligan, and their equipment into view of the audience. The Pilot's coming-out party was about to begin.

Jeff reached into his shirt pocket and dramatically pulled out the palmtop, pointing it with raised arms toward the audience.

"It's called the Pilot," he said. The crowd reacted with a soft "ooh" and a little clap, an unusual reaction for the jaded digerati.

"Let me show you how it works." He put the Pilot down on the Elmo projector. For a second the Pilot appeared on the screen high above the stage, exactly as planned—and then the screen went dark.

The audience's reaction told Hawkins immediately that something was wrong. He looked up and around, and then understood: Nobody in the audience could actually see the Pilot.

Time was ticking down; the presenters stood for a moment on the stage, frozen. An audiovisual technician ran out from the wings and began to inspect the Elmo projector.

"Ed, do you know any good jokes while we're waiting?" Hawkins asked.

"I don't feel very funny right now," Colligan responded. The crowd laughed.

Hawkins turned to plead with David Coursey. "We need more time—stop the clock! This isn't our fault—this is an AV problem."

As his precious minutes evaporated before him, Hawkins pulled himself together. He walked to the edge of the stage. "I am going to *describe* to you what you'd be seeing if that projector was working right now," he said. And that's exactly what he did.

The audience clearly enjoyed Jeff's bravado. Ironically, his verbal description only made the audience crave the live demonstration even more. "It was almost like you teased them," Hawkins recalls. "You're showing them this cute little thing, and they really want to see the rest of it."

A few minutes later, the screen came back on. "Should we give them more time?" asked Coursey of the crowd. The audience cheered in approval, and the host agreed to reset the clock at eight minutes. Hawkins picked up his demo where he had left off five minutes earlier, and put the Pilot through its paces. "See, just like I told you," he pointed out as he pressed the date book button to reveal the schedule screen.

Then he handed the talk over to Colligan to show the desktop software and the true miracle of Pilot—the synchronization feature called HotSync.

"Let's say you want to have lunch with David Coursey," Colligan joked to the audience. "Now you enter your lunch date." Colligan typed "Pizza with David" on the PC, whose image was also projected behind him. "And then you synchronize by just pressing this button on the cradle."

On the two screens behind him, a tiny animated, spinning double arrow appeared, indicating that the Pilot and the desktop PC were now communicating, bringing each other up-to-date—synchronizing their data. The audience broke into applause.

"Now you could do a 'repeating event,' but you wouldn't want to have lunch with David Coursey very often," Colligan went on, grinning.

The audience cheered when Hawkins mentioned the Pilot's $299 price, but Hawkins had even better news at the conclusion of his demo: Demo attendees would be allowed to preorder the Pilot for $149. "We got a huge round of applause," Colligan remembers.

As the audience streamed out of the auditorium during the break, they found a table set up where Rob Haitani, Kate Purmal, and Joe Sipher were on hand to provide close-up, personal demonstrations of the Pilot. Over 400 of the attendees, half the group, took Palm up on its discount offer.

That evening, the Palm team celebrated. U.S. Robotics' Jon Zakin bought several bottles of champagne, which they drank, jubilant, in the cool desert night air.

On the last day of Demo, the attendees cast their votes for the prestigious and comic Demo God award for the best presentation. The winner: Jeff Hawkins, for his grace under pressure. The award was especially gratifying considering the cause of the technical snafu, which came to light shortly after the presentation: Jeff himself had bumped into the power switch on the side of the projector, turning it off.

Back at Palm's Los Altos offices, Pat McVeigh had taken inventory of his situation. Not only did he have no customers for Pilot, Palm wasn't even set up to receive orders even if there had been customers.

So far, a company called Rush Order had manned the company's 800 number, taking orders for Graffiti and PalmConnect. But now McVeigh hoped for a large number of orders, which would be shipped from Salt Lake City to the retailers; as he soon discovered, the only system Palm had to receive these orders was a single fax machine. If a fax came in while the machine was busy or was out of paper early one morning when an East Coast retailer faxed in an order, Palm would never know. It was enough to make a salesperson break out into sweat.

"You always need a right-hand person," McVeigh says. "Of course, I immediately thought of Andy."

For years, Andy Simms had worked for McVeigh at Apple, where his colleagues characterized him as an effective salesman who took success and failure in his job very personally. Andy sweated the details, too, something that Pat knew he needed.

McVeigh mapped out their next steps. First, they would have to come up with a sales strategy that would rely completely on a powerful and unpredictable creature: the retail channel.

Consumer products sales managers usually refer to the stores who sell their products as "channel partners." The goal of both parties is to sell large quantities of the manufacturer's product. If the product sells well, both parties are happy.

But if it does not, the two partners' needs diverge. Manufacturers need their products offered in the stores. Retailers need to make a profit on every product. If a product doesn't sell well enough, retailers remove it from their shelves without much thought of their "partners." Shelf space is precious, and hundreds of other products are waiting to take the open space and provide better profits.

McVeigh and Simms decided to sell Pilot, at least at the outset, through only a handful of national retail chains, which would make it easier to focus their small launch budget on those stores. At this stage, the game was to make the retailers carrying the Pilot feel that it was a successful product.

If the Pilot proved a hit, they would still have enough inventory to fill the retailers' reorders. In that case, they would have no trouble signing up additional stores in a second phase, when Palm had more leverage to negotiate. "In the retail marketplace, good news travels fast," says Simms. "And the idea is: If you don't want to get burned too bad in retail, have them call you, versus you knocking on their door."

If the product didn't sell, on the other hand, then the number of retailers stocking the Pilot didn't really matter, because the game would already be lost. "If you can't make a couple of people successful," figured Simms, "you sure weren't going to be able to make a hundred partners successful."

U.S. Robotics reacted strongly to Palm's sales plans. "We had yelling matches over it," says Michael Seedman, who ran the modem division.

A self-described "street fighter" when it came to sales, Seedman had aided USR's astonishing ascension to dominance by distributing its modems through as many outlets as possible. He didn't like Palm's strategy. "That's the kind of approach you take if you want single-digit market share," he says. "We, on the other hand, wanted a huge hit. And my point was, you have to distribute products where people want to buy them. It's that simple."

Dubinsky and McVeigh argued that the modem business analogy wasn't appropriate. The Internet explosion—an external factor—drove the demand for modems, but only Palm's marketing efforts would drive demand for the Pilot. "There was nothing that happened on the outside that suddenly said 'OK, we are ready to buy handhelds.' It was all *us*. The right marketing, the right PR, the right product," McVeigh says. Besides, even if Pilots were distributed through just a few national chains, a store that carried the Pilot would still be a reasonable drive away for most potential buyers.

For the moment at least, the USR executives let Palm's distribution strategy stand.

McVeigh and Simms's tour of the country's top retailers got off to a rocky start in Eden Prairie, Minnesota, a suburb of Minneapolis. They wanted to get in the door at Best Buy, despite the disappointing meeting McVeigh had had with the chain's modem buyer several weeks earlier. This time, they had an appointment with the buyer of organizers, a man who had seen a lot of products fail miserably in this category. Still, the two Palm salesmen weren't entirely without confidence; they knew from Colligan's stories that even the biggest skeptics usually came around to liking Pilot once they saw the prototype.

It didn't work. The buyer turned them down flat.

"He felt that what customers were waiting for was essentially a subnotebook computer," Simms remembers. The buyer insisted that his customers wanted more features, not less—and that the Pilot's price was too high. "*How* much? Are you crazy?" the buyer said. "Let me show you something." Here, the buyer grabbed a cheap pocket organizer from the shelf. "It's got all these features, and it's $19.95! You guys are dead." The bottom line: Neither he nor Best Buy wanted anything to do with the Pilot.

McVeigh and Simms trudged out of the building, tails between their legs. In the parking lot outside, Andy turned to Pat. "Is this what it's going to be like?"

In fact, the Best Buy buyer's response wasn't unreasonable. First, buyers in his position all over America had gambled on handhelds many times before, and lost. Furthermore, different product categories earn different profit margins. Organizers generally fell in a 40 percent profit margin bracket for retail stores, but Palm couldn't afford to sell it at nearly that high a discount. Therefore, from the buyer's perspective, the Pilot looked like an unprofitable proposition when compared with other pocket organizers (never mind that they couldn't compare with the Pilot in terms of software elegance, features, and PC synchronization).

Buyers of PCs, on the other hand, were used to far lower margins. In fact, next to the 9 to 15 percent profit that stores earned on each sale of a computer, the margin of about 20 percent on the Pilot that Palm could offer (plus 5 percent for marketing programs) was very appealing.

The experience taught them a valuable lesson. "We learned that we didn't want to deal with the organizer buyers," says Simms. "We started immediately after that to position it as a PC accessory."

Their next stop was the Circuit City headquarters in Richmond, Virginia. They indulged in slightly greater optimism this time, in part because Circuit City's CEO, a Flextronics board member, had already heard about Pilot. With any luck, Circuit City, with over 350 electronics stores nationwide, was already favorably disposed toward the new Palm product.

Sure enough, the buyer liked Pat's Pilot demo, especially when McVeigh offered to let Circuit City be the exclusive consumer electronics chain to stock Pilot. The buyer ordered 5,000 Pilots, half of the initial batch.

Now McVeigh and Simms could relax a little. In the dog-eat-dog world of retail, this order gave them a lot more leverage for their next appointments.

With Circuit City on board, they had little difficulty signing up the number one and two computer chains, CompUSA and Computer City. By launch time, they had added three local chains and Ingram Micro, a distributor who could sell Pilots to the numerous small independent computer stores across the United States.

Now there was only one question: Once 10,000 Pilots were in the stores, would anyone buy them?

Soon after the Pilot debut at Demo, the first press reviews appeared. "Last week I had a religious experience with a telephone. This week, I'm having one with a computer. A really tiny computer," wrote columnist Stewart Alsop in *Infoworld,* whom Ed Colligan had briefed on the Pilot weeks ahead of time; Alsop went on to give the product a glowing review.

Colligan's guerrilla marketing strategy relied heavily on reviews; Palm simply didn't have much money for advertising.

He therefore needed to get actual Pilots into journalists' hands, quickly, so that they would continue to publish reviews of the Pilot, in effect providing free publicity.

In these early days before the official product launch, however, the Pilot assembly line at the Flextronics plant in Singapore had yet to begin rolling. The only Pilots in existence had to be hand-built—and they were brutally expensive.

Ed Colligan had ordered 40 of these units from the factory at a cost of several hundred dollars apiece. Each of these so-called design validation test (DVT) units was carefully handed out to an influential analyst or journalist for a few days, whereupon he fervently hoped that it would be returned so that the PR agency could send it to the next journalist in line.

Each time a positive review appeared, Andy Simms faxed it to his retail buyers. Circuit City, among others, responded just as he had hoped: Its buyer upped his order to 10,000 units. At the next company meeting, Andy got up and announced the order to his colleagues.

He had only been at Palm for a month, a newcomer amid the tightly knit group of 28 people who had worked together for over three years. Some of them still looked at him askance, seeing him as a big-company guy experiencing small-company culture shock, a guy who occasionally complained about the start-up's lack of infrastructure.

On this day, however, he could bask in a moment of triumph. "I think that order blew everybody away, because that basically sold out our first build," he says.

Still, in the back of his mind, he knew that Circuit City's order didn't guarantee the success of Pilot. The retail chain orders mattered only if consumers then went into those stores and bought that inventory. The real measure of success wouldn't be initial orders; it would be reorders. Palm wouldn't know whether there would be any until a few weeks after the Pilot started shipping—a day that was much more distant than anyone at Palm expected.

ELEVEN

THE ELEVENTH HOUR

In early February 1995, Jeff Hawkins stood up at one of Palm's all-company meetings to deliver a warning. He'd launched hardware products many times, he told his staff, and major problems often emerged at the eleventh hour, just as the product was nearing production. There might be problems in the manufacturing, the software, or the hardware. He couldn't predict what exactly was in store, but Palm should be braced for it.

It was fortunate that he made the speech when he did. Not long thereafter, whatever could go wrong with the first manufactured Pilot units—did.

The Flextronics factory in Singapore had started to build Pilots in early February, pressing ahead to build 10,000 units by the end of the month. Flextronics workers tested every single Pilot organizer at the end of the production line, then packaged 150 at a time into special boxes that were designed to protect their precious cargo during the ride across the Pacific to Salt Lake City. There, the Megahertz factory workers took over, testing the units once more and then packaging them with the cradle, software diskettes, and manuals into individual retail boxes.

Jeff Hawkins, Rob Haitani, testing manager Shawn Ford, and a few of the engineers were among the first to receive these early, prerelease units. They used the early Pilots incessantly, testing them for possible flaws.

One day, while changing the batteries in his test Pilot, engineer Chris Raff noticed that the springs that held the batteries seemed to be bent and shortened, so that the batteries were no longer being held tightly. The danger was that if the springs lost contact with the batteries altogether, the Pilot's memory would be erased, and all of its owner's appointments, addresses, and other information would vanish.

Raff walked over to Rob Haitani's cubicle and showed him what he'd found. They determined that when the Pilot was dropped or bumped against a surface, the weight of the batteries compressed the springs. However, the springs didn't then return to their original shapes.

They showed Hawkins what they'd found. "Look," Rob said. He took Jeff's Pilot in hand, banged it against the desk, held the unit in front of Jeff's face, and then shook it gently. Right away, they all could hear a slight rattling sound from the loose batteries—a tiny death rattle.

"It sent chills down my spine," Haitani says. "You try to remain calm, but it was obvious this was a catastrophic problem. This wasn't some tiny crack in the plastics, some minor nuisance that would develop over time. This was a showstopper."

Clearly, Palm couldn't ship an organizer that gave itself a frontal lobotomy every time it was bumped or dropped. The problem would have to be fixed, and fast. Bill MacKenzie and Malcolm Smith from Palo Alto Design Group (PADG), the company that designed the Palm's case, spent days searching for replacement springs that didn't contract and that could be retrofitted into the units that had already been built.

When he finally found a supplier, Bill MacKenzie brought a shoebox full of the new springs to the Palm offices for testing. "Look at these," he said, as he passed the shoebox around. "These little guys are holding up the future of the company."

The springs cost no more than a few cents each, but they cost Palm several weeks. Under the circumstances, there was no way Palm could meet its original shipping date, February 28. The schedule was reset: The Pilot's first shipments would leave the factory in mid-March.

Unfortunately, the fun had only just begun. In late February, the Megahertz factory managers reported a far more troubling occurrence: Every once in a while, a Pilot that had been certified in Singapore to be in good working order arrived in Utah dead as a doornail. Pressing the organizer's On button did nothing at all.

There was no time to lose. Testing manager Shawn Ford flew to Singapore. After 19 hours in the air, Ford took a cab directly from the airport to the Flextronics factory to pluck 100 Pilots from the assembly line. For the next four days, he sat at the factory, switching them on methodically in hopes of figuring out the cause of the sudden-death syndrome.

Sure enough, each day, a small number of units simply wouldn't wake up, despite having worked the day before.

The first crucial step in fixing any bug is to reproduce it so that the engineers can study it—but this bug wasn't easily reproducible. It kicked in on an unpredictable schedule.

Ron Marianetti solved the problem by writing a software program that did nothing but switch on the Pilot. Working with electrical engineer Karl Townsend, he hooked the Pilot to a function generator, a machine that could generate the necessary signal to start the Pilot automatically a thousand times per second. "At that rate, we could make the bug show up within a few minutes," Marianetti says.

Once the engineers could isolate the glitch, they were able to track down the problem: a bug in the Motorola Dragonball microprocessor chip itself.

This mess was worse than they'd thought. They could always fix a bug in their software, but only Motorola could fix a bug in the Pilot's chip. Worse, because Motorola would actually have to fabricate new chips, the fix could take months.

Palm simply didn't have the time. Jeff and Ed had announced at Demo that the Pilot would be shipping in late February, and it was now early March.

Once again, Ron Marianetti came through with a solution.

Over the course of several days, he wrote a *patch*—a software Band-Aid—that, when installed in the faulty Pilots, overcame the effects of the Dragonball bug.

Palm would have to install the software patch in the RAM (memory) on the 10,000 palmtops that had already been manufactured. Unfortunately, if one of these Pilots ever lost its battery power, the RAM would get wiped clean, taking down both its owner's data and the software patch, which would make the Pilot vulnerable once again to the permanent-sleep problem. Still, the software-patch approach was the only one that would work in the time Palm had left.

One morning, while Marianetti was fine-tuning the patch, Shawn Ford came to his office, puzzled. "A giant furry hamster just ran across the screen," he reported.

Ron laughed. Ford had found the secret Taxi Easter egg that Marianetti had planted in the Pilot's software months before. However, the little cartoon taxi didn't just drive across the screen infrequently, as Marianetti had intended. In fact, once it showed up for the first time, it scurried across the screen *repeatedly* at random intervals. By the end of the day, it wasn't funny—it was annoying. Ron Marianetti, master programmer, had produced a software bug of his own.

Soon after, the taxi made an embarrassing appearance right in the middle of a demonstration by Jeff Hawkins himself. "It showed up in front of all these people, and Jeff had no idea what it was. Looking back now, I should at least have made it show up during testing, so people weren't too shocked." Marianetti felt terrible. "I couldn't sleep a couple of nights."

Hawkins and Haitani talked to Marianetti. Their biggest concern was that the taxi wasn't the kind of hidden Easter egg that engineers and Pilot fans might delight in calling up, but that it buzzed across the screen unbidden. Businesspeople would surely find the uninvited apparition startling.

There was only one solution: Marianetti would have to write a second software patch, one that made the Taxi show up at the infrequent, irregular intervals he had originally intended—and only when called up by the Pilot's owner.

Marianetti was lucky this time; he could roll his fixes for the wake-up bug and the Easter egg into the same software patch. He could only imagine how he would have felt if Palm had had to shoulder the cost and delay of putting in a software patch just to fix his silly Easter egg.

The time that it took to implement these eleventh-hour fixes threw Palm into crisis mode. The marketing and sales teams, in particular, were worried that the entire launch would self-destruct.

Rush Order, the fulfillment house whose agents answered Palm's 800 number, had begun taking orders for Pilot starting in mid-February. In addition to the 400 orders from the Demo conference attendees, many of the industry movers and shakers had told their friends about the product, and the advance press reviews had also created demand.

The Demo attendees expected to get their Pilots by the end of February; starting on about March 1, they began to call Palm's 800 number with a single angry question: "Where is my Pilot? You *promised* it to me by late February."

When the battery springs were the Pilot's only problem, Rob Haitani and Bill MacKenzie had expected that the first thousand packages would be ready to ship in mid-March.

"I'm afraid there's been a slight delay, sir," the telemarketer would say. "We will be sending your Pilot on March 15."

"But that's *two* weeks late! Jeff Hawkins said, 'end of February!' "

During the next two weeks, Rush Order took hundreds of new orders. The phone reps told customers that their Pilots would be shipped in mid-March. When the middle of March rolled around, and their orders still didn't show up—now because of the wake-up bug—those early customers called Palm's 800 number again.

"I'm very sorry, sir, but there's been another delay," the telemarketer would have to admit. "We expect to have inventory in two weeks, and we'll send you your order as soon as we can. Your Pilot will be in your hands the first week of April."

"But that's what you said *the last time* I called!" the enraged callers replied. "Why should I believe a word you say? Let me talk to your supervisor!"

For Palm, offending these people was suicidal. Ed had created the low-cost Pilot offer for Demo attendees precisely because they were so influential. If they liked their Pilots, they would spread the word about its merits. Instead, the ever-receding shipping date threatened to have the opposite effect.

In late March, Colligan's PR efforts started to pay off—at exactly the wrong time.

On March 25, *Business Week*'s Steve Wildstrom dedicated a full-page review to the Pilot, bearing the headline, "The Little Dynamo." Only a few days later, on March 28, influential *Wall Street Journal* technology columnist Walt Mossberg wrote: "I can say it is by far the best little computer I have ever seen and the only one I can imagine incorporating into my daily life."

The glowing reviews were a dream come true and a disaster rolled into one. Although Ed read the reviews aloud at the weekly company meeting, fighting to project his voice above the applause and hooting, the positive press also meant that hundreds of new customers—now 1,500 of them—would be subjected to unfilled and delayed orders.

Just as it seemed the situation couldn't get any worse, a phone call from Salt Lake City brought even more bad news. Pilot organizers had begun showing up dead on arrival in Utah *again*, even though they had been working fine when they left the plant in Singapore. And it wasn't just a few in each shipment this time—it was many.

The transoceanic phone lines were buzzing. The manufacturing experts in Singapore and Salt Lake City investigated every angle they could think of. Did the units get damaged in transit? Had Palm received defective components? Was the humidity in Singapore causing the failures? Had the software patch been installed incorrectly?

Days passed, yet nobody could find the cause of the failures.

Finally, Dubinsky ordered the production line shut down. There was no point in continuing the production until the problem was identified and fixed.

She called an emergency meeting of everyone even remotely connected to the Pilot, including electrical engineer Karl Townsend; Ron Marianetti for the OS; representatives from manufacturing; PADG designers; and, of course, Jeff Hawkins, Rob Haitani, and Shawn Ford. The crisis team crammed into the small conference room next to Donna's office.

"We are going to sit here with every possible theory until we crack this problem," Donna announced. "What is every single change we've made to the product from the time it was working to the time it stopped working?"

The cross-functional group combed through every detail of the production process, probing every step involved in putting a Pilot together.

Finally, Rob Haitani remembered a tiny change that had been recently made in the production process: a small red sticker, warning Pilot owners not to dawdle when replacing the batteries, was now being affixed to the inside of the battery door.

The label had not gone through any testing program; how complicated could a sticker be? But once the group scrutinized a few of the dead units, it became clear that the humble sticker had set off an elaborate chain of mechanical, electrical, and software failures.

It went like this. The sticker added a millimeter of thickness to the battery door. When the door was slid into place now, the sticker pushed the batteries against the springs, which made them lose touch with the contacts on the opposite end. After a few minutes, the unit lost power, erasing both its data and Marianetti's software patch. In the most insidious cases, some batteries later reestablished contact, making the Pilot appear OK to the assembly-line testers. But having lost the software patch, the wake-up bug could then kick in at any time.

The solution was as simple as using a different paper thickness for the label, but the damage had been done. Thanks to a simple sticker, the Pilot's shipping date had to be reset yet again.

Finally, on April 9, a few hundred Pilot packages were ready to ship to customers. What Palm needed, of course, was several *thousand* finished packages, which could be sent to the direct customers as well as the retail stores that Simms and McVeigh had worked so hard to bring on board. Instead, the company could ship out only what the factory could produce: a few hundred Pilot packages a day.

The allocation game began. Each morning, Chuck Corbett, Palm's operations manager, got together with Andy Simms in a conference room.

"They finished 387 units last night," Chuck would say to begin the meeting. "Where do you want them to go?" It was a hand-to-mouth existence; if Ed Colligan had requested 30 for sending to journalists, for example, he would get 10 today, 10 next week, and then 5, and then 5.

A full day's build often was barely sufficient for just *one* of Palm's retail partners. Simms had no option but to ship the entire day's yield to whichever retailer had an advertisement running. After the meeting, he'd have to call the buyers of the other stores, deliver the bad news, and get raked over the coals. "Whatever the voice mail from Megahertz said could make or break his day," Corbett remembers.

Slowly, the factories in Singapore and Salt Lake City ironed the kinks out of their systems, increasing their yield of finished Pilot packages. The little handhelds were pieced together with replacement springs and fragile software patches, but they worked, and they were finally reaching the customers who had waited so long. As April 1996 drew to a close, direct customers received the Pilots that they had ordered up to four months earlier—and an apology letter signed by Dubinsky.

It had been nearly five years since Jeff Hawkins first captured the imagination of two venture capitalists and a handful of employees with his ideas for a small, handheld computer and the millions of consumers who would buy it.

Now, at last, the Pilot would put Jeff's predictions to the test.

TWELVE

INSIDE THE TORNADO

O nce they finally reached the store shelves, the first few thousand Pilots practically flew off the shelves. Rave reviews poured in. "The Pilot 1000 is an outstanding product: It's fast, easy to use, and inexpensive," *PC Computing* magazine told its readers. "If you're searching for the ultimate palm-size organizer, look no further." At each company meeting, Donna Dubinsky read still more glowing letters and e-mails from customers.

At first, the Palm team didn't dare to think that the Pilot was a surefire hit. After all, Apple enthusiasts had snapped up the first batch of Newton within days, too—and then Newton's sales had petered out to a mere trickle. What marketers called *sell-in* (how many the stores ordered) didn't count. Only sustained *sell-through* (i.e., purchases from those stores by living, breathing customers) would indicate a true measure of Pilot's acceptance.

Chuck Corbett was the first to suspect that the Pilot was selling through. Palm still didn't have the kind of fail-safe ordering process that a "real" company would have; instead, orders from retail stores came in by fax, which Corbett typed into a temporary order entry program. After each day of operations work, he sat down at 6:00 P.M. and spent hours typing in the orders.

"We were a no-name company; we had no clout," Corbett

remembers. "CompUSA wasn't going to order twenty per store, they were going to order *two* per store." After a few weeks of entering orders, he was intimately familiar with each chain's ordering pattern, and that pattern indicated a small-scale success. "Both the frequency and the volume of orders increased. That was telling me that demand was going up."

He told Donna of his hopeful suspicions, and lobbied her to increase the forecast—to ask Megahertz to build more Pilots than the scheduled 10,000 units each month.

Dubinsky inevitably replied: "These are the early adopters. I want to wait and see sell-through in Tuscaloosa, Alabama." In the weekly forecast meetings, she took to prefacing her final decisions with the clause, "despite what Chuck says."

The failures of previous handheld computers gave her an extra measure of caution. Until Palm had sold at least 40,000 Pilots without a slowdown, nothing was certain. In addition, summer was coming, when retail sales are typically at their lowest. So Donna stuck to the plan: to build 10,000 the first month, 20,000 the next, and then 10,000 per month thereafter.

In May, however, Pilots continued to sell briskly. In fact, stores began to sell out, creating a shortage that the early Pilot fans eagerly reported on Internet bulletin boards. Customers, the press, and even Palm's retailers interpreted the shortage as an indication that the Pilot was a runaway success, hardly suspecting that the shortages simply meant that the manufacturing plants were not producing very many Pilots.

In June, the Pilot was featured on *Good Morning America;* shortly thereafter, four employees demonstrated the device in the U.S. Robotics (USR) exhibition booth at PC Expo in New York. Caitlin Spaan, Palm's new channel marketing manager, was among them. "We were always swamped," she remembers. "You couldn't take a break. I was losing my voice, because you talk and talk and talk."

On the plane ride home, in fact, the man sitting next to Spaan saw Caitlin's USR shirt, and asked her if she knew anything about the Pilot. Caitlin pulled out her Pilot and launched into her demo. "There are four main applications. . . ."

The USR executives in Skokie were well aware of the Pilot buzz, which only intensified the simmering battle over Palm's limited chain-store distribution strategy.

Sales VP Pat McVeigh was more convinced than ever that his strategy was on target. "If we had authorized more retailers, that would have meant that the average location was selling one or two a month," McVeigh explains. "If you call up any given retailer and say, 'Hey, how's the Pilot doing?' he'll say, 'Yeah, it's okay.' It's like the movie *The African Queen:* The river flowed swiftly, but at the end it came to a wide swamp, where you could hardly detect that the water was flowing through. Humphrey Bogart was pulling the boat through the leeches. If you put too many retailers on, that's the swamp." McVeigh had no wish to have to pull the Pilot boat through the retail equivalent of leeches. "We said, 'Let's make this a narrow gorge,' and the retailers said, 'Oh man, this product is *hot!*' If we had put 20 times the number of retailers on, they would never have said that."

But the USR executives in Illinois weren't buying Palm's argument. At each monthly meeting in Skokie, they pressured Dubinsky to expand distribution; each month, she returned to Palm, worn out from having to defend Palm's strategy yet again. In fact, she was starting to have doubts about her long-term ability to work with U.S. Robotics. The company's confrontational decision-making style, beloved by the tightly knit team of USR executives in Skokie, exhausted and upset her.

Sales director Andy Simms also found his patience wearing thin. He, too, considered quitting his job. "Look, either I am right or they are right," he told McVeigh, "but I can't keep having the same conversation every week."

Hoping to change his mind, Pat and Jim Obot, Palm's recently hired VP of operations, took Andy to the nearby El Territo restaurant and bar, so that he could take a deep breath and rethink his decision. They also assured him that Donna supported his distribution decision 100 percent, and was willing to continue to fight USR on the issue.

"And that's what mattered," Simms says now. He decided to stay.

In July, Pilot sales dropped by about 10 percent; in August, sales slowed even more. Retailers now not only had Pilots reliably in stock, but inventories were rising.

Palm held its breath, not knowing whether it was witnessing a standard summer sales slowdown that would end in September, or whether all the early adopters had now bought all the Pilots they were going to buy, leaving Pilot sales to peter out, the way they had for the Newton. "To be honest," says Pat McVeigh, "you can sell 30,000 of anything. We had hit that group of people. The real question was if the word of mouth was going to start kicking in."

Great press coverage, however, continued. "The Pilot is terrific," the columnist of *Network World* had gushed in July. *Boot* magazine declared in August, "Having lived with the tiny powerhouse for a week, my feelings definitely go above and beyond lust. This is love." The Pilot was even mentioned in *Rolling Stone* magazine in August: "You'll attract plenty of envious 'Hey, what's that?' attention from your friends."

With contradictory evidence before her—stellar reviews, flat sales—Donna had to make two agonizing decisions: How many components Palm should buy, and how many Pilots it should manufacture. With the Christmas season approaching, these were crucial decisions.

Not surprisingly, the U.S. Robotics executives had a strong opinion. Unfazed by the failures of other handheld computers and the summer slowdown, they expected the Pilot to be a fast success. "We were extremely bullish about the concept," says Chief Operating Officer John McCartney, who was now Dubinsky's boss. "Probably more bullish than Donna and Jeff."

Over dinner in a restaurant in Skokie a few months earlier, Jon Zakin had at once delighted and startled Donna with a question. "How are we going to sell a million of these?" he had said. She had laughed off the suggestion. "At that point, that estimate was outrageous," Dubinsky says, "but he was obviously thinking big, and that was really refreshing."

Neither Andy Simms nor Dubinsky felt sure that consumer demand for the Pilot would increase in the fall, but the big Christmas season was approaching, and decisions had to be made. "We sort of rolled the dice and said, 'This is either going to sell at Christmas, or it's not. So let's go for it,' " Simms says.

Moving into phase 2 of his distribution plan, he signed up three office-supply superstores (Office Depot, Office Max, and

Staples), increasing the number of stores carrying Pilots from 2,000 to 5,000 by October. With more than double the retail locations, Palm would have to build a lot more Pilots just to stock the extra stores.

Based on the expanded distribution, Dubinsky set the build forecast high—but still not high enough for USR. At a meeting with John McCartney and Rick Edson, the head of USR's manufacturing, Edson proposed to build tens of thousands of Pilots more than Dubinsky wanted to manufacture. Edson forecast much higher Christmas sales than Dubinsky and her team were forecasting. "No product can take off that fast," Dubinsky countered.

She pointed out that Palm was already working on an enhanced version of the Pilot (eventually called the PalmPilot) for release in February 1997. If Palm built many more Pilots than it could sell during the Christmas 1996 season, the company would be stuck with tens of thousands of obsolete machines when the new model arrived, and would have to swallow the loss.

To Dubinsky's dismay, however, COO McCartney sided with Edson. The USR executives essentially ordered Palm to ramp up factory production of the Pilot.

"That was one of those moments when I said to myself, 'How can I stay?'" remembers Dubinsky. "If my feelings as general manager of this business are 'X' and I get overridden, then I clearly don't have responsibility for this business." (In the end, her instincts proved correct. Despite a stellar 1996 Christmas season, Palm had manufactured far too many Pilots. In the spring, Palm had to write off thousands of unsold handhelds.)

Now that the Pilot was shipping, hiring lots of talented new employees quickly became crucial—yet it was nearly impossible. U.S. Robotics applied its Midwestern pay scale to Palm, but salaries in Silicon Valley were significantly higher than in Chicago. The pay-scale problem was compounded by Dubinsky's continued frugality, and the Palm managers were reticent about paying new employees more than their Palm old-timer peers. The upshot was that the best offer Palm could make to a job candidate was often far lower than what other firms were offering.

While most of Palm's managers struggled to add new staff, the sales department had managed to hire four sales managers practically overnight, thanks in large part to the failing fortunes of Apple Computer, whose demoralized employees were eager to jump ship. "I had the luxury of cherry-picking Apple at a weak moment," Simms says. He hired people he knew well. "I knew they were great people first, with wonderful integrity, and they were good salespeople."

Andy Simms's emphasis on hiring good people echoed a statement that Ed Colligan was fond of making: "Avoid the bozo explosion." Ed had experienced the rapid growth of a small company many years earlier at Radius, and had observed that in that growth-spurt phase of any company, one hiring mistake led to many more. "If you hire one bozo, he'll soon turn around and hire people just like him," he explained to his staff.

Clearly, for those who took jobs at Palm during this period, money wasn't the primary attraction. More often than not, it was Palm's unexpected corporate culture—an open, idealistic, and genuinely fun work atmosphere—that appealed to them.

"My interview with Ed was just hilarious," says Caitlin Spaan, who joined Palm in late May. "He acted like I was a shoo-in, but it was clear that he was just very, very friendly. Once I was at ease, then he started to ask the harder questions. I was getting the feeling that this was a pleasant place."

Carolyn Malestic, an American who worked as a product manager in USR's French office, had a similar experience. Even though she had no intentions of moving back to the United States, she had sent her résumé to Palm, who was in desperate need of a multilingual product manager for the French and German versions of the Pilot. "I was looking for a free weekend in San Francisco," Malestic admits.

The Pilot bug had already bitten her; she used hers daily. Now, as she sat in Palm's tiny conference room, she found herself growing nearly as fond of the people who had created the Pilot.

When she emerged from Palm's offices in the late afternoon, after hours of meetings that seemed more like a spirited, witty conversation than a business interview, she turned to her brother, who was waiting in the parking lot. "I've got a big problem," she told him. "I really like those people."

In the end, Palm's idiosyncratic culture indeed proved irresistible. Malestic accepted Rob Haitani's job offer and moved to California.

Like all new employees, Caitlin Spaan received a Pilot on her first day at Palm. Bill Woodruff, her fiancé, picked her up at the end of the day. "For some reason, I was two hours late," he remembers. "Under normal circumstances, this would have been about the biggest mistake I'd ever made. So I arrived, ready to answer some serious questions, like 'Where have *you* been the last two hours?' But Caitlin was sitting on the railing out in front of the building. She had this Pilot box open, she was playing around with this thing, and she was in a perfectly happy mood. And she said, 'You know, this thing is really neat.' "

By the end of May, less than two months after Pilot had started shipping, Palm had somehow grown to over 40 happy employees—but that wasn't nearly enough.

For her part, Kate Purmal soon encountered a people shortage of crisis proportions. It was her responsibility to enlist independent programmers to write add-on software for the Palm platform.

Before the Pilot had shipped, large, established software companies had been uninterested in devoting resources to writing Pilot conduits. As Palm sold its first 10,000, then 20,000 Pilots, however, software companies began fielding hundreds of calls from customers seeking software links to their favorite desktop programs. The sudden customer interest worked wonders. Within months, both Lotus and Symantec put engineers to work on creating links between Pilot and their software.

In the meantime, Purmal counted on the hundreds of hobbyist programmers and the motley crew of small-time software companies who were struggling to make a living in the meager handheld market. ("If you give me a big enough user base, I'll crawl on my stomach through broken glass to develop software for you," one desperate programmer had told Chris Raff before the Pilot launch.)

Just as Purmal had hoped, these smaller operators descended on Palm like fans at a rock concert as soon as Raff completed the software development kits (SDKs) in mid-June. In principle, the programming community's enthusiastic response was good news. In practice, Kate and Chris soon drowned in their workload fielding the programmers' questions.

Purmal found herself answering hundreds of e-mail messages and phone calls each week from prospective software developers from around the world, who wanted to know how big the Pilot's market was and how hard it was to develop software for the Palm OS. One developer wanted to discuss his plans for an e-mail application. Others wanted to write financial calculators, music synthesizers, or graphics programs that turned the Pilot's touch screen into a living sketch pad. One gentleman called to express his intention to write a program for tracking bull semen for a bovine sperm bank.

Two days after Palm shipped its SDK, a Pilot version of the arcade game Space Invaders was posted on the Internet. The Palm engineers marveled. How could a developer possibly have created this program in two days? It seemed impossible.

It turned out that the game's programmer hadn't used the Pilot SDK from Palm at all. Instead, he had used rudimentary PC-based development tools that his hacker friend Darrin Massena had created.

Massena had simply grown impatient waiting for Palm to complete its development kit. He took it upon himself to figure out how the Pilot applications were structured, and built the first available development tools. Within a few months, several other hackers had posted development tools. "The guys who were writing third-party tools amazed me," says Purmal. "They were building these tools as shareware, for fun. That's when the explosion started."

Shareware games for the Pilot seemed to multiply almost overnight, with commercial applications not far behind. By August, Purmal, Raff, and their two summer interns were in deep trouble. To field the technical and administrative questions of such an army of programmers, they would need far more help.

However, developer support positions are notoriously hard to fill. After all, people who know enough about programming to qualify for a developer support job could just as well be software engineers themselves, and would probably be happier writing their own software than helping others. It would take Purmal until October to find the next employee for her department.

One of the biggest differences of opinion between the Palm and U.S. Robotics executives concerned how much profit USR should make from each Pilot. Hoping to turn Palm, still an unprofitable division, into a money-making operation, John McCartney favored higher product prices and reduced spending.

Donna Dubinsky and Ed Colligan took the opposite tack. A lower price meant more Pilot users, a greater market share, and therefore more software developers writing Pilot applications. Dubinsky didn't intend for Palm to remain a low-margin, struggling company forever; her master plan was to produce a family of Pilot products at various prices once the Pilot had established itself, resulting in a very profitable business.

Part of the problem, no doubt, was that USR's core modem business was slowing; the general managers of its various divisions reported faltering results. "Then I would get up, and I'd show great results, month after month, really good news," says Dubinsky. "And they would just beat me up mercilessly. I felt like I got nothing but criticism every time I went out there. Every time on the airplane, on the way back, I was quitting. I was writing my resignation letter."

After a few such trips, she made a promise to herself that she wouldn't quit within 48 hours of a Skokie staff meeting. "Because every time I was back for 24 hours, I'd be fine. I was back in our environment, at Palm, with people I liked and wanted to work with."

Though USR yielded on many of the biggest issues—"Donna got most of what she wanted because we really did want to build the business," Jon Zakin says—she couldn't help feeling like a battered bulwark that kept Palm from getting derailed.

The employees were usually oblivious to the stress on Dubinsky, but one day, in late summer, Donna Gafford, Palm's office manager and Dubinsky's assistant from her Claris days, noticed that Donna slammed down the phone after a conference call with the manufacturing staff in Salt Lake City. Gafford had been watching through the glass wall that separated her cubicle from her boss's office, so that she could give Donna an important message as soon as the conference call was over: The nanny who took care of Dubinsky's five-year-old daughter during the day had to return to Russia on short notice.

Donna broke into tears. "She just fell apart. It was very human; she needed to let go," says Gafford. "She needed to be told, 'Don't worry, it'll be okay.' " Gafford pushed aside her paperwork, hit the phones, and managed to find a temporary replacement for the nanny, so that Dubinsky could finish the day focusing on her job.

By the fall of 1996, Pat McVeigh had hired a few sales managers to sell Pilots to the enterprise market—that is, to corporate buyers who could buy thousands of Pilots at a time for distribution to their employees. However, these sales managers couldn't just sell Pilots in a vacuum. They needed marketing programs to first make the corporate buyers receptive.

One of McVeigh's friends was well connected with The Gartner Group, a leading technology research and consulting firm that advised corporate clients. Better yet, two of Gartner's senior execs were already Pilot fans. Pat persuaded Gartner to let Palm somehow participate at Gartner's symposium in October—a conference attended by 5,000 senior information technology (IT) executives who hoped to learn about the latest technologies for their businesses.

For Palm, this was a chance to get the IT executives to *use* a Pilot. A very work-intensive idea emerged: Palm would enter the entire conference schedule—five packed days of concurrent sessions—and other useful information into Pilots, and let the attendees use the organizers during the conference.

Pulling off this program proved a monumental task. How, for example, could Palm's marketing staff ensure that these thousands of Pilots would be returned at the end of the conference? How would they keep the Pilots that weren't used during the conference from "wandering off," as Palm's worried operations manager put it?

The planning took months. In the end, Palm rented a large ballroom that could be locked securely each night and staffed each day, next to the conference's check-in. There, Pilot boxes were stacked along one wall, in rows 50 long and 15 boxes high. As the conference attendees entered the conference hall, each was handed a Pilot in exchange for a credit card number. At the end of the conference, each executive could either return the Pilot or keep it at 50 percent off; Palm would charge his or her credit card.

The conference was a huge success. 2,500 Pilots wound up in the hands of executives in America's largest corporations, to be seen and admired by everyone else in the company. For years to come, information systems execs would tell Palm that the Gartner event had introduced the Pilot into large corporations.

In the meantime, Ed Colligan had taken the idea of getting executives hooked on the Pilot to a new level. He had struck a deal with the organizers of Agenda, which, like Demo, is a fancy, invitation-only gathering of the who's-who of the high-tech industry. Agenda '97 was to take place in late October, only two weeks after the Gartner symposium. Larry Ellison, the CEO of Oracle, was scheduled to speak. So was Bill Gates of Microsoft.

Instead of just lending Pilots loaded with conference information to the attendees, Ed wanted to stress the Pilot's simplicity—and make it fun. He cooked up a theme: "Moms love Pilot."

The scheme would work like this: The mothers of Ed, Jeff, and Donna would attend the event at Scottsdale's posh Phoenician resort. Armed with demonstration Pilots, their task was to persuade high-tech executives to try out Pilots on the spot. In fact, it was set up as a competition. Each mother carried a stack of cards that said: "Mom Colligan ____, Dubinsky ____, Hawkins ____ (check one) made me a deal"; when one of the moms had convinced an Agenda attendee to give the Pilot a try, the executive was to check off the appropriate box. After the conference, Palm would tally the forms and declare a winner mom. (The results: Ed Colligan's gentle, soft-spoken mother fell behind the two other, more battle-ready moms. But in the spirit of good morale, Palm's Caitlin Spaan cheated, declaring the competition a three-way tie.)

The Agenda attendees were much amused by the three

ladies' sales tactics. And no wonder: even the wealthiest, most high-powered, high-tech executive has a mom.

Letting influential people try and buy a Pilot proved to be a most effective marketing tool. Years before Internet marketers coined the term *viral marketing*, the Pilot proved the ultimate viral product: At business meetings, on the golf course, or in a thousand similar situations, a Pilot owner would proudly show off his new gadget's uses, thereby winning over new enthusiasts. (In 1999, a *New Yorker* cartoon lampooned PalmPilot owners' propensity to rhapsodize about their toy at every opportunity. In it, a prostitute leans into the open window of a car and says to its driver: "For an extra fifty bucks, I'll let you show me your PalmPilot.")

By October 1996, Palm had long since outgrown the two rooms it occupied at 4410 El Camino Real in Los Altos. When another building tenant, a rental-property pamphlet publisher, went out of business—a victim of the booming Silicon Valley economy, which reduced the number of available apartment spaces down to almost nothing—Dubinsky was able to add first one, then another room adjacent to Palm's headquarters as the number of employees swelled to 35, 40, then 50.

By now, with 57 employees occupying the four scrappy rooms, Palm was bursting at the seams. Groups of three and more employees crowded in bullpens (extra long cubicles where the employees sat shoulder to shoulder), and managers doubled up with their new employees in their own cubes. It was high time to move.

U.S. Robotics leased a two-story building in nearby Mountain View for Palm. Even though parts of the building were still under construction, Palm moved into the two finished areas it could find, one on each floor, in October.

Those employees assigned to work on the ground floor of the new building were aghast when they arrived at their new office space. U.S. Robotics had installed six-by-eight-foot cubicles throughout the first floor—a substandard allotment in Silicon Valley, where eight-foot-square cubicles were the norm. Some of the programmers argued, in fact, that they would need more space just to accommodate the double computer systems they kept on their desks.

By comparison, the cubicles on the second floor, at the standard eight-by-eight size, seemed spacious. Enclosed offices lined the walls for Palm's directors and VPs—another shocking departure from the Silicon Valley norm, in which even vice presidents work in open cubicles (though usually larger ones).

The cubicle-size difference of 16 square feet might not seem justification for mutiny, but in the red-hot Silicon Valley job market, where companies dangled before their staffs such perks as Friday afternoon beer busts, on-site gyms, and trendy office designs, it was a distinct problem. When it came to hiring and retaining employees, Palm was already at a financial disadvantage; the last thing Dubinsky needed was inferior cubicles.

Doug Haslam, in charge of Palm's one-person human resources department, immediately placed a call to USR's headquarters.

"In the Valley, people place a high value on these things," he tried to explain to the USR facilities staff. "The workforce looks at them and says, 'I want an informal environment, I want to come and go as I please. The size of my cube and my ability to make it individual is important to me.' It's not just that 'We're from California, we're a little different.' There's a real cultural difference between how you operate and how we operate."

When the USR facilities managers were unwilling to change Palm's cube size, the argument escalated to the USR executives. To them, the issue seemed ridiculous.

"Our HR person told me there was a battle about the size of the cubes," Jon Zakin remembers. "I thought it was a joke. But she said 'No, this is a big battle. It's a fight for corporate identity.' It was a funny conversation because at USR, we were so much into *not* thinking this was important. USR literally grew up in a warehouse; we were a true garage start-up. Casey and the original partners sold magazine subscriptions to finance the business initially, and they started out above a dance studio and above a pizza parlor. We used to joke that while everyone else was squandering money on heat and air conditioning, we were kicking the hell out of the marketplace."

The six-by-eight cubicles stayed.

Although USR's idea of the standard employee cubicle was smaller than usual, its concept of an executive office was much too lavish by the egalitarian Silicon Valley standards. U.S. Robotics' remodeling had included moving a wall to enlarge Dubinsky's office space, making the conference room next door smaller.

"We need the conference room space," Dubinsky protested. "I don't need a bigger office. I can't believe you did that!" From her perspective, things only got worse when she saw the regal wood furniture that USR provided. "It was gorgeous, but it wasn't me, and it wasn't Silicon Valley."

Once again, she got on the phone to Illinois. "This reflects badly on me," she said. "It makes me look like I want these trappings of title, which I don't want. You can't do this here—this is not the standard in Silicon Valley." But it was too late for any changes. Dubinsky would have to learn to live with her luxurious office. As a reminder of Palm's less splendid past, she hung the Market Meter on the wall next to her desk.

The marketing staff had also installed a link to Palm's earlier days: the basketball hoop that Ed Colligan had brought with him three years earlier. It now stood in a wide-open space among the upstairs marketing cubicles, ready for the next impromptu game.

The Pilot's first critical Christmas season, when sales of consumer goods can go through the roof, was fast approaching. Jon Zakin knew that an increased marketing budget could accelerate the Pilot's sales momentum. Practically overnight, he allocated additional marketing budget to Ed Colligan. "That first holiday season was really important," Colligan says. "We needed to knock it out there, we needed to hit another level. Zakin gave us $1.2 million more to go. He said, 'Go blow this thing out!' "

Colligan had never let up on his PR efforts, and positive reviews continued to pour in. With the additional budget, he could add more advertising to the mix. The ad agency produced a four-page magazine insert that included a Pilot-size fold-out brochure that readers could pull out. The insert ran in business magazines, including *Fortune* and *Forbes*. "There's only one gift you won't want to give away this year," the cover page read. When readers turned the page, they read: "Pilot. You'll buy it as a gift, but keep it for yourself."

As Christmas approached, Pilot sales took off for good. In November, *Computer Retail Week,* whose readers are retail channel managers, told the retailers what they already knew in a review of 1996's hottest products: "Pilot has plenty of useful appeal, and customers have been flocking to stores to purchase them." Inevitably, those retailers who weren't carrying Pilot wanted to more than ever. The orders that poured into Palm doubled from November to December.

By the time the 1996 Christmas season was over, Pilot had reached over 70 percent market share in the United States—nearly three-quarters of the handheld computers sold in America were Pilots. (Keyboarded handheld PCs, such as the Hewlett-Packard 200 LX, the HP OmniGo, and the Psion duked it out with organizers like the Sharp Zaurus for the remaining 30 percent of the market.) Palm had sold five times as many Pilots as it had dared to forecast only six months earlier, and the Pilot had received 21 "Best Product" awards from magazines and newspapers.

Over 1,000 developers had purchased Pilot SDKs to write software for the product, and about 100 third-party software applications had already been published (75 of them were shareware). Pilot customers could now buy conduits for 12 of the most popular PIM desktop programs.

"God save U.S. Robotics. They have recently introduced the Pilot 5000, the hottest, smallest, simplest machine in the Valley," wrote *Forbes FYI* magazine in its December issue.

It had been a good year.

THIRTEEN
MICROSOFT 1.0

In the fall of 1996, Jeff Hawkins was worried. According to rumor, the moment the Pilot was announced, Bill Gates had directed his company to come up with a stripped-down Windows operating system (OS) code-named Gryphon, to compete with the Pilot. Gryphon was supposed to be ready some time in 1997.

Jeff had anticipated that Microsoft would compete for the handheld market even when the Pilot was little more than four design goals on a notepad. "People would ask me who I worried about; my answer would always be Microsoft," he says. "People thought it would be Sharp and Casio, companies that build devices. We said, 'No, it's really going to be Microsoft.' "

With Microsoft's Gryphon OS (which computer magazines called "Pilot killer") still on the drawing board, the software giant had been plowing on with an earlier OS, code-named Pegasus (designed for clamshell-style devices with tiny keyboards) that had already been in development.

Despite every effort of secrecy by a computer industry company, bits of information about new products always reach competitors well before the product is for sale. As details leaked out (from component suppliers, retail buyers, and analysts, for example), Hawkins analyzed every shred of information about

Microsoft's Pegasus. His gut told him that Pegasus wasn't anything consumers would be interested in.

Still, he says, "I worried that I was wrong. That I either judged the market wrong, what the market wants, or the ability of Microsoft to muscle its way in with marketing dollars. They could come up with a product that I would think wasn't good, but would turn out to be great."

His cycle of doubt fell into an old pattern. "The first thing that happens with Microsoft is that they announce they're going to do something," he says. "At that point, you used to get all the analysts saying, 'These guys are going to kill you. You can't succeed.' Everybody is telling you you're a loser!

"Next you learn some details about the product, and you say, 'OK, now I'm beginning to understand their strategy; maybe I can handle this.'

"The next thing is that you get the full details on the product. And you go, 'Oh, great! It looks like they're really screwing this up . . .'

"Then you get one in your hands and play with it. You confirm your impressions. The final thing is that you see how it does in the market, and how people write about it.

"It's worst at the beginning. Because everyone's assuming it's going to kill you. And each step along the way, you get a little more confident in your ability to succeed."

It was, and is, typical of Microsoft to announce products long before they're ready. Microsoft has nothing to lose by doing so—to the contrary; its preannouncements often succeed in stalling competitors' current sales. In that tried-and-true fashion, Microsoft announced the Pegasus OS under its official name Windows CE (for Consumer Electronics) in September 1996. Two months later, seven hardware companies, among them Hewlett-Packard, Philips, and Casio, would introduce Windows CE products at the Comdex computer tradeshow in Las Vegas. *PC Week* reported that Microsoft's traditional hardware partners, Compaq and Toshiba, had "backtracked on their original plans to launch Pegasus 1.0 devices," and speculated that Microsoft's announcement was designed "to stave off additional defections to the competing Pilot effort."

Palm was playing in the big leagues now.

At an off-site marketing meeting, Ed Colligan and his team

discussed how to prepare for this new threat. Even if Jeff was right, the Microsoft marketing machine could still do much damage if it aimed its efforts directly at Palm.

Ed Colligan reminded his team of Palm's strategy to stay out of Microsoft's crosshairs. As far as the press and the public were concerned, he said, "We're not competing with Microsoft, we're competing with Casio, and HP. Don't turn Microsoft into a competitor. Let's not get into a PR battle with them." His argument was to let Microsoft battle Newton and General Magic, companies who were marketing handheld *operating systems*. "We purposely downplayed the platform," Colligan recalls, "and we played up the product. We were just these little guys off in a corner, selling thousands of units."

Even armed with Hawkins's reassuring analysis and Colligan's communications strategy, the Palm team waited with trepidation to see the new Windows CE products. Rob Haitani was Palm's resident expert on competitors' products. Over the years, he had loaded his own personal data into a succession of handheld devices and used each until he felt that he fully understood its benefits and shortcomings. He and Colligan set out for Comdex 1996 to observe the new competing products up close.

For the unveiling, Microsoft had rented the arena where the Canadian circus Cirque du Soleil performed. After Bill Gates's introduction of Pegasus, the audience of several thousand was to be treated to a performance by the extraordinary troupe. Colligan and Haitani tried to crash the unveiling, but were turned away by security.

Instead, they had to contain themselves until the doors opened on the Comdex exhibition hall the next day, where Microsoft's seven hardware partners exhibited their products in Microsoft's giant pavilion.

"I was pretty freaked out," admits Haitani. "Before that, I was just too busy to really worry about it, frankly. But then going to Comdex when they launched, just going into that pavilion, the size of a football field . . . I felt like, 'Oh my God! These guys are going to crush us.' "

"It was the big Microsoft marketing juggernaut and money spent up the ying-yang," says Colligan. "We were thinking, 'Geez, how are we going to compete with this?' Fortunately, the products sucked beyond our wildest dreams."

The Windows CE 1.0 products were shaped like clamshells that opened to show a screen and a keyboard. Especially when compared with the Pilot, they were clunky, slow, expensive ($500 to $800), and hard to use. The complicated Windows user interface (UI) from large-screen PCs, Start menu and all, had been shoehorned onto the small screens of what Microsoft was calling HPCs. (The acronym stood for *handheld personal computer,* a Microsoft effort to suggest that they offered all the features of a small PC.) The intention was to give the user the familiar Microsoft UI, with nothing new to learn; but the result made for a frustrating user experience.

"They were so easy to attack, it was unbelievable," says Colligan. "They were just sitting ducks. They didn't sync as well as us, they didn't have the same software support, they weren't as fast, they weren't as easy, they didn't work very well."

During the weeks before Comdex, Colligan had readied Palm's PR defense against the Pegasus products, preparing for the likely questions of how Palm intended to compete with these products.

Sure enough, reporters and analysts descended on him. "It was the big talk at Comdex. 'How are you going to compete with CE?' "

Haitani remembers a reporter testing a CE device and saying, "This is great!" "All right, let's look up a phone number," Rob replied, suggesting a head-to-head race that simulated Palm's favorite challenge: the phone test. "Imagine you're at an airport phone booth . . ."

With just two steps (one touch on the address book button and one stroke of the stylus), Haitani's Pilot jumped directly to the specified phone number. The whole process took less than three seconds. The same steps on the Windows CE device took the reporter many more steps—and closer to 30 seconds. Rob's carefully devised user interface had won that race.

Anticipating the slew of Microsoft-powered products rattled the Palm sales team. They were the ones who would have to convince the retailers to keep stocking Pilots in the face of pitches from Windows CE device makers HP, Philips, and Casio.

Nor did these reps, who periodically flew into Palm for

meetings from all over the United States, have the benefit of the "don't panic" message the Palm executives spread in meetings and hallway conversations. But they were painfully aware that Microsoft had won almost every market it had ever pursued. Palm's only hope was to be an exception to this rule.

Haitani prepared a presentation that was designed to calm the sales force. It began with a slide titled "Microsoft Strategy." A nasty Borg alien from the TV series *Star Trek* illustrated three bullet points:

- You will be assimilated.
- Resistance is futile.
- Have a nice day.

This, of course, was exactly what everybody expected of Microsoft. But Palm, Haitani insisted, wouldn't just roll over. The sales reps should remind everyone in earshot of the Pilot's benefits, which could easily be summed up in three compelling words: *Smaller. Faster. Cheaper.*

When Windows CE handhelds finally came to market, the press gave them mixed reviews. *Byte* magazine: "At last: Pocket PCs That Run Windows." *San Jose Mercury News:* "Windows CE not ready for public use." *Infoworld:* "Windows on a tiny hand-held computer? Give me a break! Everything I ever hated about Windows 95 seems even more ridiculous on a miniature PC."

Press coverage notwithstanding, the real proof of a product's success is its sales numbers. Each month, as Colligan pored over market share data, a pattern became clear: As each Windows CE manufacturer launched its product, its market share spiked in the first month—and then dropped to almost nothing in the following months. The seven CE models combined achieved less than 20 percent market share in the United States, even as the Pilot's market share climbed to over 70 percent.

In fact, the Windows CE marketing onslaught wound up helping Palm in sideways fashion: Most of the Windows CE reviews included discussions of the Pilot, giving the Pilot additional publicity. It wasn't long before Internet wags began referring to Windows CE as "Wince" for short.

In December, *Windows Sources* magazine summed up the episode like this: "With Pilot, USR really taught Microsoft something."

The Microsoft scare was over—for the moment.

Jeff Hawkins was in charge of keeping Pilot ahead of its competition. Even before the Pilot was launched, work on the next version of the Pilot was already under way. This improved model went by the code name Striker; the accompanying desktop software that synchronized it was code-named Shirley. (Both were named for characters in the movie comedy *Airplane.*)

"Fix what's broken" was the motto for Striker, which meant that this new model would have a backlit screen, so that its owner could check the calendar or phonebook in the dark, and slightly upgraded calendar and address book software for the desktop PC.

There would be two Striker models: one targeted at the cost-conscious consumer, the other a high-end model with features designed to make the Pilot more attractive to corporate customers, like more memory and a built-in e-mail program.

Meanwhile, Jeff was already weighing ideas for future breakthrough products, new Pilot models that featured radical steps forward rather than incremental improvements.

For some time, U.S. Robotics executives had begun pushing Hawkins to develop a wireless version, one that could send or receive information without the need for a phone line and a modem. "I had a much broader conception [than Palm] of what the Pilot could be in terms of a communications device," says John McCartney.

Over time, the USR team grew more insistent. The Megahertz team had just finished one wireless product, the Allpoints PC card, and had a team of engineers and product managers raring to go.

Jeff felt certain that all handheld computers would one day have wireless features, but that day was a long way off. The basic problem, as he saw it, was that the wireless networks and the technology available were too immature for a satisfying wireless palmtop. "I didn't know what the right technology to use at that time was, and I didn't want to be a pioneer with arrows in my back," Hawkins explains. "I didn't feel at the time that the right sort of wireless networks existed, or that I could build a great product. I just didn't know what to do. There was too much uncertainty for me, so I was reluctant to commit."

Wireless circuitry would impose a dramatic battery drain, would make the device far bulkier, and would deliver the Internet at snaillike speeds, which customers would find unacceptable. Jeff wanted to wait until the technologies had improved.

Ultimately, however, the USR managers issued an ultimatum: Unless Jeff put a wireless radio into the Pilot, they would do it.

With his back to the wall, Hawkins relented.

"All right, if you really want to have a wireless product, I'll do a wireless product," he told the USR brass. "But I think it's too early, and we may get some things wrong. If I had my druthers, I'd wait a little while longer until I was more certain."

Despite having argued passionately against a wireless Pilot, now Hawkins threw himself into fleshing out ideas for a Pilot that would be able to go online, wirelessly, from almost anywhere in the country. "Once you commit to something you have to be behind it 100 percent," he says. "I was very excited about the product. It's hard to look at a product objectively when you're in the middle of development. Once you have teams of people working on it you can't sit around, saying 'I don't know if this is the right thing to do.' You have to be gung-ho and go for it."

Ed Colligan assigned Joe Sipher to be the product manager of the new device, which was code-named Blue Sky ("because it was sort of way out there," Sipher says). Megahertz's team of wireless experts in Seattle became part of Palm's staff.

Hawkins figured that it would take two years to come up with a wireless Pilot. In the end, he underestimated the staggering complexity of the project; it wound up taking three years, finally seeing the light of day in May 1999, bearing the name Palm VII.

Hawkins and Sipher weren't the only ones working on secret new product ideas in the fall of 1996. Rob Haitani, too, was kicking around ideas for another generation of products, which he had code-named Limbo.

"Initially we thought, 'How low can you go?' . . . for cheap, inexpensive. Then it became another conversation at the same time, about how *small* can we make this," says Hawkins.

"We had made a breakthrough in form factor," says Haitani referring to the Pilot's size and shape, "but we needed to continue making breakthroughs in form factors." He commissioned an industrial-design study of different sizes and shapes that could accommodate the Pilot's evolution.

"One day, someone came in with a proposal where they had a picture of a thinner unit," says Hawkins. "They had made it thinner by putting the batteries on the side. It had a thick edge to it. I didn't like the design. They had another one where they were using six button [batteries] cells, like cameras. And I didn't like that at all. They weren't good designs."

They were, however, exciting enough to stir up a keen interest in the Palm staff, which worried Jeff. "Sometimes I'm spurred into action when I see something bad happen," he says. As in the wireless handheld debate, he didn't want to stand by while a proposal he considered seriously flawed gathered steam; once again, he preferred to look for a superior solution himself.

He started thinking about better ways to make a slim design Pilot rather than a low-cost one. "I set the parameters of it to be the most elegant, beautiful product we can make. Thinness is part of it, but also materials and finishes and that stuff," Hawkins says.

As he had done when creating the original Pilot, he began with a stack-up sketch on paper. Of course, the AAA batteries used in the Pilot wouldn't fit into a thinner design. "I did some research on lithium-ion batteries, and I called a couple of battery vendors, because no batteries existed at the time that would work." The battery vendors doubted that they could come up with the right kind of battery for Palm, but Hawkins was unperturbed. "I convinced myself that this battery would work," he says. Palm's sole hardware engineer at the time, Frank Canova, would spend the next six months persuading battery makers to work with Palm.

To work on the design and mechanical engineering of the new project, now code-named Razor (and ultimately called the Palm V), Haitani hired IDEO, a cutting-edge firm that had developed thousands of products, including Apple's first mouse and virtual-reality headsets for Sega.

Jeff and Rob also reconsidered an earlier product idea: a Pilot with a keyboard. Even though Pilot was selling briskly to early adopters, Graffiti was a lingering worry. Would people who didn't buy into the latest technologies be turned off by the concept?

Hawkins commissioned a plastic model of the Pilot that had the same shape and dimensions, but also a cover, which opened on a hinge to reveal a laptop-like arrangement: screen on top, a tiny keyboard on the bottom. The setup had some logic, but Jeff was only half-heartedly interested.

In the end, the decision was an easy one to make. When Hawkins, Sipher, and Haitani mapped out all the projects in Palm's pipeline against the number of engineers, it was clear that something would have to go. They cut the keyboard model.

Even so, it was a difficult time for Rob Haitani. He was responsible for the German and French versions of Pilot and version 3.0 of Pilot (which would one day become the Palm III). Now, with the Razor project before him, he had added another major project to his plate.

He had started working 12-hour days in the summer of 1994; by now, he was worn out. He was the first employee to arrive at the office, by 7:00 A.M. ("I turned on the lights and the coffee machine"), and now he routinely left his desk well after 9:00 P.M.

Palm had hired many additional programmers in the efforts to ease the crunch; but in a strange paradox of computer engineering, the influx of new workers made little difference. In theory, doubling the number of engineers on a specific project should mean that it will take half as long. In practice, adding more engineers doesn't produce such a straightforward equation. "We had all those projects going," says engineer Ron Marianetti, "so we started hiring more engineers, which made it even worse. Because now the three or four of us who knew anything about all the software were hounded by a dozen other people who knew nothing about it and had all these questions."

While Hawkins assessed the likely threat from Microsoft, Dubinsky and Colligan encountered problems from an utterly unexpected source. A few months after the introduction of the Pilot, the mail had brought a cease-and-desist letter from the lawyers of the Pilot Pen Corporation. It demanded that Palm stop using the name Pilot, a trademark that the pen company owned.

Colligan flew to Trumbull, Connecticut, to resolve the issue with Ron Shaw, the president and CEO of Pilot Corporation of America. To the management at the Pilot Corporation's Japanese headquarters, the source of potential confusion was obvious. By using the name Pilot, Palm had "misled our customers and consumers into thinking that their products are somehow made, sponsored, endorsed or licensed by Pilot Pen," Ron Shaw told a reporter.

Ed hated to give up the name Pilot. His PR efforts so far had resulted in over 250 million impressions (a PR-industry statistic—the number of articles that mention the Pilot times the number of readers). The headway that Palm had made toward making *Pilot* a household word would be thrown out the window if the company were forced to choose a different product name.

Pilot Corporation, however, was threatening to sue Palm (or rather, U.S. Robotics), a proceeding that would drag on far beyond the approaching April 1997 release of Pilot 2.0, code-named Striker.

If a name change were absolutely necessary, then the time to do it was with the Pilot 2.0 version. For all the lost opportunity a name change would cause, the damage would be relatively contained (Palm had sold only about 100,000 Pilots). Colligan was confident that the next version would sell many more.

He and his team began to brainstorm. The ideal replacement name would retain the word *Pilot*, but combine it with another word in some way that would pacify Pilot Pen.

PalmPilot seemed the obvious, if slightly unwieldy, choice. If Pilot Pen were to reject any name containing the word *Pilot* (and if a judge were to agree), then Palm could use PalmPilot as a transitional name. On its next-generation product, Palm could drop Pilot altogether, using Palm alone.

Pilot Pen Corporation filed suit against Palm, first in the United States, then in Japan, and in France, where the laws concerning trademark infringement cases were known for favoring plaintiffs. While the lawyers prepared their arguments in three countries, Colligan, with little alternative, proceeded with the product launch using the name PalmPilot. If Palm won the case, the name change would turn out to have been unnecessary. If

Palm lost the case, at least all of its efforts to publicize the name Pilot wouldn't have been for nothing.

A year after Jeff Hawkins's and Ed Colligan's tour of analysts and journalists to launch the Pilot, Ed was back on the road.

In a two-week sweep of East and West Coast media, he lined up articles that would appear in the months after the two PalmPilot models (Personal and Professional) were announced.

"We met back-to-back with *Newsweek* and *Time*," he remembers. "And as we were walking out at the end of the meetings, both of them asked us whether they could run it on Monday, and we acted kind of, 'Sure, OK.' And when we left, we said to each other, '*Time* magazine is asking us if they can run it? Wow!' We were just high-fiving each other in the elevator."

Colligan continued with the marketing strategy he had devised in the face of Microsoft competition: promoting the PalmPilot itself, not its operating system. When analysts asked why Palm didn't consider it important to be the standard handheld platform, Colligan answered, "It's very important. But standards are built, not announced." Companies like Apple, General Magic, and Microsoft had each declared their new operating systems to be new standards in handheld computing—but calling something a standard doesn't make it one, as their failures clearly showed.

On March 10, the day Palm unveiled the PalmPilot models, the company found out just how much its customers loved their original-model Pilots. The Pilot had, from the beginning, been designed for easy upgrading; the plastic panel on its back could be removed, revealing the memory card inside. All a customer had to do was replace the original memory card with a new one purchased from Palm, that contained the software and added memory of the new PalmPilot, and presto: the older unit had now had a brain transplant that turned it into the newer PalmPilot model.

No other organizer manufacturer offered this kind of do-it-yourself upgrade; in fact, such a money-saving deal was unheard-of in the consumer electronics industry.

But Ed and the marketing department hadn't factored in the backlight.

The new PalmPilot models included a backlit screen—the feature that, despite Colligan's lobbying, had been missing in the original Pilot. Unfortunately, no simple memory card swap could bring a backlit screen to the older Pilot models. The only way to get the backlight was to buy a brand new PalmPilot.

Within hours of the PalmPilot announcement, several hundred angry Pilot customers stormed Palm's 800 number, expressing their anger. They didn't want a memory board swap; they wanted to trade in their old Pilots for a large discount on a brand new PalmPilot—something neither Colligan nor his product managers had even considered.

The uproar, which continued for many weeks, caught the Palm executives off guard. Ed tucked the experience away for future product launches. "It changed my thinking in a couple ways," says Colligan. "One, make sure you take care of your core customer base. Even a small upgrade offering is better than nothing, and supports the loyalty those customers have shown you. Second, bring the prices of the older products down with sufficient lead time in front of a new product's introduction, so the desire for an upgrade is tempered by the pricing differential of the new products."

Despite the furor surrounding the upgrade offer, the PalmPilot launch was a smashing success. The monthly spiral-bound booklet of press clippings prepared by Palm's PR firm was over an inch thick in April. Under the headline "U.S. Robotics PalmPilot. Love is in the air . . . again", *Boot* magazine pronounced the new handheld computer a "kick-ass product."

To celebrate the successful launch, Donna invited Palm's now 135 employees to an afternoon of finger food, PalmPilot-shaped chocolate cakes, and games at a bowling alley near Palm's former Los Altos offices. Jeff, having been nicknamed Mobile Man by a small analyst firm, showed up in an appropriate caped costume that Ed's wife Lisa had sewn for him. Between his turns bowling, the gangly Jeff leapt through the alley in the bright yellow cape and shirt with the large letter *M* sewn on its front.

To the outside world, Hawkins was now known as the father of handheld computing, but to his employees, he could still be just Jeff.

January 2, 1992: Jeff Hawkins (*center*) and his two software engineers, Ain McKendrick and Art Lamb (*right*), gather at the offices of venture capital firm Merrill Pickard to celebrate Palm Computing's first day. (*Photo courtesy of Art Lamb.*)

Spring 1992: Jeff Hawkins, product marketing director Kate Purmal, and jack-of-all-trades and business development director Joel Jewitt work on the Zoomer project in one of the two Palm Computing rooms of the Merrill Pickard offices. (*Photo courtesy of Art Lamb.*)

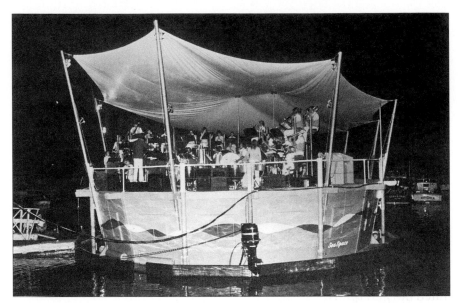

Jeff Hawkins wasn't the only inventor in his family—his father Robert built a gigantic, 50-ton, 16-sided boat with eight retractable legs. Nicknamed the Bubble Monster, the boat is shown here after its sale to a touring orchestra. (*Photo courtesy of Jeff Hawkins.*)

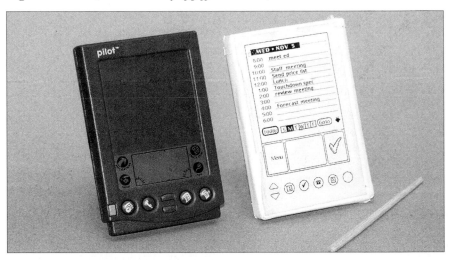

Right: The balsa-wood model that Jeff Hawkins carved in his garage workshop on the night he was inspired to create his own handheld computer—and the chopstick he whittled down to stand in for the stylus. *Left:* The original Pilot, whose dimensions matched the original model almost precisely. (*Photo by Mike Tobias, courtesy of Handspring.*)

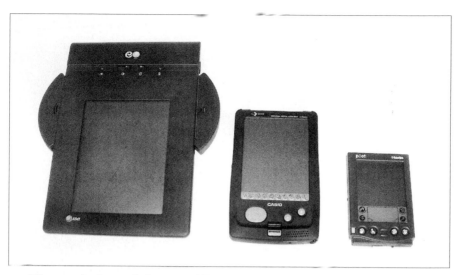

The evolution of the steadily shrinking handheld computer, illustrated by (*from left*) GO Corporation's spin-off EO (1992), Casio's Zoomer (1993), and Palm's Pilot (1996). (*Photo by Robert Baxley.*)

Twice in Palm's history, designers considered building a clamshell-style model that would feature a tiny keyboard. (With the lid closed, the dimensions would be the same as the original Pilot.) The keyboard design flunked in focus-group tests, however, and was abandoned. (*Photo by Robert Baxley.*)

December 1993: At the Palm holiday party, executives Jeff Hawkins, Donna Dubinsky, and Ed Colligan entertained the Palm employees with rewritten Christmas-carol lyrics. (*Photo courtesy of Donna Gafford.*)

Palm Computing, 1993. *Back row, standing:* Monty Boyer, Jeff Hawkins, Shawn Ford, Carl Chen, Donna Dubinsky, Kate Purmal, Greg Kucala, Roger Flores, Joel Jewitt, Art Lamb, Stuart Meyer, Bob Lemay. *Middle row, kneeling:* Joe Sipher, Ain McKendrick, Andrea Butter, Vicki Barklow, Chris Raff, Maryann Donolo, Donna Gafford, Ed Colligan, Vitaly Kruglikov. *Front row, seated:* Jody Schreiber, Suzanne Jacobs. (*Photo by Michael Dubinsky.*)

The earliest plastic, nonfunctional model of Touchdown (later to be called Pilot) and mocked-up cradle that Palm showed to potential investors and corporate collaborators.

January 1996: Product managers Joe Sipher and Rob Haitani at crunch time, backstage at Demo, preparing for the Pilot's worldwide unveiling. (*Photo courtesy of Donna Dubinsky.*)

Ed Colligan and Jeff Hawkins backstage at Demo, testing the equipment before presenting the Pilot. (*Photo courtesy of Donna Dubinsky.*)

Following the successful Pilot presentation at Demo 1996, U.S. Robotics executive Jon Zakin (*seated, left*) treated the Palm team to champagne. *Back row:* Maxine Graham (*seated*), Donna Dubinsky, Rob Haitani, Tina Owenmark (*seated*), Jeff Hawkins, Joe Sipher (*seated*), Ed Colligan, Pat McVeigh, Kate Purmal. (*Photo courtesy of Donna Dubinsky.*)

October 1997: Donna Dubinsky poses with her mother at Agenda, the industry conference where the Palm executives' mothers demonstrated the simplicity of the Pilot. (*Photo courtesy of Donna Dubinsky.*)

July 1998: Donna Dubinsky in the bustling offices of the newly founded Handspring, Inc.: three desks and a plant, in borrowed office space. (*Photo courtesy of Donna Dubinsky.*)

The regular company-wide communications meetings at Handspring carry on the tradition that Jeff Hawkins and Donna Dubinsky (shown speaking) began at Palm. (*Photo by Dennis Burry, courtesy of Handspring.*)

March 2000: Palm goes public. At Nasdaq (*from left*): Palm executives Judy Bruner, Carl Yankowski, and Alan Kessler. (*Photo by Al Perlman, courtesy of Palm.*)

FOURTEEN
SWALLOWED WHOLE

Although the PalmPilot was far from being the household name in Tuscaloosa, Alabama, that the Palm team hoped to make it one day, it certainly was familiar to technology executives. Ed Colligan's strategy to place Pilots into the hands of this influential group had been a resounding success. At Demo '97, a year after Hawkins's nerve-wracking Pilot demonstration, a *San Jose Mercury News* reporter noted, "Everywhere, attendees were pulling [Pilots] out of pockets, purses, briefcases and shoulder bags."

As a result, opportunities for new markets, new partners, and new products were blossoming. Marketing managers from other companies called daily with proposals for joint promotions. Techies called hoping to license bits of Palm's technology.

Palm's executives fought the temptation to pursue them all. "We were constantly struggling with the tension between trying to take advantage of this opportunity we had created, which seemed limitless and very broad, and trying to remain a small, focused organization that could deliver," Dubinsky says.

Even though Palm had sold a few hundred thousand PalmPilots, the executives were keenly aware that the handheld market was still in its very earliest stages. One hundred twenty million people owned PCs; at least, in theory, every one of them was a potential customer for Palm—or for Microsoft's Windows CE partners. Palm needed only consider the cell phone—a gadget with over 100 million customers—to see how far the handheld computer had to go.

Yet many companies had been the first to establish a new industry, only to be overtaken by competitors and relegated to the status of mere footnotes in technology history. Dubinsky, Hawkins, and Colligan were determined to do everything in their power to prevent this from happening to Palm.

On a Monday morning in early February 1997, following a worldwide meeting of U.S. Robotics managers in Chicago, the executives back at Palm compared notes. They had all come to the same conclusion: The parent company's days of unfettered success were over. U.S. Robotics' flagship modem market was slowing; in fact, it was becoming a commodity business with decreasing profit margins. New technologies like cable modems were emerging from rival companies. USRs' once undisputed lead was vulnerable.

Over the past six months, the U.S. Robotics executives and Dubinsky had clashed with increasing frequency over Palm's profitability. Palm was still operating at a slight loss; USR's John McCartney wanted Palm to turn a profit.

But it was commonplace, Donna argued, for early-stage technology companies to remain unprofitable at the beginning, as they spent more money to invest in their future. "We've got to invest in this today," she had said, "going over the top on marketing, on building the organization. We have the chance to be the real, true leader for years."

Now, as she saw USR's business struggling, Dubinsky realized that pressure on Palm to be profitable would only rise. Looking ahead, all she could see were battles yet to be fought with her USR bosses. In fact, bruised to the bone from the constant conflicts over the past year and a half, Dubinsky was again ready to resign—and this time, no 48-hour cooling-off period seemed likely to soothe the damage.

She was in a bind. Quitting meant abandoning everything

she had worked so hard to achieve. But the current situation was untenable. The more she thought about it, the more she saw only one way out: a spin-off from USR.

In a spin-off, Palm would become an independent company. Independence wouldn't just put a stop to the never-ending battles over strategy; it would also make Palm stronger. Instead of having to live by budgets that were set by a parent company with its own profitability requirements, Dubinsky would be able to invest more in Palm's growth. A spinout would mean that Palm would once again be able to offer its own stock options, making it far easier to attract and retain employees.

Over dinner one night, she consulted an old friend, Frank Quattrone, a Stanford-educated investment banker, about how spin-offs worked. Having taken companies like Netscape and Amazon public, Quattrone had become one of the Valley's movers and shakers.

Quattrone understood that this was no theoretical question; clearly, Donna was really asking about a spinout of Palm.

"I told her that I thought it was a good idea," he says, "because generally spinouts work when a company has a business that's very different from its base business, and where, if it were separate, investors would value it differently than if it were a small part of a big company."

When investors consider buying a stock, they generally consider the company's profits and its rate of growth. In established, slow-growing industries, highly profitable companies have the highest market value. However, investors also pay a high price for a company's stock if its business is in a new, fast-growing category like the Internet, or handheld computing—even if the company isn't yet profitable, as long as they believe that the company has a bright future. If it's part of an established company in an established industry, on the other hand, the same fast-growing but unprofitable business may actually reduce the overall company's value.

By separating the two entities, the parent company can in fact become more valuable, because it no longer has to report losses from the spun-out business. In other words, U.S. Robotics' stock value might actually increase if it didn't carry the booming but unprofitable Palm on its balance sheet. Meanwhile, the spun-out company can become highly valued on its own. Indeed, Quattrone estimated that investors might value Palm at somewhere between $0.5 billion and $1 billion.

Thrilled that her plan made financial sense, Dubinsky scheduled a follow-up phone call with Quattrone for Tuesday, February 25, 1997. But she never got the chance: A few hours before the appointed time, her phone rang. It was John McCartney's administrative assistant, requesting her participation at a conference call with McCartney and all of USR's general managers—now.

When she joined the call, McCartney's news stunned her: U.S. Robotics was about to be sold to 3Com Corporation. The announcement would hit the airwaves the next day.

Although USR had been working on the merger for months, it was the first Donna or any other USR manager had heard of it. Because merger rumors would rock the stock prices of both companies, the deal had been kept utterly secret. "I knew there were meetings that I wasn't a part of," says Dubinsky. "But I assumed it was a reorganization. Partly because these guys seemed like such diehard independents, I couldn't imagine them wanting to sell their company."

She also knew nothing about 3Com. Even as McCartney, on the conference call, continued to explain the imminent merger, Dubinsky cradled the phone on her shoulder and logged onto the 3Com Web site, in hopes of finding familiar faces among 3Com's executives and board of directors. Sure enough, the flamboyant Frenchman Jean-Louis Gassée, who had run Apple's product development in the mid-1980s and knew her well, was on 3Com's board. This, she thought, could be useful.

Even before the call was over, the next steps were clear to her. First, she postponed the scheduled phone call with Quattrone; she couldn't possibly talk with an investment banker while she carried this insider information. Then she hopped into her Chevy Blazer and drove to 3Com's campus, where McCartney had said that the USR and 3Com executives were meeting at that very moment, surrounded by lawyers and hammering out the fine points of the merger. ("John McCartney made fun of me because I didn't even know where 3Com was," she says. As it turns out, 3Com was only 15 minutes away.)

She found the company along Highway 237, not far from the semiconductor giant Intel in the town of Santa Clara. The 3Com campus was a series of white buildings that looked as if huge children's building blocks had been scattered randomly between parking lots.

McCartney had told her to ask for the meeting rooms of "Project Sport," the code name the two large companies were using for the merger activities. A USR manager escorted her to the conference rooms filled with USR and 3Com execs, bankers, and lawyers for both companies. In the hallway, her escort stopped two people rushing between conference rooms and introduced them to Dubinsky: Eric Benhamou, the CEO of 3Com, a short, quiet man with dark, bulging eyes and a slight accent that was hard to place, and Janice Roberts, a 3Com Senior VP and Benhamou's much more extroverted right hand in the merger. Her accent was quite clearly British.

Both Benhamou and Roberts had come to 3Com themselves as a result of mergers. Born in Algeria and raised in France, Benhamou had been the cofounder and vice president of engineering of Bridge Communications, which 3Com bought in 1987. He clearly thrived at 3Com; by 1990, at the age of 35, he was appointed CEO, in an era when 3Com had fallen on rough times after years of rapid growth. He was widely credited for turning the troubled company around, partly through a series of smart acquisitions. Roberts had been the managing director of a British networking hub manufacturer, the first company that Benhamou acquired for 3Com. After the acquisition, Roberts stayed in the United States and quickly rose through the ranks to run both business development and marketing for the company.

With annual revenues of $3 billion, 3Com was the world's second-largest networking company (the much larger Cisco was No. 1). In 1997, the Internet had taken off in a big way, and the hot new thing in networking was remote-access equipment, which companies like America Online and AT&T purchased to connect their customers to the Internet.

Benhamou wanted to get 3Com into this new, fast-growing business. The fastest way to do so was to buy a company that was already in it—either Ascend or USR, whose remote-access business was overshadowed by its reputation as a consumer modem company. "Ascend was very expensive," says Bill Slakey, 3Com's director of investor relations at the time. "Ascend had about $250 million in revenue, and a market cap of $8 billion. U.S. Robotics, which also had $250 million in [remote-access] revenue *plus* a billion-dollar modem business, had a market cap of $8 billion. So for the same price, they could get what they viewed as a better remote access business—plus all the modem business."

Wall Street, however, felt otherwise. When the merger was announced, 3Com's stock fell by 10 percent the next day, and continued its downward slide. Two months after the merger announcement, 3Com stock had lost a third of its value. "To the outside world, to the investment community, getting U.S. Robotics' modem business was a huge negative. It was viewed as a business on the verge of commoditization, a business that was going nowhere," Slakey says.

Benhamou believed he could take that risk. For years, analysts had been telling 3Com that its own network interface cards (NIC), the hardware that adapt a PC for use in a network, were going to become low-profit commodity products, too—and yet 3Com's NIC business was still going gangbusters.

Through all of this discussion and analysis, one element of the acquisition was barely even mentioned: Palm Computing. The Pilot, a consumer product only 10 months old and accounting for less than 5 percent of USR's sales revenue, wasn't even on 3Com's radar screen.

Dubinsky entered the meeting room where most of the U.S. Robotics executives huddled over documents. She spotted John McCartney and Jon Zakin, and sat down with them. Faced with the prospect of being a tiny speck in a networking company's product portfolio, Dubinsky wasted no time in getting to her point: "Spin us out! We don't want to be part of this!"

From USR's perspective, though, a Palm spinout made absolutely no sense. Since the fall of the previous year, USR executives had decided to sell the company, found a suitor, and completed three months of negotiation. The merger with 3Com was valued at about $7 billion, one of the biggest in the high-tech industry to date. The executives weren't about to endanger the smooth conclusion of the transaction by introducing a new, loose-cannon factor like a Palm spinout one day before the merger was to be announced.

In fact, a spinout of any part of USR at this point would have a negative impact on the merger. 3Com intended to acquire USR using a special accounting practice for corporate takeovers called *pooling of interest*. This accounting method offers substantial tax savings to the merging parties, but there's a catch: According to the rules of pooling, the acquiring company may not dispose of significant assets of the combined firms for two years after the deal. Clearly, spinning off Palm just after the 3Com-USR merger "would have killed pooling for us," Jon Zakin explains. "If we had spun off Palm, we wouldn't have been poolable."

"At that point, we were a $100 million business," Dubinsky says. "We were really little. So here is this little squeaky wheel, saying, 'Do something special for us.' They said, 'Look, this is too big a deal. It's too complicated, and there's no way we'll complicate it further.' There was going to be no more discussion on it, and that was that."

Even so, by evening, Donna began to think that perhaps the merger was good news even without a Palm spinout. For one thing, 3Com was a Silicon Valley company; at least she would no longer have to contend with a California-Midwestern corporate culture clash. There also was the chance to work for a different management team. Clearly, a spinout was still everything she and Palm longed for. However, if a spinout had to wait, the merger might be just what Palm—and Dubinsky—needed.

Just before the public announcement of the merger, Donna pulled her executive staff together to tell them the news. "We don't have a lot of information, and we don't know what this will mean for Palm," she said, "but I think it's very positive."

She repeated her assessment to the full company after the stock market had closed. "The reaction was pretty positive," remembers Doug Haslam. As the man in charge of human resources, a negative employee reaction would have made his life miserable. "3Com had been successful, and it was a California-based company. It helped that Donna and Jeff were positively inclined, saying, 'This will be good for the business.' That really helped."

In an effort to make 3Com a recognizable brand name, the company had paid $4.5 million for the right to put its name on Candlestick Park, home of San Francisco's Giants and 49ers, six months earlier, in September 1996. Even so, many Palm employees had never heard of the company. Ron Marianetti, mistaking 3Com for 3M, wondered: "Why are we being bought by a company that makes Post-it Notes?"

For Dubinsky, the merger offered both the chance and the threat of a new organization within the parent company: a chance, because she wanted to report to a new manager who might see Palm's challenges her way, and a threat, because 3Com might want to fold Palm into 3Com completely. 3Com had a long history of acquiring companies—and assimilating them completely into the corporation. If Palm were to be similarly assimilated, its employees dispersed into innumerable corporate departments, she was sure the Pilot's success would fizzle out. She decided that, at the first opportunity, she would ask Eric Benhamou to let Palm operate separately from the other 3Com businesses.

Her chance came only a few weeks later at a personal meeting with the 3Com CEO. Whereas USR provided lavish offices for its executives, there were no private offices at 3Com at all. Even Benhamou used an open cubicle equipped with the same sparse furniture as all other 3Com employees. For meetings and confidential telephone calls, Benhamou used a private conference room that was filled with his books, office equipment, and mementos of 3Com's successes.

Over a lunch of catered sandwiches in "Eric's conference room," as the 3Com employees called it, Dubinsky gave Benhamou an overview of Palm's business, stressing the importance of managing it independently. "Keep us on the side; don't integrate us. If you do, you'll kill Palm."

Benhamou said he would think about it.

The merger between 3Com and USR proceeded with the upheaval and turmoil that's typical when two companies are integrated. "From a people standpoint, the integration plan was a disaster," wrote a *Chicago Tribune* reporter after interviewing U.S. Robotics management and employees. The deal had been announced as a merger, but 3Com was clearly acquiring USR— and calling all the shots. A small layoff of overlapping positions was expected, but many USR managers left the company voluntarily, anticipating the chaos that lay ahead.

But Palm was the eye of the storm. At Palm's communication meetings (which were now monthly) and in myriad hallway conversations, Donna, Jeff, and Ed assured the employees that Palm would remain independent. ("Stay in your cubes! No need to panic!" Rob Haitani joked.)

As insurance, Dubinsky had enlisted Casey Cowell, the CEO of USR. As vice chairman of the merged company's board of directors, she felt that he would be an important ally. "Casey, I need your support on this," she asked him. "Please do me this one favor: Separate this business. If it gets caught up in this whole mess, it's going to drown us."

Jon Zakin and Casey Cowell went to bat for Palm. "Casey and I felt that Donna wouldn't get the resources she needed within John's group at 3Com," says Zakin. "She and John [McCartney] fought a lot because of the accounting orientation that John brought to decisions. So we proposed that Janice Roberts take it over. We felt that Donna would have a better shot at having a free hand reporting to a 3Com person and a marketing person in Janice."

In May, Dubinsky approached Benhamou again at a dinner during the biannual business review gathering of all 3Com executives. Though the merger wouldn't be wrapped up until July, the structure of the combined organizations was being worked out, and Donna was anxious for the decision on Palm's fate.

Benhamou asked for more time. As the headaches of a massive corporate merger showed little sign of abating, he had much bigger problems of his own. "I have too much going on," he told her. "I promise I'll take care of you, but you have to give me six months."

"I don't have six months," Dubinsky responded. "I need to know now."

The urgency came, in part, from her impression that 3Com's

managers intended to absorb Palm completely. A few 3Com executives had made it clear that they wanted to assimilate Palm into 3Com's NIC group, because NICs, like modems and the Pilot, were sold in retail stores (unlike most of 3Com's products). At a meeting with 3Com sales executives, Pat McVeigh also discovered that the 3Com sales force expected to merge his team into its own organization.

Fortunately, Donna could show 3Com a superb example of the chaos that could result when a sales force wasn't exclusively focused on Palm: When USR in Europe had managed Pilot sales in combination with its modem business, it had failed miserably. Dubinsky and McVeigh pointed to the experience as a clear example of how Palm would suffer if it were assimilated completely.

Fortunately, not all 3Com executives hoped to see Palm absorbed into the bigger company. Others questioned that wisdom, pointing out that Palm didn't actually fit into 3Com's existing business very well.

Journalists and analysts questioned Benhamou, too. "They said, 'Why don't you just sell off Palm? It has nothing to do with your business,' " remembers Elisabeth Cardinale, who worked in 3Com's PR department. Even 3Com's largest investors pointed out that Palm seemed to have little in common with the networking company.

Soon enough, other high-tech companies attempted to turn Palm's poor fit with 3Com to their own advantage. "Many people, before even the U.S. Robotics transaction had been consummated, called me up and said, 'Well, when you finish the purchase of U.S. Robotics, I'd like to buy Palm from you,' " Benhamou says.

However, Eric Benhamou did think that Palm could fit into the business strategy of his networking company. 3Com's business was to deliver information over a network, whether to a PC, a laptop, or a handheld computer. With the Pilot, users could carry the network, and the access to the Internet, in their hands.

On the other hand, he agreed that Palm should not be completely absorbed into the networking company. When the merger closed in late June, he confirmed that Dubinsky would report to Janice Roberts, the British executive who also ran

3Com's marketing and business development. "Eric recognized that the best thing for Palm was to leave it and let it thrive as a separate business," says Roberts. "But it was unusual for 3Com. We hadn't really done that before."

Even though Palm wasn't spun off, Dubinsky had at least saved the company from assimilation into a networking behemoth and secured a spot under a marketing executive who might understand Palm's special needs.

For his part, Jeff Hawkins recognized that the merger had provided an unexpected benefit: It kept Donna at Palm. "It was an immediate lift for her; she was optimistic again. If that had taken another few months, I think Donna might have left." And that, he says, would have been a disaster of another kind. "I don't know what would have happened at Palm if she had left. I don't think we would have made it."

FIFTEEN

OMENS

In the year following the launch of the Pilot, a lot had changed at Palm. The tiny, unknown band of 28 who had once played hoops among the cubicles, eaten bag lunches in the company kitchenette, and discussed an engineer's engagement plans well before the intended fiancée even had an inkling, had become a company of 135 people. They joined various outside contractors on two floors of a brand-new office building (with six-by-eight-foot cubicles on the bottom floor). Palm Computing and its PalmPilot were now household names in Silicon Valley. New employees arrived so quickly that Jeff Hawkins and Donna Dubinsky no longer knew everybody's names. Despite Ed Colligan's warnings, bozo explosions had already erupted in several departments.

Because each day brought a new sales record, the Palm cash dance tradition soon died out; there was little call for the kind of celebration that a $10,000 day had warranted only 13 months earlier. Besides, what had seemed innocent fun among friends in the small Palm no longer felt appropriate for a mature senior manager with her own team of employees.

The old-timers watched Palm become a real company with mixed emotions. They had believed in Jeff's vision through long years of failure, and they were thrilled that their labors had placed them on a trajectory straight into orbit. But with departments growing by leaps and bounds, the fun of working at Palm became a matter of geography. The people on the second floor missed the sound of Donna's booming laughter, which now reverberated in the first-floor offices, and the employees working in the tiny first-floor cubicles missed Ed's irreverent wisecracks. Art Lamb, Ron Marianetti, and the rest of the engineers disappeared into a dark corner of the building, emerging in small groups only for lunch.

Jeff Hawkins now came to his office at Palm only three days a week, spending the remaining days of the week on a book about his brain theories. Meanwhile, the day-to-day management of the product development was in good hands with Rob Haitani and Joe Sipher and their growing team of product managers; Marian Cauwet ran the engineering team.

Still, despite his reduced schedule, the product managers turned to Jeff whenever technical obstacles, or too many conflicting opinions, threatened to stall a project or derail it from the direction Hawkins had set.

For some managers, his control over product design took getting used to. "[In my previous jobs,] I worked for VPs of marketing who said, 'Run the show. You know what you need to do. Define the product from beginning to end,' " says a senior product manager. "When I came to Palm, it was very different. There was a Chief Product Officer, Jeff, who had tremendous ideas, and the job was to 'productize' his ideas and bring them to market."

For Donna, the personality clashes that had marred her relationship with her USR bosses were gone. "I liked Eric Benhamou," she says. "I liked Janice Roberts. On a personal level, I felt a much better connection with the 3Com people, throughout the company."

Even the heavy wood furniture was removed from her office once the U.S. Robotics/3Com merger was consummated in June 1997. "I felt so much better the day I got the same furniture as everybody else," she says.

At a company-wide communications meeting, Janice Roberts reassured the employees about Palm's ongoing independence, pointing out that her own former company still produced a thriving product line despite having been bought by 3Com. For many of the female managers at Palm, the fact that the company was run by a woman who would now be reporting to a woman even felt like a little bonus.

Roberts herself enjoyed having Palm as part of her responsibilities. "I became very enamored of Palm," she remembers. "I really liked the team from the start."

However, Dubinsky's enthusiasm dropped as the months passed. Keeping Palm on the road to handheld greatness, it quickly became clear, could turn out to be even harder under 3Com than it had been with USR.

For one thing, the union of the two corporations was stumbling over two all-too-common corporate merger roadblocks. First, combining the two companies' infrastructures and IT systems proved challenging; in fact, it would take 18 months to complete. Second, the two companies' corporate cultures could not have been more different.

The cultural mismatch was arguably the bigger problem to solve. "U.S. Robotics was very entrepreneurial, and 3Com really wasn't. They were a little more structured and a little bit slower moving," says Jon Zakin. John Petty, a USR director who left soon after the merger, later put it less diplomatically in an interview with the *Chicago Tribune:* "If Robotics was an army, we were so aggressive we were outrunning supply lines, while 3Com was stuck inside the tent looking at maps while the enemy was destroying the villages."

Slowed by the kind of corporate bureaucracy that's inherent in most large companies, 3Com's democratic, all-inclusive culture only exaggerated the sluggishness. "If I'd stayed, it would've been slow death by conference call," says USR director Petty.

The Palm managers, too, found their time taken up by an increasing number of cross-divisional meetings. Struggling to keep up with its own growth, understaffed and overrun by opportunities, the Palm team had no time for corporate groupthink. Nor did Palm have any interest in the networking business, an enterprise-oriented, extremely technical field. Yet there were Palm's executives, called in to participate in all-day, cross-divisional meetings, sitting through discussions of strategies for routers, switches, and hubs. From Palm's point of view, it was a colossal waste of valuable time.

Colligan had been nervous about the merger from the beginning. "I always felt that USR was one step removed from us, so there was a reasonable possibility that they would leave us alone," he says. 3Com, on the other hand, was close by. "My first reaction was: 'Oh no, they're right around the corner. Oh boy! A lot more contact.' I didn't know what would happen, but my sense was: 'That's not good.' "

The problems began with phone calls. Used to absorbing acquired companies completely into the corporate structure, 3Com managers and executives began to call their counterparts at Palm; almost immediately after introducing themselves, these 3Com staff members declared themselves to be in charge.

In many cases, Donna had to call on Janice Roberts to call off the relevant 3Com manager. "Janice really protected us," Dubinsky says. "There was a long period where time after time after time, she really protected us. I don't even think I knew half of what they were coming after."

She was increasingly concerned, however, about a heated debate over a strategy that started to emerge between her and her new 3Com bosses. It was a battle with high stakes; as far as Dubinsky and Hawkins were concerned, picking the right strategy was tantamount to ensuring or losing Palm's future as the leader in handheld computing.

3Com CEO Eric Benhamou believed that Palm should license its OS to other companies. "This was clearly a point where we had fundamental business disagreements," he says. "Jeff and Donna thought about their business as primarily a device business. I thought that if this was all they were going to do, it was going to be far short of the potential of that business. And I couldn't conceive of a device business that would really, really change the face of computing. We had to create an OS business."

The idea would be to let other companies manufacture Palm-compatible handhelds of their own, paying Palm a royalty on each unit sold. This strategy, the 3Com executives argued, would place handhelds running the Palm OS into the hands of many more customers than Palm could reach on its own, thereby expanding the large platform that would attract even more software developers.

To drive the point home, USR and 3Com executives pointed to Apple's failure to license the Macintosh OS early in its existence. The common industry belief was that, by refusing to let other companies manufacture Mac compatibles, Apple lost its chance to turn the Mac OS into the standard. Instead, Windows, which Microsoft licensed to any computer maker who was interested, became the most predominant OS—and made Microsoft the most powerful force in the industry.

As far as USR, 3Com, and many analysts were concerned, the lesson for Palm seemed to be: License early and license broadly, before Microsoft takes your market away.

Palm's executives didn't find the Apple analogy apt, however. Dubinsky and Hawkins agreed that Palm should license its OS, but in a very focused way. Donna argued that the handheld market was still in its infancy. At this early stage, licensed PalmPilot clones would simply compete for the relatively small pool of potential palmtop customers. Instead of expanding the handheld market, broad licensing would only reduce Palm's income, and its ability to invest in improvements to its technology. Dubinsky could point at the example of Microsoft's CE licensees: Seven companies sold devices based on Windows CE 1.0, competing with each other fiercely for customers, and yet Windows CE's market share had not grown, and none of the licensing companies were able to make a profitable business.

"Licensing will come later," Dubinsky argued. "Today it certainly won't add value. What *will* add value today is investing in product development, getting the next generation and the next generation out, advancing the category, and building intellectual property."

Donna wasn't against all forms of licensing, however. She was all for licensing to companies who catered to markets that Palm itself could not reach. For example, Symbol Technologies, a maker of bar-code scanners, wanted to create an extra-rugged PalmPilot that would contain a bar-code reader. Doctors and nurses could reduce medical errors by scanning the bar codes on medications, hotel personnel could check in guests at the curb, and police officers could check a vehicle's warrant status from anywhere on their beat.

Once Palm and Symbol signed a licensing agreement, Palm engineers wound up spending months modifying the Palm OS to accommodate Symbol's scanner, but Palm had gained an important partner in its effort to expand handheld computing.

Dubinsky also pursued another, quicker way to expand Palm products into new markets: original equipment manufacturer (OEM) agreements. That is, Palm could manufacture PalmPilots that carried the logos of other companies, which would sell the palmtops under their own brand names. In this approach, Palm could reach new markets much more quickly than through licensing, and make a profit it would have missed without the OEM partner.

Kate Purmal had drummed up such an agreement with Franklin Quest (now Franklin Covey). The company was a natural partner for Palm; it sold its famous Franklin planner, and the organizational theories behind it, in seminars and Franklin's own stores, places where Pilot would otherwise not be available.

Steve Brown, Palm's director of business development, was responsible for striking up more such deals for Palm. Brown, an appealing young up-and-comer who had played basketball for Stanford, set out to elicit interest in PalmPilot from companies who were strong in the corporate market, where Palm was traditionally weakest. The first name that came to mind was IBM.

IBM executives agreed to meet with the Palm team at the Admirals' Club at Dallas airport, a geographical spot halfway between IBM's Raleigh offices and Palm's West Coast home.

The three IBM executives must have experienced a minor culture shock when they rose to meet the Palm contingent: the outspoken Dubinsky, the wisecracking Colligan, and the young black professional Brown. "Later, Donna said we were like the Mod Squad walking into the room," says Brown. "They were pretty classic IBM guys. You could just see the look on their faces: 'What *is* this company?' That's what I liked about Palm—it was just a little bit off-beat."

The IBM representatives recovered quickly and, over the coming months, negotiated an agreement that resulted in IBM-branded versions of the PalmPilot and many of Palm's future products.

In the summer of 1997, Palm redoubled its effort to entice developers to write the thousands of software programs that would make the PalmPilot an even more useful device. Donna hired Mark Bercow, a young executive from 3Com. As VP of strategic alliances and platform development, Bercow would be in charge of partnerships, both with other companies and with the world's programmers. ("I expected Jeff Hawkins to be a pompous ass," he says. "So many technical visionaries are like that. I was surprised by his humility and his almost childlike inquisitiveness.")

Of course, Kate Purmal's group had long worked toward cultivating a developer community, now numbering 2,000 programmers, for the Palm platform. Her efforts culminated in early October, just weeks after Bercow's arrival, at Palm's first Developer Conference: a gathering for geeks, designed to make developers enthusiastic about writing programs for the Palm OS.

At the time, most of Palm's developers were either tiny companies or solo programmers who were moonlighting evenings and weekends writing applications for the Palm OS. In the PC world, where big companies like Microsoft, Lotus, and Symantec were the leaders, independent software developers had little chance for success on their own. In the new handheld industry, however, there were no established leaders yet; any developer with a good idea had the chance to become a household name. Therefore, the conference theme, which would be printed on carrying bags and everywhere in the auditorium, was "Think Big."

To open her keynote speech, Dubinsky commissioned a video that lampooned the history of handheld computing. She enlisted John Doerr, the high-profile Silicon Valley VC who had started the pen computing frenzy of the early 1990s by funding GO, to play himself in the video; in it, he reenacted his "invention" of the industry by throwing his pen across the room in frustration. Jeff and Donna's fruitless search for start-up money was illustrated by a sequence of VC doors slamming shut on Jeff's dismayed face, and film clips shot in Depression-era style showed pen computing programmers begging on the streets, holding cardboard signs that read, "WILL CODE FOR MONEY."

All in all, Purmal and her team had spent nearly $1 million on the conference—for Palm in those days, a lot of money.

Unfortunately, only weeks before the show, only about 100 programmers had signed up to attend. This was grim news, indeed. Without the enthusiasm of independent programmers, one of Palm's key strategies to defend its lead over Microsoft stood on shaky ground.

For several weeks in a row, the Monday morning executive staff meetings centered on whether Palm should cancel the conference altogether. Colligan argued that Palm should give the event its best shot and hope for the best.

In the two weeks before the conference, the trickle of registrations picked up slightly. But Dubinsky wanted to take no chances: She decided to stack the deck. In an e-mail to the entire company, she requested that every single Palm employee attend at least the first day of the conference, so that the large auditorium would be at least moderately filled during the keynote addresses.

On the conference's opening day, October 15, Purmal's heart raced as she surveyed the lobby: It teemed with hundreds of walk-in attendees who had not bothered to register. By the time Dubinsky opened the conference with her speech, the auditorium buzzed with over 500 programmers and the 150 Palm employees.

The crowd roared with laughter at Dubinsky's video. Next, Donna called the surprised Hawkins onto the stage to present him with a gold-plated PalmPilot—the one-millionth unit off the production line. One million PalmPilots had been sold in 18 months. Palm's little invention had been accepted faster by America than any other computer—and faster than VCRs, cell phones, TVs, or almost any other consumer electronic product.

Despite the worries only a few weeks earlier, Palm's first developer conference was ultimately a huge success. For Palm, there was only one disappointment: Few large software companies had sent representatives. Like everything else in Palm's world, though, that would change.

In the fall of 1997, 3Com's business hit a hard bump. Unsold USR modems were piling up in the retail channel. Benhamou applied the brakes: 3Com would sell far fewer modems to the nation's stores until they cleared out the inventory they already had in stock.

The result was an immediate, steady slide of 3Com's stock price from the mid-50s to the mid-30s only a month later. (The following summer, it would fall still further, into the 20s.)

Palm's executives applauded Benhamou's decision. He'd showed that he could take the right steps.

His next step came as a shock, however. Now that he was expecting lower sales, Benhamou had to cut his company's expenses. One approach might have been to drastically cut the budgets of underperforming product lines, leaving the budgets of promising product lines like Palm untouched. But Benhamou didn't have the time. Half of his company's product lines were new to him; he decided to cut the budgets of all 3Com divisions evenly.

Unfortunately, Palm could ill afford such belt-tightening. It needed to spend money and invest in its future. "When you have a business such as Palm, you want to grow fast and realize the opportunity," says Janice Roberts. "Naturally, you want to be able to put money into it to build your position, build your brand, build the market. And then you become part of a bigger public company that has to meet its expectations. It's really hard to bring any two companies together like that," she says. But there was little she could do for Palm. 3Com's needs were her first priority.

Instead of gaining strength by the large corporation, Palm's growth was stunted by its large, and now flailing, parent.

Donna Dubinsky, for her part, hadn't given up on the idea of a Palm spinout. In fact, the 3Com merger made her more insistent than ever. Donna wasn't the only one who wanted 3Com to spin off Palm after the merger—her employees were also obsessed with the thought.

The frequent calls from 3Com managers who professed to "be in charge" or to "want to help" had taken their toll. Just as in the USR days, Palm's employees were hypersensitive to requests from their parent company that they interpreted as "not good for Palm." "The culture at Palm was nearly dysfunctional in some ways, in that it was an amazing esprit de corps and focus on the product, the market, on growing quickly, on proving that this idea was right and on building this huge business," remembers Bill Slakey, who came to Palm as its controller directly from 3Com, where he had been investor relations director. "Palm was very, very focused in that way. But very distracted—and this is what I mean by almost dysfunctional—by the merger. The most reluctant acquirees you can imagine."

The 3Com backlash at Palm was exacerbated by the crash of 3Com's stock price. Silicon Valley's Internet gold rush was heating up; everyone at Palm knew somebody (or knew somebody who knew somebody) who had just become an overnight millionaire on stock options in a start-up nobody had even heard of. The Palm employees' USR stock had been exchanged for 3Com's stock during the merger, however. Now that 3Com's stock price hovered in the mid-30s, with little imminent prospect of rising again, most of the employees' stock options were worthless.

Jeff, Donna, and Ed enjoyed tremendous employee loyalty. Still, Palm was outgrowing the small-company atmosphere that so many of the employees had cherished. It maddened the Palm employees, too, that their work contributed to what was by now recognized as the fastest-selling product in computer history, yet their salaries, bonuses, and stock options were tied to the failing fortunes of an unloved parent company. Sooner or later, money would become an issue.

"3Com was under attacks from all sides, and they seemed to be incompetent to do anything about it," remembers engineer Art Lamb. "I actually wanted to leave at that point. I talked to Rob [Haitani] and Ron [Marianetti] about trying to start something [a start-up company]. But we didn't really have the business savvy to pull it together."

The executives' worries about a talent drain were compounded by the increasing urgency to hire *new* employees. The Internet bubble had triggered what would soon be recognized as the biggest hiring boom in history; hundreds of start-ups had begun to woo employees with the lure of instant millions. Even successful companies like Oracle and Cisco were having trouble competing with the start-ups for talented workers. "We started to get more and more name recognition, more and more 'Wow, this is neat!' " says HR director Doug Haslam. "People wanted to come because they wanted to work on the technology, the product, the vision."

Faced with a choice between stock options in an Internet start-up, a successful technology firm, and 3Com, job candidates often declined the offer from Palm.

With little alternative, Haslam began to circumvent 3Com's HR salary guidelines, offering job candidates for crucial positions higher salaries than the 3Com pay scale allowed. Predictably, each such infraction got him into trouble with 3Com's own HR department.

There was nothing Donna could do about the stock price or about the instant millionaires at other companies. She did, however, come up with an idea that she hoped would compensate her employees for the success they were creating: rich bonuses. She made a proposal to 3Com's executives: to calculate the bonuses for Palm employees based on Palm's sales results, not 3Com's.

3Com's HR executives, sensitive to equal treatment of all employees, balked. Unwilling to give up, she pressed the issue until a compromise emerged: Half of the bonus would be paid based on Palm's sales, the other half based on 3Com's.

Sure enough, for many quarters to come, Palm's employees received far higher bonuses than 3Com's employees, who often got no bonus at all.

While 3Com's business struggled, Palm's fortunes continued to skyrocket.

The PalmPilot was becoming an American icon. Palm fan Web sites had sprung up all over the world. The little device made guest appearances on TV shows (like *Murphy Brown* and *Just Shoot Me*) and in movies; an opening shot in *Wag the Dog* featured a close-up of Robert DeNiro's character's PalmPilot. Al Gore used one. At each monthly company meeting, Dubinsky read letters from enthusiastic customers, and the sales executives showed off the latest sales charts. "Now *that's* a beautiful picture," Andy Simms would comment each time. In December 1997 alone, over 100,000 people bought PalmPilots.

Only Palm's continued chafing against its corporate parent spoiled the celebration. After having come so far, worked so hard, and endured so many setbacks, it galled many at Palm to have to share the credit for its best-selling creation with a parent company who had had none of the vision, done none of the work, and now seemed an obstacle to further success. It had been bad enough to see their product called "the USR Pilot"; now the press wrote about 3Com's PalmPilot. It just didn't seem fair that Jeff Hawkins's creation wasn't called "*Palm Computing's* wildly successful PalmPilot."

After much discussion, 3Com had agreed to let Palm describe itself as "Palm Computing, Inc., a 3Com company." But as 3Com's businesses continued in the doldrums and Palm's sales rose ever higher, Palm employees started to joke that soon enough, the name would be "3Com, a Palm Computing company."

To Palm's executives, however, it wasn't a joke. "I always felt that Palm would be bigger than 3Com," says Hawkins. "I never told Eric that directly. The first time I met him, I told him it would be his biggest division. I don't think he believed me."

By December 1997, every instinct told Dubinsky that Palm didn't belong with 3Com. Never mind the minor cultural differences; Palm's business just didn't fit. If Palm stayed in 3Com's stranglehold, it might never achieve its real potential. She arranged for a meeting with Benhamou to talk, once more, about a spinout of Palm.

The topic wasn't new to Benhamou. Dubinsky had hinted at it in more or less subtle ways from the very beginning; so had Frank Quattrone, her investment banker friend (and a long-time adviser to Benhamou himself).

His arguments to Benhamou had been straightforward: "There's a lot of value there. The people are really focused on building a big business. Inside 3Com, it will be a drag on earnings; outside, it could be worth a lot."

At the time, Benhamou indicated that the time wasn't right for him to seriously think about a spinout. He had more important issues to deal with: specifically, the enormous task of integrating the two large companies.

Now, in December 1997, Dubinsky sat down with Benhamou in his private conference room and went over her list of arguments, which by now she could have recited in her sleep. First, Palm could not reach its potential as part of a networking company. "It has different dynamics. It requires a different type of recruiting. It requires different business models to report to Wall Street." 3Com couldn't afford to invest in Palm's growth without hurting its bottom line, yet without more investment, Palm could fall prey to Microsoft, she argued. Furthermore, a spin-out would "unlock value" for 3Com's shareholders, who would receive the proceeds of the sale of Palm Computing.

Benhamou agreed to ask investment bankers to analyze the spinout issue. When she left the meeting, Donna was elated. She was confident that he would arrive at the same conclusions as she had.

As promised, Benhamou asked two investment banking firms who regularly did 3Com work for analyses of the case for a Palm spinoff: Deutsche Morgan Grenfell, led by Frank Quattrone, and Goldman Sachs. They had till March to give him their recommendations.

Dubinsky threw herself into the task of supplying the two banking firms with all the Palm business information they'd need for their analysis. She was determined to leave no stone unturned in her quest to set Palm free.

SIXTEEN

MICROSOFT 2.0

3Com's budget cuts in the fall of 1997 came at a particularly bad time for Palm. Not only was Ed Colligan's marketing department gearing up to launch the next version of the PalmPilot (the Palm III—having lost the Pilot Pen suit, Palm dropped the term *Pilot*), but Palm was also bracing for stiff competition: the second version of Windows CE, code-named Gryphon, due to be announced in January 1998.

The rumors about CE 2.0 had become concrete during the summer months. The new Microsoft-driven handhelds no longer looked like clamshells; they looked like PalmPilots, complete with buttons and handwriting recognition software. They would sport 4 MB of memory or more, built-in modems, voice recording, and a slew of other features.

"A lot of people thought we would get clobbered by Microsoft. It was a foregone conclusion that Palm would be put out of business," Hawkins says. "I refused to accept that."

At the first rumors of the CE 2.0 products, a small "compete with Microsoft" movement formed inside Palm. They told Jeff that Palm should match at least some of Microsoft's features in Palm's next product releases.

"Senior people on Donna's staff said, 'We must change our

strategy; we'll have to do something.' Here were smart people telling me we were going to lose," says Hawkins. He worried about the upcoming battle, but refused to veer from the focus on simplicity.

For months, Jeff found himself in arguments over his decision, in product design meetings, in random encounters in the hallways, and even in the executive staff meetings. In the old days, decisions like this one would have been made quickly in discussions with Colligan, Haitani, and Sipher. But many of Palm's 150 employees were new, and hadn't yet internalized the Hawkins/Palm philosophy of simplicity. Most had come from other technology companies, and despite the PalmPilot's success, the conventional technology thinking that had shaped most of them was hard to shake off. To *not* try to match Microsoft seemed crazy, especially in the features, such as more memory, that were relatively easy to add.

Hawkins refused to do even that. "I could have added more memory, but that would send the wrong message to the market," he says. Microsoft, with its roots in the desktop PC world, would promote Windows CE handhelds as though they were tiny desktop computers. Microsoft would tout bits and bytes, MIPS and chips, memory size and processor speed. Yet, all these features would accomplish, he insisted, would be to make a handheld slow, clutter its user interface, and make it expensive.

"The way to compete is not going head to head with these guys; that's a losing proposition," he told his colleagues. "I want to go some place where they can't go. I want to prove that this isn't a little computer."

Jeff intended to leapfrog Microsoft with the two more dramatic product overhauls that were in the Palm pipeline: (1) the ultrathin fashion statement, code-named Razor (Palm V); and (2) the wireless, antenna-equipped Blue Sky (Palm VII).

"I was a little Jobsian in this, because I refused to put any new features into Palm V," Hawkins says, referring to Steve Jobs, Apple's legendary autocrat. "Some new features wouldn't have hurt, but I wanted to make it clear to everyone what the goal was. The goal was beauty. Beauty, beauty, beauty. I didn't want any distraction with other things. I didn't want the people who would review the product to say, 'They've come out with a product that has twice as much memory.' I wanted them to say: 'They've come out with a new product that's just beautiful.' "

In his pursuit of the slim, chic Pilot he had in mind, however, Hawkins was still running into mechanical obstacles.

One such problem had just surfaced: attaching the front and back of the metal case. Hawkins wanted to use glue. Screws, he felt, would destroy the sleek look he wanted.

He faced opposition from many sides. Palm's manufacturing experts favored screws, because gluing was a messy process that didn't use the same assembly equipment as the other Palm-Pilots. The hardware designers didn't believe that there was a gluing compound suitable to the task. In fact, when they exper-imented with different glues, the prototype palmtops popped open in drop tests; the glues weren't strong enough to hold the casing together.

Even the repair team had its say. Their concern was that in order to repair a glued Palm V, they would have to rip apart and destroy the case, making repairs much more expensive.

With stubborn determination, Hawkins brushed all con-cerns aside. The goal was to produce the slimmest, most elegant and sophisticated-looking palmtop, and for that, only glue would do. Besides, he had spent his childhood building con-traptions under his father's direction, using any imaginable material. The right kind of glue existed somewhere in the world, he insisted; his team just had to find it.

Work on the other Palm sibling, the wireless Palm VII, was proceeding in parallel. The idea was to build in a two-way radio, which would communicate, via flip-up antenna, with the Bell-South wireless data network, so that the customer could tap into the Internet or send e-mail without a modem or a phone line.

Unfortunately, the rate of data exchange was excruciatingly slow: about 8 kilobits per second. (The modern desktop modem is about seven times as fast.) Most Web pages were staggeringly huge. A single stock-quote page could take several minutes to download. A customer would never put up with such a wait. Worse, Web pages are designed for PC screens, not the small screens of a handheld computer. Browsing and clicking through these Internet pages on a handheld were out of the question.

The solution was typical Hawkins. "He kept saying, 'Can't

you put a form on the device?' or 'Can't you only send the stuff that fills the form?' " Joe Sipher says. When Joe finally understood what he meant, the idea seemed simple. Instead of trying to display a complete, downloaded Web page on the tiny screen, the Palm VII would be preloaded with mini–Web pages, complete with graphics, blanks, pop-up menus, and so on. Data from the Web would appear in the appropriate blanks: stock prices, news articles, movie schedules, sports scores, phone book information, and so on. Because only tiny snippets of text would be transferred (something Palm called *Web clippings*), each Web lookup would take only a few seconds.

Making this work, however, took Sipher and his team well beyond the technical ground with which Palm was already familiar, including designing a tiny two-way radio and server software that would strip out all of the data that typically make Web browsing so slow: the graphics, frames, Java, ads, and animations, leaving only the pure text to stream onto the Palm VII. They investigated a number of server software technologies that could play that role, with no luck; most, unsurprisingly, had been designed for use by PCs.

"Then we'll have to do our own," Jeff told Joe. He put Ron Marianetti on the task.

On January 7, 1998, at the Consumer Electronics Show, Microsoft launched its new handheld OS. A slew of companies, including Casio, Philips, and obscure names like Palmax and Uniden, announced new handhelds that would run Windows CE 2.0, though none were expected to ship until April or May.

The rumors had been true: The new products looked remarkably like PalmPilots. *Wired* magazine said in June, "The physical resemblance between the two is so striking, you can't help but conclude that Microsoft, sensing a successful product that it hadn't yet driven out of the market, copied the PalmPilot's look and gave it a Windows feel."

To add insult to injury, Microsoft came up with what seemed like a deliberately confusing name for the new devices: *Palm PCs*. The battle between Microsoft and Palm had officially begun.

"**W**e immediately started getting all sorts of calls from people trying to understand if we had licensed our software to Microsoft," Dubinsky says. "We had just renamed the entire product line heavily with the Palm name. We had Palm OS, we had Palm Computing, and here they were with Palm PC! There was clearly going to be massive confusion in the market."

"I remember seeing it in the paper the day it came out," says Colligan. "We went to Eric and the whole team at 3Com and said, 'We want to send a letter of cease-and-desist to these guys. We have a registered trademark on Palm Computing. We're going to fight this. They're clearly trying to trade off our brand position in the marketplace!' "

Now that Palm was part of 3Com, suing Microsoft wasn't a decision Donna could make on her own. This was a tricky situation: Microsoft and 3Com were already collaborating on two large networking projects that 3Com considered of major importance. A 3Com employee, nicknamed Microsoft Bob, even worked in Microsoft's headquarters, the better to react quickly to Microsoft's every wish.

To Palm, the need for a lawsuit seemed clear; to 3Com, it was clear that such an action could have dire repercussions. Even Microsoft Bob got involved. "He was flipping out," Dubinsky says. "He would call me every other day, saying, 'Why are you doing this, don't you know this is ridiculous?' I said, 'This isn't ridiculous to me.' "

After days of agonizing, the 3Com executives agreed with Palm. "It didn't matter that we had other collaborative projects in other parts of the business. Microsoft still crossed the line," says Benhamou. "We said, 'Listen. Both of us are large, multi-faceted companies. We're not necessarily going to collaborate across all fronts, nor are we competing against all fronts. We should just be clear as to which are the areas in which we compete, and which are the areas in which we collaborate, and make sure that we understand where the boundaries are. In this particular case, you have been a bad competitor, and we're going to call you to the mat on that.' And the conversation was extremely structured; it was not a highly emotional conversation."

The Palm executives breathed a collective sigh of relief. "3Com's head attorney was very sober about this," Dubinsky remembers. "He basically said, 'Look, if we don't show Microsoft that we're going to defend our rights in the area of intellectual property, then they are not going to respect us. We have to do what is right, regardless of who it is. Let's try and settle and work on a compromise.' In the end, we got to defend our property."

Microsoft responded that the word *Palm* was simply a generic term for a device held in one's hand, and that anybody could use it.

While Benhamou placed phone calls to his contacts high in the Microsoft organization to mediate, Palm prepared to prove that the Palm PC name caused confusion in court. The lawyers gathered evidence of Palm's long-time use of its trademarks, and the 800-number representatives kept track of how many customers called to express confusion about the name *Palm PC*.

Having learned a little something from the Pilot Pen episode, Palm filed suits in Europe—in Italy, France, and Germany, where the rules of trademark infringement had proved so cut and dried only six months earlier. Dubinsky's timing was impeccable: News of the lawsuit hit the airwaves only days before CeBIT, the largest computer show in Europe, was to open its doors to half a million visitors in Hannover, Germany. Microsoft and its hardware partners were sure to showcase the new CE devices there.

On the clammy and cold opening day of CeBIT, Palm's attorney searched out the booths of Microsoft and its hardware partners to make sure the companies had complied with the injunction. The bigger companies had done so. But the smaller, unknown firms hadn't taken the warning seriously (or just hadn't had the manpower to make the rapid changes). "Basically, the marshals came in and had to pull any literature with Palm PC on it out of the CeBIT show," says Dubinsky. "It was a bit of a scene," Colligan says with satisfaction.

Accused of stealing ideas, Bill Gates angrily defended Microsoft's actions at a roundtable with reporters in San Jose, California, and repeated Microsoft's public line: Palm PC was merely descriptive; it wouldn't confuse anyone. Any suggestion to the contrary was "beyond bizarre." (After his appearance, Gates left the room—and accidentally left behind his palmtop. To the amusement of the assembled media, Gates's assistant rushed back into the room, saying that she had to retrieve "Bill's PalmPilot.")

In the meantime, Eric Benhamou continued his careful conversations with Microsoft VP Paul Moritz. "We knew that if it was mishandled, it could have negative repercussions on the other relationships we had," says Benhamou.

Rather than press on with the lawsuits in Europe, 3Com's executives started settlement talks with Microsoft. By April 8, six weeks before the first CE 2.0 products would ship to stores, they had reached a compromise: Microsoft agreed to drop the use of the term *Palm PC* and, instead, use *palm-size PC*. In return, 3Com agreed to drop its lawsuits.

Colligan didn't consider the compromise ideal. Protecting the Palm brand was a top priority; *palm-size PC* was still too close for comfort. "If I were Palm Computing as a stand-alone company, I would have kept fighting."

Benhamou, on the other hand, believes that an independent Palm wouldn't have stood a chance. "I think that the fact that 3Com had a relationship with Microsoft helped Palm a great deal, because had Palm been an independent company, Microsoft would have moved 25 cannons aiming at Palm, and would have just shot them out of existence. They couldn't do that with 3Com. They had to deal with us."

After months of legal skirmishes, it was a relief for Ed Colligan to enter the battle with something tangible and exciting: the new Palm III, which Palm unveiled in March along with an upgrade for PalmPilot and Pilot models that included the new infrared beaming feature. This time, there was no firestorm of anger from Palm's now 1.5 million customers. Having learned from the PalmPilot announcement a year earlier, Ed had made sure to offer a trade-up for the original Pilot models.

Unsurprisingly, the Palm-Microsoft battle caught plenty of attention. The business magazines covered the expected struggle with special interest, observing that Microsoft considered winning the handheld market vital to its future. "Microsoft's master plan is to control—or at least put Windows inside—every access point to information and entertainment, whether it's a desktop computer, telephone, TV, or handheld device," *Time* magazine reported in a three-page article titled "Palm-to-Palm Combat."

Microsoft had been dominant in a world that centered on the PC, where it was to most users' advantage to use the same OS as everybody else. However, the world was changing. The center of gravity was shifting away from the PC, which was Microsoft's undisputed domain. Since the mid-1990s, much of the focus of personal computing had shifted to the Internet, where Microsoft was not a clear winner. And a new category of mobile, Palm-like devices was further shifting computing away from the desktop PC. Winning the handheld war, in other words, was critical if Microsoft was to maintain its power.

Little wonder, then, that Microsoft had already spent as much as $250 million developing Windows CE, employing 600 employees in its CE group and directly related projects—more than twice the number of Palm employees, even though Microsoft didn't manufacture, sell, or market any devices of its own.

Within days of the Palm III launch in March 1997, Palm's PR agency rep Allen Bush passed a warning to Colligan. Bush was getting the impression from tech journalists that Microsoft was pushing them to write comparative reviews, Palm III versus Windows CE, rather than giving the Palm III stand-alone reviews. Microsoft was sure to tout the Palm-size PCs' features, claiming superiority over Palm's products in a more-is-better message. Ed's job was to dispel that myth before it could take hold.

Part of that job was figuring out how the Windows CE products really performed. The day that the first CE palmtops were for sale in stores, Palm product manager David Christopher tested the various models side-by-side with a PalmPilot. As soon as he had loaded the data from his own Palm III into the CE handheld, he found that, even with twice as much memory, the Windows-driven device couldn't hold as much data as the Palm III. Next, he found a hilarious warning in the Casio user manual:

"Refrain from playing back recordings or turning on the back-light except when necessary"; those functions would drain the batteries extremely quickly. Sure enough, as he continued putting the Windows CE handhelds through their paces, the batteries on some didn't last even an hour.

The next day, Dubinsky told the assembled company about Christopher's test results, to roaring applause. "[Windows CE 2.0] was a classic overpromise and underdeliver," Christopher says. Now Colligan and his team had to be sure that the world at large also saw it that way.

Christopher and fellow product manager Greg Shirai set out across the country—Shirai on the West Coast, Christopher on the East—for a two-and-a-half-week trip they called the FUD Tour. (FUD stands for *fear, uncertainty, and doubt,* which tech executives often accuse Microsoft of trying to instill in the minds of businesses and consumers about Microsoft's competition.) Their mission was to demonstrate to journalists and analysts how the new Palm III held up to its rivals—and that Microsoft's wouldn't win in the end. Palm's PR agency suggested that the Palm duo open each meeting with: "What is Palm doing to compete against Microsoft? We're here to tell you."

It was the largest press and analyst tour Palm had undertaken to date. In six to eight meetings a day, they repeated Palm's mantra of simplicity to every analyst and journalist who would listen. Palm focuses on the user, they said, whereas Microsoft focuses on lodging Windows everywhere. They conceded that Microsoft's approach worked in the desktop computer world: In a PC, all the bells and whistles caused no harm because ever faster hardware made up for the sluggish software. In the handheld world, however, simplicity ruled. Pressing one button on the Palm III instantly showed the day's schedule—processor power had nothing to do with it. Windows CE, they pointed out, just meant "the complexity of Windows in the palm of your hand."

The eight testers from *PC Week*'s lab weren't convinced; they wanted to focus on features, specifically on those that the IT managers in corporations demanded. The two Palm product managers compared notes every evening on the questions and objections they had gotten that day. "They said, 'Microsoft is going to crush you, they have the enterprise connections, the hooks to Outlook, and the hooks to Exchange, blah, blah, blah,'" Christopher told his colleague. "And we don't really have very good answers to that." Palm had focused most of its efforts on consumers, and still didn't have a solid strategy for selling into corporations.

When the *PC Week* review was published, it didn't surprise Christopher. "The first palm-size PC to hit the streets is going to give 3Com Corp.'s PalmPilot PDA a run for its money." But the article was a victory for Christopher nonetheless. In two of the evaluation criteria he had suggested, Windows CE came up short—the reviewers found both synchronization and navigation easier on the Palm III.

Most journalists, however, received Palm's "simplicity matters" message with more enthusiasm. As soon as the Palm presenters got around to showing that it took 25 times longer to search for a name on the Windows CE handheld than on the Palm, the journalists' reaction was immediate. "Really?"

"Yes, here, check it out for yourself," Christopher would answer, pushing the Palm III and a Windows CE model across the table.

But while the press focused on products their readers could buy now, industry analysts were skeptical about Palm's long-term outlook. Because these analysts could influence both the press and their corporate clients, Palm's executives had to try to change their minds.

Therefore, soon after the product managers returned from their trip, Palm Platform VP Mark Bercow left the office to meet with the most influential industry analysts, in hopes of offering tangible proof that Palm was capable of staying ahead of its competition with innovative new products. He could point out that over 8,000 developers had written over 1,500 add-on software titles. Palm was making inroads into corporations, he said, through alliances with companies such as Computer Associates, Remedy, and Sybase, who supplied enterprise software. Furthermore, Palm also had signed four OEM agreements and licensed the Palm OS to Qualcomm for a combined cell phone and organizer.

Industry analysts agreed that the current Palm handhelds were superior to those based on CE, but they were unwilling to predict Palm's success in the future. Like everybody else in the computing industry, they had learned long ago that most markets that Microsoft wants, it eventually gets.

By summer, though, it was clear that the Palm marketers had earned their pay. Sales of PalmPilots and Palm IIIs continued to increase each month, while all CE products together failed to take more than 20 percent of market share. In fact, Palm now sold three times as many handhelds as it had only a year earlier, when Palm had become a small part of 3Com.

In the *Wall Street Journal,* Walt Mossberg wrote a column titled "The Palm Pilot has some new rivals but no competition" that concluded: "If its parent firm, 3Com, gives Palm the money and leeway it needs to keep innovating, it could become a major force in all kinds of new digital appliances."

For the moment, the Microsoft scare was over. But other battles lay ahead; of that the Palm executives were sure. What was less sure was whether 3Com would indeed give Palm the money and leeway it needed to stay ahead.

SEVENTEEN

THE FIGHT FOR INDEPENDENCE

3Com had lowered Palm's budgets just as the threat of aggressive competition from Microsoft was looming; Donna Dubinsky needed no further reminder as to why Palm needed its independence. The time to grow Palm quickly was now, before Microsoft-powered products got much traction in the marketplace. Within 3Com, Palm's budgets would be too small to fund rapid expansion.

With the date of the bankers' presentations on a possible Palm spin-off quickly approaching, Donna stepped up her efforts, feeding the bankers and lawyers every scrap of information she could put her hands on concerning the handheld industry. She, Jeff, and Ed had concluded that a spinout wasn't just important— it was critical to Palm's chances for retaining its lead in the handheld computing industry. So critical, in fact, that they were determined to resign if Palm wasn't spun out. The experience with Zoomer had taught them that they could not let a business partner's conflicting agenda cause Palm's failure. They never wanted to have to think: "Well, we would have been successful if we hadn't depended on someone else," as Hawkins puts it.

But quitting would be a last resort; Dubinsky had high hopes for the spinout talks. She'd discussed her arguments with some of the people who would advise Benhamou, including his friend and 3Com board member Jean-Louis Gassée, and her boss, Janice Roberts. "I'd walk out of every meeting and feel like, 'OK! We got it! I'm going to make this happen'," Dubinsky says.

For Benhamou, the spinout issue was an irritation he didn't need. Throughout 1997, one major problem had followed another. 3Com's roller-coaster ride had started in late January, when a price war with Intel caused 3Com's stock to plunge. Then the merger with U.S. Robotics became a hornet's nest.

Benhamou and his executives had expected that merging the two large companies would entail a great deal of work, but no one had been prepared for just how badly the integration would proceed. 3Com's troubles continued through the fall of 1997, with the discovery of unsold inventories in the channel and worsened with slow sales of several product lines. Two class-action lawsuits filed in late 1997 against both the company and Benhamou personally (and other top 3Com executives) added to the agony. The suits alleged that 3Com and its executives had manipulated 3Com's stock price by concealing its USR integration problems, weak demand for its products, and the state of its channel inventory.

Now, in spring 1998, 3Com's finance department forecast a disastrous fiscal year: The company's income would be less than half what it had been the year before.

In short, Benhamou had much more urgent issues on his mind than bankers' presentations on a Palm spin-off. He needed to refine the company's strategy, streamline its operations, and shift its sales from the slowing product lines to fast-growing categories—like the PalmPilot.

On March 11, 1998, Hawkins, Dubinsky, and Palm's controller Bill Slakey drove to 3Com to join Benhamou, Janice Roberts, and 3Com's chief financial officer Chris Paisley for the first of the two investment bankers' presentations. Frank Quattrone's team, made up of several of Deutsche Morgan Grenfell's (DMG's) most senior analysts, arrived shortly thereafter.

3Com could achieve its objective—"maximizing the value of Palm"—in several ways, the DMG bankers said, such as selling Palm to another company or forming a joint venture with a partner. But in the bankers' opinion, only one option unequivocally met both 3Com's and Palm's goals: a spin-off.

Donna and Jeff left the meeting energized. "It seemed like it was the right thing to do," says Hawkins. "I just assumed it was going to happen. It made sense, so it should happen."

Goldman Sachs, the other banking team Benhamou had asked to analyze the case for a spin-off, presented a less clear-cut picture two days later. "They took a much more on-the-fence position of saying, 'If you want to do it, you can do it. You certainly can keep it, too. It's a nice business,' " says Dubinsky.

The decision over Palm's fate was significant enough for Benhamou to involve members of his board of directors before reaching a verdict. Of the subcommittee members, the colorful Frenchman Jean-Louis Gassée, had the most intriguing vantage point. He had been a long-time friend of Benhamou's and a member of 3Com's board of directors since 1993. As vice president in charge of Apple's research and development in 1987, he had overseen the start of Apple's Newton project. Moreover, Gassée was an entrepreneur himself, having run his company Be, Inc. for nearly eight years; he certainly understood Hawkins and Dubinsky's frustrations. "It's difficult for entrepreneurs like Jeff and Donna to flourish inside a large organization," Gassée says. "It's not natural. To be an entrepreneur, you've got to be driven, stubborn, focused. You are used to getting your way, at least inside your organization. The 3Com acquisition no longer enabled that to some extent."

Hawkins and Dubinsky argued their case for a spin-off directly before the board subcommittee in mid-April. As the meeting came to an end, Hawkins made an impassioned plea to the assembled group. He was tired of fighting never-ending battles with people who thought they knew more about Palm's business than Palm's own executives, he said. He explained how the disastrous Zoomer experience had given him the conviction never again to compromise his control over a project. If Palm failed, it had to be because he and Dubinsky had failed, not because corporate parents or business partners had interfered.

"The battle with Microsoft will be very hard," Hawkins declared. "I won't commit years of my life to it with one hand tied behind my back."

The meeting ended without a verdict. "In the end," says Dubinsky, "they turned to Eric and just said, 'You know, it depends on whether you view it as strategic or not. If you view this as strategic to the future of the business, then we should keep it. If you don't think it's strategic, then it looks like it's a very possible thing to spin off.' " Nevertheless, Donna remained optimistic. The logic for a spin-off, she thought, was still on her side.

While Dubinsky waited for a decision from Eric Benhamou, she received another reminder of Palm's value in the form of a phone call from Steve Jobs, Apple's founder and, at the time, Apple's interim CEO. Dubinsky had known Jobs during her years at Apple, but hadn't spoken to him in over a decade.

"Steve, congratulations!" she said when she recognized her caller. "What a tremendous job you're doing." Jobs had only been in charge of the ailing Apple for a short while, but already signs of a turnaround were visible.

Without much small talk, Jobs cut to the chase: He had called Eric Benhamou expressing Apple's interest in buying Palm from 3Com. Jobs was looking for ways to expand Apple's product lineup with a low-cost portable computer. Dubinsky listened with amusement as Jobs suggested to her that Palm could use the kind of help that a great product design company like Apple could give her. She knew that Jobs was sounding her out on the idea. While it was clearly up to Benhamou to decide if he wanted to sell Palm, Jobs expected that if he could get her excited about the idea, Dubinsky would lobby Benhamou to consider the sale.

"Guess who I just talked to—Steve Jobs!" Dubinsky called out as she approached Ed's corner office.

"What did he want?" Colligan asked, stepping out of his office.

"He wants to buy Palm," Dubinsky explained.

"What did you tell him?"

"I told him that I was getting too cranky to work for anybody!"

For Eric Benhamou, the spinout decision rested on a number of interrelated issues.

"I first had to convince myself that there was a strategic reason why it should happen, that there was enough fundamental difference between the handheld business and the rest of the businesses that it should be even more separate," Benhamou says. "Second, I had to convince myself that there was a potential to create shareholder value.

"But the first question had to be: Why? And then after that, How? And When? But early on, there were no good answers to: Why?"

Where the bankers and the Palm executives had seen certain success of a Palm spinout, Benhamou saw a lot of risk. "If it was a flop, not only would it be bad for Palm, it would be bad for 3Com."

Meanwhile, his management team was still struggling to integrate U.S. Robotics. "It could have been a lot of attention diverted on the part of the 3Com team and neglecting the rest of the business, which was 95 percent of the revenues. I couldn't afford to make that kind of call," he says. "I would have been sued for the rest of my life for this if it had flopped!"

In the end, despite the presentations by lawyers and investment bankers and Palm's executives, Benhamou made his decision alone. "It was so many people trying to influence me in very self-serving ways, I chose not to listen to them," Benhamou says.

His decision was no.

The news devastated Donna. She had been hoping to extricate Palm from its parent company's embrace for well over a year, from the eve of the merger between USR and 3Com in February of 1997 to now, the early summer of 1998. Gaining Palm's independence was the most important thing she had to do for Palm, she thought.

"I felt like such a failure," she says. " 'Why am I so unable to convince people of the right thing to do? Am I such a bad communicator?' " Here she was, having built and run the company with the fastest-selling computer product in computing history, a company that had sold nearly 2 million devices where previous companies had failed, a company that had become the center of an entire new industry. But for all her astonishing achievements, 3Com's management seemed to give her business opinions little weight. "I feel like I have a very good case here. Is it me? Am I doing something wrong?"

Unwilling to give up, and with Janice Roberts's help, Dubinsky began investigating other ways of gaining Palm at least the lure of a thriving stock to retain employees. One possibility was the creation of a *tracking stock* for Palm, a then-new financial instrument. If 3Com issued a tracking stock for Palm, the new Palm stock could then attract investors who were interested in the high-growth handheld business, and 3Com would have "unlocked" Palm's value.

Benhamou rejected the option. Tracking stocks were both too complicated and, because they were so new at the time, unproven.

There was one glimmer of hope. Benhamou had said that timing was a key issue in his decision against the spin-off; 3Com, Palm, and the financial market weren't ready. Furthermore, a spinout in 1998 would be impossible because of the "pooling of interest" bookkeeping method used in the USR-3Com merger. Under U.S. tax law, the acquiring company in such mergers may not dispose of a significant part of the assets of the combined firms within two years, except for "disposals in the ordinary course of business." Spinning out Palm within two years of the 1997 date of the USR acquisition could incur big charges against 3Com.

Whether the pooling of interest rules were relevant in the Palm case was a matter of interpretation. For one thing, it was a stretch to call Palm a significant part of 3Com. Palm's revenues that year accounted for $272 million out of 3Com's total sales of over $5.4 billion—about 5 percent.

Even though it would have been extremely risky for 3Com to sell any of its assets and still qualify for the pooling treatment during the first year after the merger, the deal was approaching its first birthday; the rules were less clear-cut for transitions in the second year. "You could absolutely get around it," says one finance industry insider.

However, having been burned by the lawsuits and accounting problems that resulted from the USR merger, Benhamou was in no mood for any further risks. "I didn't feel there was any reason at all to try and operate close to the edge of what was allowed from a regulatory standpoint," says Benhamou.

In other words, a spin-off during the next 13 months was out of the question.

Determined to leave no stone unturned, Dubinsky hit upon another idea, one that would eliminate the concerns about the timing of a spinout.

She had been a founding member of Claris, the software company Apple had set up with the expectation of spinning out after a few years. Claris executives had negotiated an agreement with Apple that gave all Claris employees stock in the company even while it was still owned by Apple. If Benhamou's main concerns were really the timing of a spin-off and the two-year post-pooling period, then, Dubinsky figured, 3Com could do what Apple had done.

She turned to an old friend, Randy Komisar, who had been Claris's legal counsel and was therefore familiar with the minutiae of Apple's commitments to Claris. He and Donna had been fast friends ever since the two were colleagues on Claris's executive staff ("I like really smart, strong-willed women," Komisar says), and Dubinsky found herself calling him for his advice often.

Komisar wasn't optimistic that Benhamou would agree to a Claris solution, as Dubinsky called it. "They'll never do it," he told her.

Komisar's reasoning had little to do with Palm, and everything to do with 3Com. Most of 3Com's business was weak; Komisar didn't think that Benhamou would let go of the one bright aspect of the company.

Furthermore, Komisar couldn't see why Dubinsky would even want to stay with Palm if it were spun out. As the CEO of a spun-out Palm, she would likely own no more than 1 percent of the company. In comparison, CEOs of independent start-ups generally owned 5 percent or more. Acquaintances all around her had parlayed their executive positions in start-ups into fortunes of hundreds of millions during the Internet boom of the past two years. She, on the other hand, would stand to earn just a few million as the head of an independent Palm.

"If they do it, you aren't going to own any of this thing," he admonished her. "Go off and build a business that you own 30 percent of, that you control!"

But Palm was her baby. She and Jeff had built the company from scratch, and turned it into the leader in an industry that hadn't even existed. She loved the product. The word *Palm* had become a great, powerful brand. She had built a team of people who were deeply loyal to her, and she felt loyal to them. Leaving Palm behind just didn't seem fathomable.

Even though he considered the Claris solution a long shot, Komisar brought reams of documents to her house. Mechanically, the Claris solution was fairly straightforward. 3Com would give between 10 and 20 percent of Palm to Palm's employees and management in the form of Palm stock options. 3Com would own the remaining stock. If 3Com eventually decided against spinning off Palm, it would have to buy the shares back from the Palm employees. The Claris solution wasn't an absolute guarantee that 3Com would indeed spin out Palm, but it would at least put a structure into place that could lead to a spin-off, a clear indication that Benhamou was really considering letting Palm go.

Benhamou's reaction was lukewarm. By this point, associates describe him as annoyed with Dubinsky's persistence. "You can push Eric too far," says one long-time 3Com executive. "Sometimes you have to back off and give him time to mull the options. If he's pushed too far too soon, then he'll just stop." (Or, as another insider put it: "From Eric's point of view, Donna was bright and talented but a pain in the ass.")

Benhamou saw Jeff and Donna as entrepreneurs with an overwhelming need to be their own masters. Later he would tell a journalist that Hawkins, who was only two years his junior, was "the classic example of a young entrepreneur who is dying to be independent and dying to do everything by himself without being accountable to anyone but himself."

Benhamou himself had come to 3Com as an entrepreneur whose company, Bridge Communications, had been acquired. Disagreements over strategies soon broke out, and most of the senior Bridge staff quit. But, as Benhamou told a reporter, "I was a little more patient. I felt 3Com had paid for Bridge and me to make a go of it. I didn't say, 'My way or the highway.' I tried to create alternatives."

At his next meeting with Dubinsky, Benhamou raised new objections. His accountants had told him that 3Com would not be able to keep such a transaction tax-free for 3Com's share-holders for more than a couple of years.

After discussing their options with Jeff and Ed, Donna offered further concessions. She suggested a Claris-like agreement that specified *no* deadline for 3Com's decision to spin out Palm or buy back the shares. Dubinsky was willing to bank on the fact that, one way or another, 3Com would have to take a step. This proposal also named sales targets that Palm would have to hit before their stock would become worth anything. "It was essentially a no-risk deal for [Benhamou]," says Colligan. "We had to create a billion-dollar business that year, or we didn't get paid nothing—nada, zip! It wasn't like 'Give us a bunch of stock and we'll try to make it happen.' "

To learn more about the Claris solution, Benhamou contacted Bill Campbell, who had been CEO of Claris and was now the CEO of Intuit. Campbell cleared his schedule on a moment's notice. When the two CEOs met, Campbell described the terms and mechanics of Apple's agreement with Claris. "I told him what made it work was that we had a very good lawyer who did a marvelous job balancing the needs of both parties," Campbell says.

Benhamou left Campbell's office with his mind made up. "It was very clear after this conversation that it was the wrong thing to do," Benhamou says.

By early June, though, Benhamou had not yet given Dubinsky a final answer. Jeff, having concluded that Benhamou had already made up his mind not to spin Palm out, wanted to meet with Benhamou one more time. "I felt I owed it to him," Hawkins says. "If I was going to leave and start another business, which looked like it was going to happen, I felt I had to tell him."

They met in Benhamou's private conference room. Hawkins laid out his predictions for Palm without him and Dubinsky at the helm. "For eighteen months to two years, it's going to do great," he began. "Without Donna, without me. It doesn't matter if we're not there."

The Palm V and Palm VII had been well defined and were capably executed by the product marketing team. He had no doubts that they would reach the market in good shape. Hawkins had also already instigated work on a Palm handheld with a color screen.

"After eighteen months or two years, I don't know. It might be very hard. It might be very hard to get someone to run the business as well as Donna, and it might be very hard to get someone to design products like I do."

Hawkins also predicted that Palm would lose some of its key players, not just its leaders. "You've got a team here that's working," he told Benhamou. "This team can really build a business. You're going to lose a good portion of the team. And it's not clear that you'll be able to replace them; it's not easy to do."

"I think I can manage this problem," Hawkins remembers Benhamou saying. "I understand what you're saying, and I'm up for the challenge."

Jeff hadn't really expected to change Benhamou's mind; but he had cleared his own conscience. "Now I thought, 'Now he knows that I'm going to go out and build a new business. I've done my duty as a shareholder and as a member of the Palm community.' So if in the end, if the new business becomes the largest handheld computing company in the world," Hawkins says, "I don't feel bad about it."

On July 1, as most employees prepared to leave for the Fourth of July weekend, Dubinsky met with Eric Benhamou again.

He gave her his final answer. It was no.

"I thought that I was most probably going to lose Jeff and Donna anyway," Benhamou explains. "When I look at all of our executives in the company, I look at them in two dimensions: leadership and membership. You have people who score very high in membership but are poor leaders. Then you have the reverse. And the people that I value the most are the people who score very high in both dimensions. These are the people that we invest in the most in the company, because they are long-term players, and they have versatile skills, and they're not high-maintenance. And neither Jeff nor Donna fell into that category, even though they were very good at a set of skills. Their set of skills wasn't broad enough. So I figured, in this configuration they're great, they're some of the best. But that's not what we need the most here. So they may actually go."

There would be no Claris solution, or any other method of separating Palm. Six months of passionate efforts had come to nothing. Timing and the tax ramifications of pooling of interest, Dubinsky was now convinced, were just a smokescreen; Benhamou simply couldn't give up one of 3Com's most valuable assets. In that case, there was no hope for a spinout left.

Dubinsky felt almost relieved. "What do they say about all the stages of mourning?" she says. "I'd gone through many of the stages already, and I was up to acceptance."

Many times during the preceding months, she and Hawkins had discussed resigning if Palm didn't become independent. This was the moment of truth. "Well, it's time for us to go," she remembers telling Benhamou. "And he said, 'Fine.' We shook hands and I walked out.

"And I walked into Janice's office and I just said, 'We're out of here!' She said, 'All right.' That was as dramatic as it was."

There was only one problem: Donna hadn't yet told Jeff that they were resigning.

EIGHTEEN

ONCE AGAIN, WITH MONEY

A few hours after her final meeting with Eric Benhamou, Donna Dubinsky sat with friends in a Palo Alto restaurant, watching the clock. Hawkins hadn't been at Palm that day; she waited to call him until she guessed he'd arrived home.

At a little past 7:00 P.M., she left the table to phone Jeff. "You know, we resigned today," she told him.

He was stunned—and not pleased. She hadn't consulted him before resigning on his behalf (and hers). During the past six months, they had spoken often enough about leaving if 3Com didn't agree to a spinout; they'd even chatted vaguely about starting a new company. However, it was Dubinsky who had led the spin-off negotiations, attended the meetings with Benhamou and Janice Roberts, and kept hopes for a spin-off alive. Jeff had had no warning that Donna would hand in *his* resignation.

"How could you do that without talking to me?" he replied.

Donna was startled. "Well, we've been going down this path . . . I just sort of assumed we were a unit."

"Well, I never really 100 percent agreed to that," Jeff replied.

He was upset. Donna should have discussed the matter with him. He was sure they'd come to the same conclusion, but it bothered him that she hadn't even asked.

"In the back of my mind, I was thinking, 'Starting a company is a big commitment,' " he says. "I mean, we had talked about it, but we never sat down and said, 'Okay, we're ready to do this.' I just thought, 'Gee, until we have done some of these things, we shouldn't have started.' "

For Dubinsky, starting a new company, an independent one that she would run, was the obvious next step. She was genuinely excited about the prospect. In 1992, she and Jeff had set out to build a large, successful company. They had succeeded, but she was itching to do it again without being hampered by outside intervention.

For Hawkins, however, starting a new enterprise was a huge setback. He hadn't been particularly fond of the idea of founding a company back in 1991, and he was no more enthusiastic about it now. It would mean a lot of work, stress, and constant worries.

Furthermore, he had just settled into a viable routine, spending a few days each week writing a book about his brain theories. A new company would set his master plan back by many years. "I wanted to work part-time on my brain stuff, and I knew initially I'd have to stop that for a couple of years at minimum," he says. "It's a multiyear, maybe a lifetime commitment to start a new business." In short, Hawkins was not pleased with the situation Dubinsky had placed him in.

"I was getting really weird vibes from him," Dubinsky says of the days leading up to her birthday on the Fourth of July. She was dismayed by the sudden turn their relationship had taken. "He was mad at me, and I can understand why."

She had wanted to found another business with him; indeed, she had expected that her professional future was closely tied to his. Now it appeared that her rash action in Benhamou's office had jeopardized their plans—and, worse, their friendship.

After two days, she could stand the tension no longer. She asked Hawkins to meet her at Java City, a tiny coffee shop on El Camino Real within walking distance of the old Palm offices in Los Altos. She wanted to admit her mistake and clear the air.

"Jeff, let's start over," she said once they'd settled with their cups of coffee at the sidewalk table. "If you want me to work with you, I'd love to. And if you don't, that's OK. We'll still be friends."

It was the opening he needed. Hawkins had decided that while he wouldn't found another company on his own, he would join Dubinsky or Ed Colligan if they wished it, because they needed his product design skills. "I felt an obligation to Donna and Ed," he says now. "If they wanted to do it, then I would be there if they wanted me to be there."

Dubinsky beamed at him across the small table, a weight lifting from her shoulders. Their friendship was preserved, and they would again work together—if they could agree on the specifics.

Starting another company had been little more than an idea they'd tossed around. It would be a handheld computing company, they'd said; they'd license the Palm OS from 3Com if they could negotiate good terms. But they had never clarified what their roles would be, or what percentage of the company each of them would own.

Specifying their respective roles in the new company was relatively easy; they settled on President and CEO for Dubinsky, and Chief Product Officer for Hawkins. The issue of ownership in the company was stickier. Ever since Dubinsky took over the reins at Palm in 1992 and instituted a consistent salary policy, Hawkins had held in high esteem the importance of fair and thoughtful compensation.

Their respective ownership in the company was by far the most important consideration, because, if the new enterprise were successful, it would dwarf their salaries. "I wanted to make sure that neither she nor I felt bad about it, or that it looked odd to anybody," Hawkins says.

The big question was—what *was* the right division of ownership?

They agreed quickly that it was not a 50-50 split. Donna threw out a suggestion. The right ratio should be 2:1, so that Hawkins owned twice as much of the company as she did.

"I felt that my skills were ultimately more replaceable than his," she explains. "If Jeff walked out the door, who would you ever get to replace him? Whereas if I walked out the door, you could find another general business person. To me, that was a clear sort of ranking."

Hawkins agreed. By the time they got up from their table to join the crowds out for the holiday weekend, the tension was gone. They had committed to working together again for years to come.

Monday mornings from 9:00 A.M. to often nearly noon was the regular time for Palm's executive staff meetings. The rest of Palm's nearly 350 employees straggled in, switched on their PCs, and settled down to the new workweek. Only people in cubicles close to the Amelia Earhart conference room were aware of the meetings; waves of raucous laughter generally rolled out from the conference room at frequent intervals. Monday, July 6, 1998, seemed no different to the Palm employees, except that it was just a little bit harder to focus on work after the long holiday weekend.

Then, just before lunchtime, an e-mail from Dubinsky titled "Important: Please Read" popped up in every employee's e-mail In box. It was cc'd to Eric Benhamou and Janice Roberts, and went like this:

> To all Palm employees:
>
> I am writing you this note to tell you that Jeff and I have decided to leave Palm. . . .
> My desire for independence and autonomy no longer matches the needs of 3Com Corporation for how they want to build this large business. Consequently, I have decided to return to the start-up world.
> . . . Jeff and I will be forming a new company (hopefully with a name that causes us fewer trademark battles!). Our intention is to license the Palm Computing environment, and to create new products on the Palm Computing platform. Eric Benhamou and Janice Roberts have agreed to the concept of our new company as a platform licensee.

Some of Palm's 350 employees were so new, they didn't have a particularly strong sense of how important Jeff and Donna were to Palm's success. All they knew was that in the communications meetings, Dubinsky made them feel included and important. "Donna showed us everything," one employee says. "Financials, product plans, forecasts. She gave us a sense of 'us-ness'—the 'us' was the entire company."

But senior managers and old-timers were plenty worried. "I was concerned," says Steve Brown, Palm's director of business development. "You just wonder: Is this the beginning of the end? I knew it would never be like it was. And then, given that we were at 3Com, there was: Can whoever is making the decisions figure this out and understand our business? It was a little bit sad, and I was concerned for the company's future."

As they approached Hawkins to say good-bye or express sorrow at his departure, more than one employee noticed that he grew visibly uncomfortable. Often, he even explained that Donna had resigned on his behalf without his foreknowledge. Clearly, he felt bad about leaving Palm, and felt compelled to explain that it wasn't entirely his doing.

Ed Colligan called the 23-person marketing team together at 2:00 P.M. in the company cafeteria. Located on the ground floor, the cafeteria could accommodate the monthly all-company communications meeting as long as the chairs were packed in tightly. Now the space seemed vast, empty, and sterile as each member of the marketing team filed in and pulled a chair from one of the tables into a U around him.

Colligan looked tired and serious. In any other marketing staff meeting, the group would quickly have turned noisy and slightly rambunctious, as Ed handed out ice cream bars, gave updates on company directions, summarized the status of key projects, and praised individuals for particularly outstanding work. But not this time.

He had little concrete information that hadn't been in the e-mail—only that Friday would be Jeff and Donna's last day at Palm. Janice Roberts would run Palm until she could find a replacement for CEO.

Somebody asked, "Are you going to leave?"

Colligan gave a half-smile.

"No," he said. "I have a great job here, and I'm committed to Palm."

He had little choice but to answer this way. Saying, "Well, I'm not sure myself," would have had a disastrous effect on his team.

In reality, though, Ed couldn't be certain how long he would stay. The resignations had taken him by surprise. Jeff and Donna had long included him in their conversations about founding a new company if Palm wasn't spun out—but Donna's e-mail had referred only to "Jeff and I."

It also wasn't entirely clear to Colligan if joining the new start-up would be his best option. He was considering applying for the top job at Palm himself.

Donna tracked him down that afternoon and explained that she hadn't really planned her rash resignation and the ensuing events. "This isn't how it was supposed to happen," she said. She added that she and Jeff still hoped he would join them.

But she also considered Colligan the best candidate for her old job. She even said as much to Roberts and Benhamou. "Give him my job," she told them. "He can do it. He'll keep this together."

Hawkins and Dubinsky's last week at Palm passed with no indication of what steps 3Com would undertake to find replacements. Janice Roberts was now officially in charge of Palm (and of finding a permanent CEO), despite having to hold down two other senior management jobs at 3Com.

Colligan had let Roberts know that he wanted to be considered for the job—but also indicated that he, too, would be pushing for an eventual Palm spin-off. If timing of a spin-off were a factor, as Benhamou had said, he was willing to be patient and wait, but the end goal hadn't changed. Sales VP Pat McVeigh also put his hat in the ring for the position. So did a 3Com executive.

With Jeff and Donna gone, many considered Ed the only executive who had the loyalty of the employees—a critical asset at a time when the greatest threat to Palm was losing valuable people, especially the handful who would be irreplaceable. Ron Marianetti, for example, creator of Graffiti and the Palm OS, could achieve engineering feats that most other engineers could only dream of pulling off. Art Lamb was not only an exceptionally good engineer, but also knew the code inside and out. Rob Haitani and Joe Sipher understood better than anyone but Hawkins himself how to make a good handheld.

Over the course of the week, a "Colligan for President" movement developed all over Palm. Within days, Benhamou and Roberts were inundated by e-mail messages supporting Colligan's presidency.

"Ed is simply a magical guy to work with. Even more so than Jeff, and I've spent *a lot* of 1-on-1 time with Jeff over the years," wrote one of the senior engineers. "Ed also commands the most phenomenal employee loyalty I've ever seen. . . . I've often said that the only meeting that I would willingly add to my already overloaded schedule would be Ed's staff meeting—because I know I'll be uniquely educated, and entertained, and do my job better for having participated."

Benhamou and Roberts were not amused. Word came down from 3Com's executive offices that Doug Haslam, who ran human resources, was to stop the torrent of employee e-mails. Haslam could only shrug helplessly. How in the world could he keep employees from sending e-mail?

As the weeks passed with no word on the CEO selection process, Colligan felt that he got the message. "I never really believed I was a serious candidate after maybe two weeks into it," Colligan recalls. "I thought, 'No. They don't want me here. They want to own this company and they want to take it over, and I am the old guard. They're going to bring in some Big Dog from some Big Company, and that's where they want to take it."

On September 8, eight weeks after Hawkins and Dubinsky had left Palm, Colligan sent an e-mail to all employees. "Today, I am resigning from Palm to pursue other interests. This has been one of the toughest decisions of my life, but in the end I think it is the best thing for me, for Palm, and for 3Com." Then, aware that some members of his own team could see his departure as a bad omen for Palm, he added: "I want to stress that my leaving is not a reflection on the opportunity at Palm. I have told people many times that I have the best job in the business, and that Palm and 3Com are great places to work. I really believe that, and I think you have to keep that in mind when you think about your own personal situation."

But it didn't matter what Ed said—the fact that he left was bad enough.

"When Jeff and Donna left, I was shocked," says Joe Sipher. "But I didn't feel like it was over, because Ed was still there. Ed will make sure everything will be okay. He's going to be the CEO. It was really when Ed left that I was struck, '*Now,* it's over. It will never, ever be the same.' "

Colligan left Palm without a plan, but with plenty of opportunities. Headhunters called him relentlessly. He had the track record and reputation that virtually guaranteed him a CEO position at one company or another, especially in the current business climate. Venture capitalists spent $4.5 billion during 1998 funding over 700 start-ups in the San Francisco Bay Area alone, and were working hard to recruit good people to run them. The biggest shortage in the Valley wasn't ideas for new ventures or money to fund them; it was good people who could turn the money and ideas into successful companies.

During the past weeks, Donna and Jeff had told anyone who asked that Ed would be 3Com's best choice as Palm's president. Privately, they hoped that he would join them in their new venture, but they weren't certain that he'd want to reprise his role as "just" a vice president. "There were just so many uncertainties," says Dubinsky. "We weren't even sure what we would be doing. We weren't sure whether we'd get the [Palm OS] license. But one of the number one issues was: Did Ed want my job? Which wasn't clear. And if he did, would they give it to him? It was a very confusing time, really, for the three of us."

The chance to work once more with Hawkins and Dubinsky, this time in an independent company, was very tempting to Colligan. Yet, despite the close relationship he had forged with them, Palm had always been "The Jeff and Donna Show"; Ed was always the next guy in line to talk to.

"Look, if I do this again, I want to be a core part of this team," he told them, "and I want to be a core part of the strategic management group, and I want to be considered a founder. I have to take that much of a next step, as opposed to just being the VP of Marketing again. That's not going to be good enough."

Dubinsky and Hawkins readily agreed and gave him the percentage of company ownership that a start-up's CEO would get, rather than the far smaller amount that a VP typically owns. "He was coming in as a partner," Dubinsky says. "He'd run sales and marketing, because that was what his center of excellence was and we needed him to run, but there was no doubt that he was coming in as a real partner. It was just a no-brainer."

It was for Colligan, too. "I loved working with these people, and we were a great team," he says. "And replicating that is really hard. What threw me over the top was saying, 'You know what, I know there is a very high probability of success here, and I know regardless: We're going to have fun together doing it.' "

Not all employees were upset about the news of Hawkins and Dubinsky's resignation. "I was actually thrilled," remembers Art Lamb. "I was really happy about it"—not because he thought Palm would be better without them, but because he might be able to join their new start-up. "I had a pretty good feeling that I would end up there at some point anyways, whether it was as one of the first employees or shortly afterwards," he says.

Upon learning the news, he and Ron Marianetti had marched to Donna's office. "I had sent out the e-mail saying we were resigning, and they were in my office as a pair within an hour saying, 'When do we start?' " she says. "A lot of people were like that."

She couldn't promise jobs in the new company to any of the employees who lined up at her door that day—indeed, soon she would strike an agreement with 3Com that she would not actively recruit employees from Palm. She could hire them only if they approached *her* for a job. So here were two of the most valuable employees asking for jobs—but she didn't yet have jobs to offer.

"First, get Palm VII into good shape," Dubinsky said to Marianetti. "Then let's talk."

Rob Haitani also assumed that he'd eventually join his mentors at their new venture. But in the days following Colligan's resignation, Joe Sipher tried to convince Rob to join him in a public pledge to remain at Palm at the next product managers' meeting. It was important, Joe reasoned, for the newer members of the group to see that the Palm old-timers were committed to the company.

Rob could only give him a tepid response. "It was awkward,

because I was also trying to rally the troops. You have a role to play, you're managing people, but your heart is telling you that you want to be with [Jeff and Donna]," Haitani says.

At this point, the new company was little more than a silly name; Hawkins and Dubinsky had incorporated it under the temporary name "JD Technology" (for their initials), but it already attracted plenty of attention. The press reported widely on the departure of "the legendary Silicon Valley entrepreneurs," as *Business Week* called Hawkins and Dubinsky in an article titled "After the PalmPilot, what do you do for an encore?", and Silicon Valley was abuzz with rumors about their plans.

For his part, Jeff was warming to the excitement of a new venture. "I was pretty optimistic that, if left to our own initiatives, as long as there were not too many outside influences hurting us, we would succeed," he says. "It may be slow, it may be fast, but it was kind of inconceivable that we would totally fail. It seems like we had proven ourselves, that we're capable enough and we are smart enough, and we know the industry well enough that somehow or other we would have some level of success. I don't know how much, but some, and maybe a lot!"

For a few weeks, he and Donna worked from their homes, meeting over her dining room table whenever they needed to get together. Then a former Apple colleague loaned them a spare one-room office space for three months. Dubinsky opened a bank account for the company, funded it with her own money, then used the new company checks to pay the rent on three office desks and chairs from a furniture rental store. Hawkins bought a plant to liven up the Spartan room. There wasn't even a computer. "We started with just me and Jeff and a plant," Dubinsky likes to say.

The division of labor between them was obvious from the start. "I had to figure out the product, and Donna was watering the plant," Hawkins jokes.

In fact, she had three clear priorities: (1) to find real office space for the arrival of employees, (2) raise money for the new company, and (3) negotiate the terms for licensing the Palm OS with 3Com.

She found workspace above a coffee shop on a lively downtown street of Palo Alto. In the process, she picked up her hew company's first employee—Lisa Lyons, the real estate broker's assistant. "It took a nanosecond before I handed her the furniture rental contract and said, 'Here—deal with this!' " Dubinsky laughs. To sign the lease on the office space, Hawkins had to write a personal check. At this stage, JD Technology didn't have a nickel of venture capital.

Funding, however, would not be a problem; of that, Dubinsky and Hawkins could be certain. Since the day of their resignation, VCs had been calling them to offer money for whatever venture the famous duo might be starting.

Randy Komisar, Donna's friend and advisor throughout the years, argued that they shouldn't raise venture capital funds at all. "You guys are far too successful and prominent to have to strike a VC deal," he told them. Instead, he suggested raising capital from their pool of wealthy friends and associates. "We'll pass the hat. We can raise ten million dollars from friends at a valuation of your choice quickly. Look, if there's one thing you learned from the last deal, it's that losing control is losing everything. If you do a VC deal, you'll lose control."

Hawkins seemed intrigued. Control over his creation without interference had been his main issue ever since the days of the Zoomer.

They debated their options, but speed was of the essence. The handheld market was rapidly growing—in September, Palm would celebrate having sold 2 million PalmPilots—and it was clear that its sales momentum was increasing. (Indeed, it would take Palm only another 10 months to sell the next 2 million units.) Even though handhelds based on Microsoft CE 1.0 and 2.0 had floundered, Microsoft was at work on another upgrade, too.

If Jeff, Donna, and Ed wanted their new company to be a major player in the exploding handheld market, they would have to come out with their first product fast—and speed has its costs. Dubinsky didn't want to have to pinch pennies in the battle for talented employees, or scrimp on low-end computer systems the way they had the last time around. Blue-chip VCs would not only invest the kind of sums she had in mind, they would also bring instant credibility and connections to other top-tier firms—leading legal firms, accountants, investment bankers—and top executives in corporations. "It could help us scale quickly much better. It could help us recruit much better; it could help us move faster; we could spend more money," she explains. "We just didn't want to be out there pinching pennies, worrying about that stuff. We wanted to go-go-go!"

In the end, her pragmatic stance won.

The environment for venture capital had changed completely since Palm's 1995 days of misery. Since then, the Internet IPO bubble had sparked an avalanche of investors, willing—even eager—to invest in risky technology start-ups, in hopes of reaping high returns on their money. Billions flooded into venture capital funds. Rather than putting just $1 million or $2 million into start-ups, VCs were prepared to pour tens of millions into the most promising new ventures (as long as they received, in return, a large percentage of the company). For a brief moment in history, money for hopeful entrepreneurs seemed to grow on trees.

Dubinsky lined up meetings with some of the Valley's top VCs to gauge their interest. Unlike the young entrepreneurs who populated the waiting rooms of the VC offices, they didn't bother preparing a business plan or PowerPoint pitch. "We walked through the lobby with all these 20-year-olds with all their slides, and we were just laughing. 'Hello, I'm Donna Dubinsky, aging entrepreneur.' "

Confident that they'd have their pick of the litter, Donna and Jeff were determined to align only with the top VCs. There was no question that they'd want to work again with Bruce Dunlevie, and that he wanted to fund them. On the very day of her resignation announcement, Dubinsky had called Dunlevie at his new venture capital firm, Benchmark Capital. He answered the call in his car—and pulled over to the side of the road when she dropped her bombshell.

"I said, 'Wow, I can't believe it! That's great! Want some money?' " Dunlevie says.

The next day, over lunch, he handed her a check for $3 million made out to "Hawkinsky Devices, Inc." The check was a joke, but also a not-so-subtle message: He wanted to fund their next venture, whatever it was.

The legendary John Doerr, who'd kicked off the pen computing wave 11 years earlier and starred in the video Dubinsky had had produced for Palm's developer conference, soon joined Dunlevie as the second investor.

Most entrepreneurs raise several million dollars in a seed round as they launch their ventures. At that time, the new company is considered to have limited value, because it has no technology, no products, no customers—just an idea and a few people willing to work hard. If VCs set the value of the start-up's idea at $5 million and then invest $2 million, the venture firms now own 40 percent of the little company. The founders aren't even left with the remaining 60 percent, because they have to set aside stock for the executives and employees they'll need to hire.

The seed money is supposed to keep the company afloat long enough to meet a few goals, such as writing software and forming alliances with other companies, which raises the value of the company. Then the start-up conducts another round of financing, which means giving up another chunk of ownership. This time, the entrepreneur and VCs agree that the start-up is worth, for instance, $12 million; to raise another $2 million, the entrepreneur has to give up another one-sixth of the company. And so it goes. Each round of financing leaves the founders with a smaller piece; if the company survives and goes public, the founders find themselves with a rather small part of the company. (Of course, if the venture is by then very valuable, even a tiny piece can amount to a fortune.)

Dubinsky's strategy was different. By the time of their new company's initial public stock offering (IPO), the JD triumvirate wanted to own a far larger amount of the company than was typical. The pitch to VCs went like this: "This is your only opportunity to invest. This is not a seed round. We are not going to *do* another round of funding." This first round, in other words, was going to raise enough money to last the young company all the way to its IPO.

They could afford to play hardball; they had other alternatives. "Look, you know, we don't need this money right now," Hawkins could say to the investors.

Playing hard-to-get worked. JD Technology may not have had a business plan, but it had the reputations of Hawkins, Dubinsky, and Colligan. The VCs considered it a "must-do deal" and invested $9 million each, in exchange for 15 percent apiece of the new company. JD Technology, a company without employees, technology—without even a license to the Palm OS—was worth $60 million.

During any other era, it would have been considered an amazing deal for the founders. During the days of the Internet bubble, however, it was considered just "good." Venture capital investments in 1998 would smash all previous records and—briefly—change the ground rules for venture funding.

Even so, the deal was good enough to get JD Technology all the capital it could need, and its founders retained a chunk of its equity that would put envy into the faces of most entrepreneurs before them and after.

The venture capital negotiation wasn't the only thing keeping Donna busy. She was also in talks with 3Com to hammer out a license agreement for the Palm OS.

When she and Hawkins had told Benhamou that they intended to found another handheld company, they said that they'd want to license the Palm OS. Benhamou had said he wouldn't oppose the idea. There was no certainty, however, that the two parties would agree on the terms of a license. The former Palm duo was determined to negotiate an unrestricted license, one that would allow them to build products that competed directly with Palm's; 3Com might not want to make such a deal.

It was ironic that Dubinsky insisted on an unrestricted license. While at the helm of Palm, she and Benhamou had argued over her licensing strategy, which was to limit licenses to companies that wouldn't directly compete with Palm, such as Symbol (with its bar-code-reading PalmPilot) and Qualcomm (with its cell phone/PalmPilot). Benhamou's position, on the other hand, had been that the Palm OS should be licensed more broadly.

Donna was in a strong negotiating position, too, because Jeff wasn't married to the Palm OS. He had even explored the possibility of working with Windows CE—briefly; once he played around with it a bit, he dropped the idea quickly. ("I just don't think I can build a good product using Windows CE," he told *Infoworld* a few months later.)

The real alternative to the Palm OS was, of course, writing a new OS from scratch. Having written the original Palm OS three years earlier, Ron Marianetti, now at JD Technologies, was itching to improve on his own creation. "I know what I did right and I know what I did wrong," Marianetti argued. "I've learned a lot since the last time around. Let's start with a clean sheet of paper." Better still, if they developed their own OS, they wouldn't be dependent on Palm.

On the other hand, developing a new OS would take time, and time to market was crucial. Also, there was the momentum of the Palm developer community; thousands of independent programmers had already written programs that ran on the Palm OS. Donna pointed out that a battle for the independent programmers' loyalty could be expensive and painful. Riding Palm's momentum had its advantages.

Jeff's primary concern, as usual, was the product. "What's the best for the customer? We're not an anti-Palm company. If we get a good license, and it lets us do what we want, and it's the right technology, then that's what we should use."

In the negotiations, Dubinsky stressed that Hawkins was going to create a handheld computer, with or without the Palm OS. Allowing the PalmPilot's creators to build their new product on some other OS would have been extremely embarrassing to 3Com. "You really wouldn't want the founders of Palm going off and building a product on another operating system, would you?" says one senior 3Com executive. "That would just have been dreadful for the company."

As it turned out, Eric Benhamou had no intention of putting obstacles in their way. "I knew it would be a competitor," he says, "but I thought it would be good. I thought one of the ways to get this somewhat immature organization that we had at Palm more focused was to give them a good competitor." Furthermore, Benhamou saw the license as a means to kick-start the kind of licensing strategy he had wanted from Palm.

On November 5, 1998, Ed Colligan issued a press release announcing the investment from Kleiner Perkins and Benchmark, the licensing agreement with 3Com—and a new name for the company. In long brainstorming sessions, the three executives had considered over 100 names, including words in other languages.

It wasn't easy to find a name. Gun-shy after their legal battles over the terms Palm and Pilot, they paid special attention to trademark searches. Sure enough, each time the founders found a name they liked, the lawyers dug up potential conflicts. One of Dubinsky's favorite candidates was nWave (for *next wave,* she explains). It, too, was taken.

Finally, during a cab ride on a business trip to Los Angeles, Dubinsky hit upon a name: *Handspring.* She liked the energy and fun that the athletic term implied, and the reference to *hand.* She soon discovered something she liked about the name even more: The trademark search came up clean. Nobody would be suing the company over the name Handspring.

Colligan commissioned a logo, and the designers came up with the stylized, X-shaped figure caught in the middle of a handspring. He nicknamed the logo person Flip.

When the media descended on 3Com and Palm to inquire about the license, the spokespeople put the requisite positive spin on the news. Palm and Handspring would be partners, said both parties. As it would turn out, the relationship between the old company and the new was far more complicated than even their most savvy executives could have predicted.

NINETEEN

SEA CHANGE

While Donna Dubinsky ran Palm, morale among the employees was high, no matter what 3Com's business difficulties were or how low the stock price went. Working at Palm was not only fun, it made employees feel successful. In only two years, the company had grown from fewer than 50 employees to 350, reached a whopping 73 percent market share, shipped well over 1.5 million PalmPilots, and signed up 7,000 developers to work on software or hardware add-ons.

But when Dubinsky, Hawkins, and Colligan left, the high spirits at Palm took a plunge. The abrupt loss of a CEO would throw any company into confusion, but for this group, losing all three leaders—a revered CEO, the company's visionary founder, and the heart of Palm's high-spirited culture—felt like a traumatic event. And they blamed 3Com for their loss.

The employee's resentment of 3Com didn't make it any easier for Janice Roberts to fill in until a permanent new president could be found. Few Palm employees knew much about her. Now Roberts, who never lost her British accent and still struggled to fit in with Silicon Valley's casual, egalitarian business culture, needed to win the respect of 350 skeptical Palm employees at a communications-turned-introductory meeting.

She started by explaining that she had worked closely with Dubinsky over the past year, and knew Palm well. Roberts's next statement, however, seemed to prove every employee's wildest fears: Before searching for Palm's next leader, she was going to take some time to get to know Palm better.

To the management at 3Com, this plan made perfect sense. Hawkins and Dubinsky's departure had taken the pressure off the 3Com executives to make a quick decision about Palm's future. For now, they could park Palm with Roberts and gain time to consider Palm's role in the context of a broader 3Com strategy.

But to Palm's staff, any delay in appointing their next CEO seemed unconscionable. Roberts already held down two executive jobs at 3Com. How could the company navigate the unknown territory of an emerging new industry and fight off Microsoft—Microsoft, for God's sake!—without a full-time captain at the helm?

Employee retention was becoming an issue. Joe Sipher pleaded with Roberts to do everything in her power to retain the key engineers, whose loyalty could no longer be taken for granted.

The responsibility to shepherd the Palm VII to completion rested entirely on him. (When, much later, he was introduced as the father of the Palm VII, he said, "*Jeff* was the father of the Palm VII. I was more like the single mother, because Jeff left after conception.") He could easily imagine his colleagues quitting, because his own allegiance was changing. "I still had loyalty to Palm, though it dropped when Ed left," he says. "Then it deteriorated rapidly."

As time passed without any visible efforts to retain employees, Sipher asked Roberts to meet with eleven of the most critical employees, mostly Palm old-timers like Art Lamb or Monty Boyer. In particular, the Palm VII project couldn't afford to lose über-engineer Ron Marianetti. Roberts's assistant squeezed a meeting for September 25, the earliest available open slot, into Roberts's schedule.

But by then it was too late. Just hours before the meeting, Art Lamb and Ron Marianetti gave notice.

Nor was that the only bad news. Another good-bye e-mail circulated shortly thereafter:

> As you may have heard, Friday I resigned from 3Com. Since I love working at Palm so much, it was a very difficult and emotional decision. I've never enjoyed a job more, and I've never worked with a finer and funner group of people. It has been an obscene pleasure working (and drinking) with all of you!
>
> And I also feel a tremendous debt to Joe . . . Whenever our phenomenal success tempted me to feel complacent or cocky, I could always look at Joe to realize that I could be better.

It was signed by Rob Haitani, Hawkins's right hand in creating the Pilot and Palm's subsequent models. He, too, would shortly join Handspring.

Roberts held the meeting nonetheless; the remaining eight key engineers attended. "I want to keep this team together," she said, according to engineering old-timer Chris Raff. "We will do whatever we have to do to keep you here." The engineers left the meeting, sure that they had just been promised large grants of 3Com stock options.

"It never materialized," says Raff. "I should have quit 30 days after that meeting when I realized it wasn't going to happen, but I still had too much faith in Palm as a company. I thought surely there was no way their effort to retain us would be nothing more than a bait-and-switch."

Terrified for his project, Sipher pressed Roberts to offer Marianetti an incentive to stay at Palm at least until the Palm VII was complete. He had calculated that losing Marianetti, and thereby delaying the launch of the Palm VII, would cost Palm millions in lost revenue and increased costs. Sipher proposed a cash incentive of $100,000 to retain Marianetti until the Palm VII shipped.

Roberts didn't offer cash, but she did meet with Marianetti. It quickly became clear that changing his mind was a lost cause. "There was no chance of getting me to stay, no matter what she did," he says. (The Palm VII was finally finished nine months behind schedule.)

The resignations of Rob Haitani, Art Lamb, and Ron Marianetti brought about the nightmare that many had feared when Ed Colligan left: an exodus of talent that could gut Palm.

It would be a grim winter for Palm's HR department, whose job it was to deal with the paperwork that every resignation causes. For months to come, e-mail messages titled "Time to move on" and "Thanks for the memories" announced the departures of what seemed like an endless stream of employees.

Many of the departing employees left for Internet companies; some of the best joined Handspring. Every departure put the same thought into the heads of the people left behind: "Do only suckers stay here?"

The product development team felt Hawkins's and Haitani's absence deeply.

One of the projects, a handheld with a color screen that later became the Palm IIIc, was stalled. Originally slated for release in the spring of 1999, it would ultimately slip to February 2000.

A master of focusing on what counted most, Jeff had always made sure that decisions got made promptly, often casting the decisive vote. "He was very opinionated and vocal about sharing his opinions. And most of the time he was right. It was good to have things move along," says Bob Ebert, a senior engineer on the Palm IIIc team. But Jeff wasn't around to keep projects on track.

Of course, the most dreaded impact of Hawkins's departure was that Palm's pipeline of innovative new products would dry up. There was only one significantly different product on the drawing board, placed there under Jeff's watch, though without much of his input: a smaller and cheaper model, targeted at a younger market that included college students. (It would be launched under the name m100 two years later, in August 2000.)

Palm would have to wean itself from Hawkins's benevolent product dictatorship, but Jeff's unique capacity of invention was hard to replace. "People look at the ingredients," says Hawkins. "They have some of them, they try to make a recipe. And it doesn't always make a good recipe. 'Well, we've got some eggs and we've got some frog legs, and we've got barleycorn—oh, we can makes something out of that!' "

Among the Palm engineers, a wistful joke made the rounds: Either Handspring would make it really big and buy out Palm, or Palm would buy out Handspring. In either case, the brains behind Palm's success, and the body of its employees, would be reunited.

Ed Colligan proved hard to replace, too. The marketing team had been split into two parts. Byron Connell ran the product marketing group, and as Palm's long-time marketing director, I was appointed VP of marketing until a permanent replacement could be found.

I agreed to the plan, even though I had already made up my mind to leave Palm. Convinced that Jeff and Donna would be next to impossible to replace, I expected Palm to hit the skids by about the spring of 2000. For five years, we had worked so hard on Palm's success—I just couldn't fathom participating in its decline. At the same time, I didn't want to let down my company in its already weakened state. Surely it wouldn't take more than a few months to find a new marketing VP, whereupon I could leave with a clear conscience.

But though there was a lot of perceived glamour in an executive position at Palm, few qualified candidates considered a division of the ailing 3Com a financially attractive opportunity, as the headhunters soon discovered. The ambiguity over Palm's future president didn't help, either. No lucid VP candidate would accept a job without knowing that he or she had a good rapport with the future boss, whose identity, in this case, was still unknown.

Little did I suspect that I would still be Palm's acting VP of marketing 10 months—and three presidents—later.

Dubinsky's absence seemed to loom largest in the Amelia Earhart conference room, where the Monday morning executive staff meetings took place. Just as Jeff had dominated product development, Donna had held ultimate control over Palm's business strategy. Her management style was to solicit input and listen closely to everyone's opinion. But in the end, Dubinsky and Hawkins made the decisions, quickly and decisively. It was the "Jeff and Donna Show," as the VPs called it.

Roberts, hopelessly overcommitted in three executive jobs, had little time to spend on Palm's premises. "You guys have to help me," Roberts told the vice presidents one Monday in November.

The vice presidents did their best to adjust from what one Palm executive called "a friendly command-and-control culture" to a "confused but more empowering culture." The result wasn't always good enough. "There was a lot of confusion," says Bob Ebert, the senior engineer on the Palm IIIc team. "Upper management didn't seem to have its act together." Palm's day-to-day decision making had stalled.

On the other hand, Roberts got the company quickly moving into two significant new directions. First, at Benhamou's request, she asked Platform VP Mark Bercow to develop a new licensing strategy for the Palm OS. Second, she saw opportunity in the Palm.net wireless Internet service, to which Palm VII buyers would have to subscribe.

At the time, the conventional wisdom had it that wireless—the ability to surf the Web or check e-mail from an untethered handheld or cell phone—would be the biggest thing since the Internet itself. VCs rushed to fund companies offering wireless services, content, or technologies. Established companies that could in some way claim to participate in the wireless boom, like Qualcomm, whose cell-phone technology could transmit data, saw their stock explode.

Palm.net was the wireless equivalent of an Internet service provider (ISP), and in the thinking of the day, it therefore held the promise of becoming as valuable as any high-flying dot-com. For Palm, a successful wireless service business had an additional benefit. The monthly subscription fees could form the basis of a high-margin revenue stream—one that might make up for shrinking hardware profits when direct competitors entered the market with handhelds of their own.

Hawkins and Sipher had developed the Palm.net service as a

customer convenience, not as a means for Palm to go into the wireless ISP business. A Palm VII owner could simply flip up the antenna and sign up automatically for the Palm.net service, without having to call a separate company to activate an account—a plan that sounds obvious, but was unheard of at the time.

There were a number of ways to make a sizable business out of Palm.net, but each would require large capital investments. Acquiring customers no matter the cost, of course, was business as usual for dot-com companies—but it was hard to see how Palm, living on 3Com budgets, would find the funds.

As I pondered the problem, I remembered the old Market Meter we'd hung in the hallway outside Jeff's office in the early days, when we'd hoped that handhelds represented the Mother of All Markets rather than a Pipedream Driven by Greed. Which was the wireless service business for Palm? Was the wireless bonanza for real? If it were a Pipedream Driven by Greed, it would distract us from much more important goals: coming up with innovative products and becoming successful in the enterprise market before Microsoft did, for example.

For the first time in my years at Palm, I found myself disagreeing with the direction set by Palm's CEO. Joe Sipher was equally skeptical. The question was: Had we Palm old-timers learned the right lessons about industry hype from the exuberant pen computing days? Or was our pragmatic attitude outdated in the "new economy" that, according to many pundits and some economists, the Internet had created?

Roberts charged Jim Obot, Palm's VP of operations, with figuring out how to turn Palm.net into a viable business. He and a small group of business managers would work for months, endlessly defining and revising business plans.

Palm's second new direction under Janice Roberts would change Palm fundamentally and forever.

Eric Benhamou had asked her to rework Palm's licensing strategy. He wanted many companies to make Palm OS–based handhelds, even if some of them competed directly with Palm's. Dubinsky had fiercely resisted this plan, of course, but she was no longer in the picture.

Palm split into two factions. The team responsible for signing licenses, under Mark Bercow, wholeheartedly supported the idea of licensing the Palm OS more broadly. Sony and other major players had expressed an interest in making handhelds. Bercow wanted to prevent these companies from signing with Microsoft, even if that meant licensing the Palm OS to companies who'd use it to compete with Palm's own products.

But a much larger number of employees felt threatened by the very thought of licensing Palm's crown jewels to direct competitors. In hallway conversations all over Palm, small groups of employees expressed angst over the business logic behind licensing. "*How* is it good for Palm if we license to a competitor?" they demanded of their managers. "If we get five or ten bucks for every unit they sell, it'll take a long time before we even make our own costs back. And if they hit a home run, they'll bury us!" When Joe Sipher heard that the Handspring license carried few restrictions, he stopped Mark Bercow in the hallway. "Why are we licensing our software to them?" he asked. "They are going to come and kick our ass!"

By this time, the Palm executives had developed a standard response: This was all part of Palm's long-term strategy against rival platforms like Windows CE. It was good for Palm, even if it came at some cost to Palm's own hardware business. Hadn't Apple lost to Microsoft because it had failed to license its OS?

But there were always doubts. Dubinsky's arguments for limited licensing had been persuasive. For many employees, it was hard to believe they were no longer relevant.

As it turned out, Palm couldn't simply turn on the licensing spigot. It wasn't for lack of interest among other companies. Ever since Bercow had signed a licensing deal with Qualcomm for a cell phone–palmtop hybrid in February 1998, his phone rang incessantly.

However, Bercow and right-hand man Steve Brown ran into resistance among Palm's own engineers. Some of them resented having to work, indirectly, on competitors' products. "There were literally engineers who didn't want to be working on the Handspring deal," says Steve Brown. "They'd say, 'I came here to work on Palm.' " Worse, Palm needed a lot more engineers—by some estimates, double the staff on hand—to handle the demands of individual licensees.

Bercow and Brown's second headache stemmed from a concern of the prospective licensees themselves: Palm's Platform group would know all details about a licensee's planned products. What assurances could Palm give that the platform team wouldn't simply turn around and tell Palm's own product teams the secret plans?

With Bercow, Roberts came up with a radical solution: to split the company into two distinct parts. The Platform group would work on the Palm OS—the "platform" that gave the group its name—and land licensees. The other half of the company, the Product group, would create and market Palm's handhelds. If Palm's licensees wanted a Chinese Wall, now they'd have it.

But if bisecting Palm's technology and engineering team was simple in concept, it was staggeringly complex in practice. It was an almost intractable issue that went to the core of Palm's past success: the tight integration of hardware and OS. Breaking those elements apart would be a gut-wrenching task.

As it would turn out, the agony of restructuring Palm's technology and people was an omen of things to come. The new licensing strategy split the company into two distinct businesses with separate goals that competed for resources, for management attention—and with each other. The difficulty of straddling the two would affect Palm and its leaders for years.

"You need to put together an analyst program," Janice Roberts told me during the executive staff meeting one day in December. 3Com's analyst-liaison group had picked up on dissatisfaction among the analysts that Palm wasn't briefing them enough.

It was important input. Microsoft had swept the country in the preceding month, making a persuasive pitch that Windows CE, thanks to Microsoft's stronghold in corporate IT departments and steady stream of upgrades, would eventually become the dominant OS for handhelds. Never mind that Palm had over 70 percent market share, while all Windows CE products combined had less than 15 percent.

If the analysts heard only Microsoft's pitch, and believed it, the press would surely follow. Already, a report from market-research firm IDC had predicted Windows CE's market share could rise to 52 percent by 2001, and to 70 percent by 2003. ("Beginning of the End for PalmPilot?" a ZDNet.com headline read a few months later.)

My team immediately started to prepare presentations about Palm's corporate sales, but we couldn't set up analyst meetings until Palm had a permanent president. This influential group would want to meet the new leader of Palm before gauging Palm's chances for a bright future. In the meantime, Microsoft's hype machine milked the IDC report for all it was worth.

To the outside world, Palm was still a star. Unaffected by the confusion over Palm's strategies for the future, the day-to-day tasks of marketing and sales still ran like clockwork. New and old customers loved their PalmPilots more than ever, and continued to recommend them to their friends and colleagues.

At the annual Comdex computer show in November, Palm was the belle of the ball. A new generation of flat-panel PC screens also captured the imagination of visitors; invariably, media coverage of the show featured headlines like "Thin Is In", "Small Is Big," and "Tiny Takes Over."

Microsoft also raised its hand to be heard—but it had little to say. The company commemorated Windows CE's second birthday and announced that the next version would be much better—when it was ready in October 1999, ten months away.

Palm's sales were soaring. As in the previous year, Palm handhelds received numerous industry awards for Product of the Year, and were featured in most magazines' holiday gift-giving guides. In December alone, over a quarter million people bought Palm handhelds, either as gifts or for themselves, twice as many than at Christmas the year before. By early 1999, Palm had sold its three millionth palmtop.

A lot was at stake at Palm's second developer conference, held in December 1998. Over 10,000 developers had purchased Palm development kits, and were therefore working on some sort of Palm software or hardware product. Therefore, Bercow's group had rented the spacious Santa Clara Convention Center for the event, and even hired San Francisco 49ers quarterback Steve Young to give a talk. Registrations once again had trickled in slowly, causing much anguish for Bercow's team, and then peaked the day before the conference. On the opening day over 1,200 programmers packed the sessions.

When Janice Roberts walked onto the stage to deliver her speech as Palm's acting president, she looked tired, as if she'd been up working most of the night. The Palm employees in the audience held their breath, wondering if Roberts would pull off a rousing speech that would do Palm credit. None had seen her speak in public, and by that time, many Palm employees no longer bothered to attend the monthly communications meetings. "It seemed the execs were just giving us a lot of pap," says an employee who left Palm a few months later.

Once Roberts started to speak, all fears were put to rest. She moved easily through her topic, presenting a strong business case to the developers to produce add-on products for the Palm platform and painting a picture of the ecosystem of thousands of companies populating the Palm Platform, for which she coined the term "Palm Economy." The previous year, most attendees were hobbyists who wrote shareware programs out of sheer enthusiasm; but this time, the 1,200 audience members in the convention hall represented small and large companies who hoped to make a business out of writing Palm software.

Since Handspring was an official licensing partner, Bercow's group had invited Hawkins and Dubinsky to speak, too, along with Haitani, who gave his "Zen of Palm" user interface design presentation.

I was angry about the decision to do so. Having a Handspring employee explain the core of our products' success was the equivalent of waving a sign that said, "Yes, we've lost our soul. It's over at Handspring now." And Jeff's presence at the show didn't make it easier for the Palm executives to present the "everything is A-OK" face to the world. By now he'd become a minor celebrity, and for two full days, CNN cameras trailed him wherever he went, attracting even more attention than he would otherwise among this crowd of tech-heads, who looked at him with awe.

Palm had planned to unveil the wireless Palm VII at the conference, even though it wouldn't be ready for sale until May.

Generally, announcing a new product before it's ready to ship to customers is a huge mistake, because it stalls sales of the company's existing products. But the Palm VII was radically different from Palm's other products, both in its higher price ($599) and wireless features. Palm was willing to bet that a preannouncement wouldn't hurt sales of the nonwireless models.

The Palm VII would be unveiled at a press conference on the first day of the conference. Jeff asked to attend. He wasn't a journalist, of course, but the Palm VII was, after all, his baby; he wanted to see for himself how the journalists reacted to his most revolutionary product since the original Pilot.

Palm's PR manager came to tell me about Jeff's request.

"What do you think?" she asked.

I stared at the white board on the wall behind her, avoiding her glance. Conflicting thoughts raced through my mind.

"There is no way Jeff can stand unnoticed in a room full of journalists. He'll attract all the attention," I said. What I didn't say, but thought, was, "Palm wouldn't exist if it wasn't for Jeff." My stomach tightened.

"We can't let him steal the limelight," I finally told her. "This is Palm's product, and Jeff is no longer at Palm. *All* the focus needs to be on Palm. Jeff can't leave the company and expect that we'll let him into our press conference."

"That's what I thought," she said.

In the early morning of December 2, an hour before the Palm VII press conference—without Hawkins—Joe Sipher paced frantically in the room that was set up for the event. He and a small crew were preparing the equipment for the first public demo of the Palm VII. Another 40 people, representatives from the 20 large companies whose Web applications were to be included in the Palm VII, were setting up to demo their applications on their own Palm VII units along the walls of the large room. Sipher silently ran through his slides, then turned to do a trial run of his demo. He would first show how the Palm VII could retrieve an address from Yahoo's People Search.

He typed in his own name, knowing that Yahoo would have no trouble pulling up his Mountain View home address. But when he tapped the Search button on the screen, and waited, no data came back. He tapped the button again, then again; with 20 minutes to go before the doors opened to a hundred reporters, the wireless device refused to retrieve data from the Web.

In his mind, Sipher raced through all the possible reasons for this breakdown. Then it occurred to him that so many working Palm VIIs had never before been amassed in a single room. Could their simultaneous attempts to go online be clogging the base station that had been set up nearby?

He sent out the word to the other Palm VII partners: Stop! Turn off your handhelds!

Sure enough, Joe could now run through his demo without a hitch. He was relieved, but couldn't be sure that he was witnessing cause and effect. What if he'd misdiagnosed the problem, and the failure was actually triggered by something that might reoccur when he was onstage?

Then the doors opened and the journalists milled in. Janice Roberts started the press conference with a prepared speech, and then turned the floor over to Sipher to introduce the Palm VII, the product he'd worked on for over two years. Joe's heart raced as his speech neared the moment of truth, the instant when he would press the on-screen Search button. "There is a 50 percent chance it won't work at all," he thought.

He also worried about how long the Palm VII might take to retrieve data. He and Jeff had originally hoped that a customer would have to wait no more than two seconds for Internet data to arrive; when they realized that this speed was impossible to achieve, they had revised the goal to five seconds. But various factors, including network capacity and Internet traffic, continued to hobble their efforts—and now, only months before releasing the Palm VII, Sipher had resigned himself to the fact that a standard Web query took about eight seconds.

Now, as Joe tapped the Search button and waited the painful eight seconds, not knowing whether any data would come back, he masked the time by talking—an old demo trick that nobody at Palm had had to use since the Zoomer days.

"The Palm VII is now sending this data via the radio to the base station, less than five miles from here. From the base station, it goes to the BellSouth wireless data center in New Jersey, and from there back across the country to the Palm.net data center here in California. From there, it goes out into the Internet . . ."

Applause interrupted him. Out of the corner of his eye, Sipher could see that indeed the data had arrived on the screen. His eyes welled up with tears of relief, and without thinking, he admitted to the assembled press, "I'm so glad this came back."

In the coming years, the Palm VII never did become a hit like the Palm III or the Palm V; even two years later, fewer than 200,000 people used one. "I was very excited about the Palm VII," says Hawkins, "but it didn't turn out the way I envisioned it. It turned out to be much slower."

Nonetheless, the machine was years ahead of its time. Whereas wireless Internet access had previously required a $4,000 laptop equipped with a $400 wireless modem that called up a $50-per-month wireless service, the Palm VII included everything in a single gadget only a half-inch taller than a PalmPilot.

In February 2000, the outside world saw Palm hitting another high note with the launch of the sleek Palm V and the Palm IIIx, which added more memory to the basic Palm III. The marketing team pulled off its biggest launch to date, loading store aisles with brochures and demo stations, and causing a minor sensation with a "Simply Palm" ad campaign that featured a nude dancer. Though the Palm V offered no extra features, yet cost $50 more than any other Palm model, it became an instant, raging success. Soon it would account for almost half of all Palm sales.

Hawkins had been right to reject adding superfluous new features that nobody would use, instead focusing on beautiful design. The headlines reflected the svelte machine's irresistibility: "Newest Palm models inspiring envy" (*San Jose Mercury News*), "This Palm deserves a high-five" (*Newsweek*), "Give these Palms a big hand" (*Business Week*), and, online: "Thinner, sexier PalmPilots" (*Wired*). Jeff Hawkins and his team were no longer at Palm, but their previous work had given the company enough momentum to sail into the new millennium.

TWENTY

REVOLVING DOORS

An executive recruiting firm had begun a search for a Palm president only in October 1998, and the quest had been hampered by lingering questions about Palm's status inside—or outside—of 3Com. So it wasn't until seven months after Dubinsky's resignation that Janice Roberts handed the reins of Palm to a permanent, full-time leader.

A press release made it official on February 2, 1999: "3Com Names Robin Abrams as President, Palm Computing."

Abrams had an impressive résumé. It included stints at Apple Computer and Unisys, which had taken her all over the United States and, for extended stays, to Hong Kong. For the past 10 months, she had been the CEO of Verifone, a subsidiary of HP. That was a point in her favor—having had experience leading the subsidiary of a large corporation, surely Abrams would know how to navigate the pitfalls in the Palm/3Com relationship.

The moment Abrams sat down for a first meeting with her executive team on February 15, she took charge, wielding a pen and recording every promise for action made by anyone in the room. She also made strong commitments for action herself. "I will hire a VP of hardware engineering by the end of March," she announced boldly.

Donna Dubinsky e-mailed Abrams and offered to meet. When the two women got together, Dubinsky was impressed. "The first thing she said was, 'Let's go through the people. That's the most important thing.' "

Within days on the job, Abrams seemed ready for action—a "decision-making machine," as one of the executives says. The recruiting firm had yet to come up with viable candidates for the Marketing VP job, so Abrams promptly fired the firm and, within two weeks, had personally drummed up two candidates. Neither got the job, but at least she was making headway. She also came through on her promise to hire a VP of hardware engineering; by the end of March, Peng Lim joined Palm's executive staff meetings.

When Abrams addressed the Palm staff at the communications meeting, she made an equally good impression. "She had presence, she seemed decisive," says Caitlin Spaan, who still faithfully attended every meeting. "She described action," says HR director Doug Haslam. "We're going to *go* and *do* and *take!*" To the Palm team, the pace was like a breath of fresh air.

"In light of the fact that there'd been no one at the helm, it was easy to come in and say, 'Okay, now's the time,' " says Abrams.

On the licensing issue, Abrams seemed willing to move mountains. Both cell phone giant Nokia and consumer electronics star Sony had contacted Palm, but for lack of the necessary engineering infrastructure, Mark Bercow's team had wondered if they should hold back. "Go out and make it happen," Abrams told them. "I'll fix the engineering. I'll take care of the rest."

There were only two problems. First, nothing much had changed in Palm's need for more engineers. Second, Palm had yet to sort out all implications of the Product/Platform breakup.

For months, a handful of executives and engineering managers had agonized over how to restructure both Palm's technology and its organization. Each time they met, they arrived at the same stalemate. "[Hardware engineering VP] Peng called it the Groundhog Day meeting," says one of the managers (a reference to the movie *Groundhog Day*). "We'd meet, talk about it for an hour, disagree, and leave again. Nothing ever got resolved."

Splitting the engineers Into two teams to create the "Chinese Wall" that the licensees required proved especially hard. Even with the bulk of the former engineering group, the Platform team would be short-staffed. Uncoupling the Palm OS from the hardware—so that it could run on handhelds designed by other companies—would be a massive undertaking. Furthermore, licensees would have special feature requests.

However, the Product engineering group also needed many more engineers. Palm's licensee/competitors would differentiate their handhelds through new, unique features. Palm's product group would have to do so, too, or else future Palm models were doomed to fall behind those of their competitors.

Whichever way the executives tried to slice the organization, there simply weren't enough engineers to go around.

By early March, the engineers had gotten wind of the plan to split their team into two. Never shy about making their opinions known, they reacted immediately—and their opinion was that it shouldn't be done at all. The technical team knew better than anyone that the tight integration between Palm's hardware and OS was at the core of Palm's past success. Many engineers insisted that there was no realistic way to uncouple the OS from the hardware and trying to do so would ruin the Zen of Palm. A few years hence, they worried, the Palm OS might be no better than Windows CE.

The engineers were never sold on the wisdom of licensing to competitors in the first place. Now, many of them worried that the strategy would do irreparable damage to Palm's technology.

The separation of Platform and Products, a crucial piece of Palm's licensing strategy, was clearly unraveling.

"Why is this such a problem?" Robin Abrams asked Mark Bercow. "What is it that people don't understand?"

"Well, they're still waiting for the organizational changes to be announced," Bercow replied.

"Hasn't that happened?" Abrams asked.

"No, we were waiting for you to do it!"

"I was told it was done!"

"No," Bercow replied. "Nobody has even sent out an e-mail."

Abrams had assumed that Janice Roberts had already announced and explained the separation to the Palm staff; but

Roberts had wanted to wait until it was clear that her successor endorsed the decision.

Abrams discussed the split at the very next communications meeting, and Bercow spent hours meeting with small groups of engineers to field questions. Even so, the engineers and many of the nontechnical employees remained convinced that Palm was heading in the wrong direction. The fragile calm that had settled on Palm as soon as Abrams had arrived was shattered.

By early April, six weeks into Abrams' tenure, the Palm VPs started to revisit their initial enthusiasm for their new leader. With Abrams moving at lightning speed, they often found themselves blindsided by events. "You started to compare notes, and it was like kids playing a game of Telephone," one of them says. " 'Where'd you get that?', 'Well, I talked to her.' 'Well, when?' "

Like the other VPs, I was losing the ability to lead my group. Leadership required knowledge, but I was often caught unaware of steps Abrams seemed to have taken.

In late April, Dawn Hannah, Palm's events manager, stopped me in the hallway. "I have to cancel the reservation for the Rainbow Room today, or else we'll lose the deposit," she said.

I stared at her for an instant, uncomprehending. We had worked for months on the plans for launching the Palm VII in New York in May. There would be meetings with journalists, promotions with retail stores, ads in the New York papers—and a party for Palm customers in Manhattan's famous Rainbow Room restaurant.

"Why would you cancel the reservations?" I asked.

"I heard that Robin is canceling the launch," Hannah said.

"What?"

I had spoken with Abrams about the launch only two hours earlier. Since then, she had apparently given very different directions to Hannah's boss.

Joe Sipher, the product marketing director in charge of the Palm VII, had had no hint about the change of plan, either. He caught up with Abrams in the hallway.

"I heard you want to cancel the Palm VII launch. You might

want to let me know," Sipher said, upset. "Why do you think we should do this?"

As it turned out, Abrams had good reasons.

Ever since Janice Roberts had seen Palm.net as a significant business opportunity, a handful of executives and managers had morphed the original Palm.net plan until it resembled that of a typical dot-com start-up: Acquire customers at all costs. Never mind that the service would lose tens of millions of dollars for years, breaking even only in 2005.

Within the standards of the Internet "new economy" business plans of 1999, this was not an outrageous proposal. Indeed, in the first 90 days of that year, VCs had already spent over $4 billion on dot-com companies whose business plans ran along precisely the same lines.

By Palm and 3Com standards, however, that business model was unthinkable. 3Com worked like any publicly traded company: Wall Street demanded earnings and profit margins comparable to those of other networking companies. Palm's budgets were established so it could feed the necessary profit to 3Com's bottom line. There was no room for launching a business that would lose millions of dollars annually for five or six years.

And so, when the Palm.net business team submitted its budget proposal, Abrams had taken one look at the figures, recognized the problem—and moved with lightning speed to control the damage.

Sipher pleaded with her for a chance to prove the real costs of Palm.net. Abrams agreed to give him one day to clarify the matter. For the rest of a frantic afternoon, Joe chased the various executives involved to gather the facts.

By the end of the day, Sipher had enough data to understand what had happened. The business managers' spreadsheets factored in the costs of acquiring new customers, but not the additional revenue these expected customers would bring in.

The bigger problem, of course, was that Sipher didn't believe in the Palm.net business plan to begin with. The question was, could he convince Abrams? If not, Joe vowed that he would resign on the spot. It was late in the evening, but he picked up the phone and dialed Ed Colligan. "Ed, I may quit tomorrow," he said. "Do you think there's a job for me at Handspring?"

Colligan said yes. Sipher was prepared for the showdown.

At 7:00 the next morning, he explained his view of the situation to Abrams. She granted him one more day to come up with a new budget for Palm.net that made sense for Palm.

Working until 1:00 A.M., he and the Palm.net managers refined the spreadsheet until the plan was very close to Palm's original strategy.

Abrams relented. The Palm VII launch went ahead as planned. Abrams's management style, however, was taking its toll on the Palm management team. "You didn't trust that you knew what was going on, and we became a dispirited group," remembers one Palm executive.

In mid-May, an e-mail announced that Marian Cauwet, VP of software engineering, would be leaving by the end of the month. Only three weeks later, long-time sales VP Pat McVeigh also resigned. The executive team was crumbling.

McVeigh was to become the CEO of a new start-up company called OpenSky (later OmniSky) that would provide wireless Internet services for Palm handhelds and Windows CE devices. Its investors were Aether Technologies, a 50-person wireless data service provider—and 3Com. Sipher may not have believed in the wireless ISP business, but McVeigh and 3Com did.

3Com's involvement came as a shock to Palm employees, who couldn't understand why Palm's parent company would fund an enterprise that would directly compete with Palm's own Palm VII and Palm.net.

Once again, the answer lay in 3Com's need for Palm to contribute to its bottom line. Spending on Palm's own wireless division would have hurt Palm's profitability. But 3Com's investment fund—which was run by none other than Janice Roberts—was a separate entity, uninvolved in 3Com's profit and loss calculations. It, therefore, *could* invest in independent companies.

Employee morale was dropping ever lower. In April, the human resources department had compiled its annual survey of employee satisfaction. The results were dismal.

To make matters worse, Abrams had signed deals with Alcatel, Sybase, Aether, NTT DoCoMo, Sun, and AOL over the course of only three months. These deals gave Palm more stature on the outside world, but the engineers, already disconcerted about the loss of Marian Cauwet, were running scared. Customizing the Palm OS for each of these business partners represented an unattainable workload. "The engineering organization looked at this and said, 'My God, we're just chasing everything, and we can't actually execute against some of this stuff,' " a Palm executive says.

But the engineering department wasn't the only place where morale was plummeting; when Abrams didn't name Andy Simms as McVeigh's successor, Simms resigned. (He joined McVeigh at OmniSky.) And the marketing team was still uncertain about its future leader. Abrams had spent a great effort on filling the top marketing position, but had so far come up empty-handed. "I've kissed a lot of frogs," she told the employees at the communications meeting.

It had only been 10 months since Hawkins and Dubinsky had left, but Palm was already in danger of losing even the remnants of its spirited culture. Abrams herself had detected "a core of original Palm employees that kept the whole Zen of Palm alive and breathing, which in hindsight is no small feat without a leader." Now those people were downcast, and most had one foot already out the door.

One of them was Joe Sipher. When the Palm VII finally shipped in May, he was ready to throw in the towel. "It just wasn't the same place, it wasn't the same culture," he explains. "I didn't have nearly as much fun—I hardly had *any* fun. It was an exercise in frustration with all the Palm.net gyrations and politics."

When he told Robin Abrams that he intended to resign, however, she came up with an idea that would keep him at least nominally with the company for another 11 months. She offered him the honorary title of "Palm Fellow," a sweet arrangement in which Sipher would be a consultant to Palm, spending about a day a week there. In return, Palm would keep some link with its product past.

(Joe used the time off to pursue a long-time dream he'd had: marketing a chocolate fudge sauce that he called Sipher's Gold. Working weekends in his kitchen, he had experimented with European cocoas, exotic vanilla extracts, and many pints of heavy cream and come up with a sinfully delicious recipe. The fudge sauce had been a smash hit with Palm's marketing staff during team meetings. But when he tried to raise investments in Sipher's Gold, he ran into a wall. Impressed by his credential as the product director of the Palm VII, investors offered to fund any kind of wireless venture Sipher might like to start—but no VC wanted to fund a food company. When Ed Colligan called to offer a job as VP of product marketing, the lure of Handspring proved stronger than any other plans. Joe jumped at the chance.)

In late June, a sizable number of Palm employees were in New York City, staffing the large Palm booth at PC Expo. Demoing the Palm handhelds to customers felt thrilling, as it had always been. All day, we fed off the boisterous energy of customers and fans thronging through the Palm booth.

In the evenings, however, our mood changed completely. Dinner conversations churned over rumors of current Palm executives suspected to be leaving, new executives Abrams was hiring against the advice of her staff, new deals signed without consultation with Palm managers, and any other negative piece of news anybody could think of.

On the return flight from New York, I made my decision. I wanted out. Ten months earlier, abandoning Palm had been unthinkable. Now my presence seemed futile. The forces that I thought were corroding Palm were far greater than anything I could fight. The next day, I gave two weeks' notice.

Two days later, on June 30, HR director Doug Haslam paced outside the conference room where I was leading a meeting; through the window, he motioned me to leave the room. "There will be a communications meeting in the cafeteria at 1 P.M.," he told me in the hallway. "Make sure everybody in marketing is there."

A group of semi-old-timers, reverting to Palm form, started to take $1 bets about the nature of the meeting.

"3Com is spinning us out." It was the perennial hope of any Palm employee.

"Benhamou got fired." Few of us had even met Eric

Benhamou, but as the head of 3Com, he had acquired the status of Enemy Number One.

"Siemens is buying 3Com." For nearly six months, there'd been persistent rumors that 3Com was a take-over target, and Siemens was the leading candidate as a buyer.

"Robin is really a man." The packaging manager was willing to place a $1 bet on his joke.

"Robin is leaving." Marketing manager Chris Weasler was weary from having spent the morning digging for details on an AOL deal Abrams had signed.

"Alan Kessler is really going to take over the Platform." Abrams had already agreed to hand management of the Palm Platform group to Kessler, a long-time 3Com VP. His appointment had not yet been announced, but the rumor that a 3Com executive was to take over a Palm group had started to circulate. The pool grew to $20.

During the morning, the facilities staff had set up chairs in the cafeteria in a giant half-circle around a small podium. Oddly, a telephone had been set on that podium, and a microphone on a stand was pointed to the telephone. Once the employees, by now numbering over 500, had settled in the tightly spaced chairs, Robin Abrams walked up through the center aisle. Doug Haslam, who already stood at the head of the room, pointed to the telephone and introduced Bruce Claflin, 3Com's COO and Abrams's boss, who was calling into the meeting from the East Coast.

Claflin's disembodied voice dropped the bombshell: Abrams had resigned. An executive from 3Com was to take her place.

The employees drew in a collective breath. Many looked confused. Were things so bad with 3Com's business outlook that Abrams was fleeing the company?

Abrams stepped behind the podium, turned the microphone toward her and explained. Kleiner Perkins, the premier VC firm, had offered her a position at an Internet start-up.

She had declined the offer, she said. "I said, 'I have a great job here at Palm," she assured the group.

Closely packed in the semicircle, the employees sat with arms folded tightly, their faces a silent sea of resentment as Abrams continued her story.

Kleiner Perkins had called her again. She'd rejected them again. Kleiner Perkins persisted. She gave in.

"My decision has nothing to do with Palm or 3Com, absolutely nothing," she assured the assembled group. Then she moved aside for Alan Kessler, the 3Com executive who was to become Palm's next president. Abrams' four and a half months at Palm were over.

All eyes were now fixed on Kessler. On many faces, cynicism showed plainly—after all, Kessler would be Palm's fourth leader in 12 months.

A very tall man who holds his head to one side as if to come down to eye level with his shorter colleagues, Kessler showed no sign of being ill at ease. He had been at 3Com since 1985 in a variety of executive capacities. After a few years in charge of 3Com's customer service department, he had become eager for new challenges. Rather than risking losing Kessler, Eric Benhamou tapped him to run the Palm Platform group.

This move had been in the works for months; Kessler had already held numerous meetings with Mark Bercow, who would be working for him. He'd also asked HR director Haslam to predict the reaction of the employees to his appointment. "A lot of it's going to be, 'You're from 3Com, and why should I think that's good news?' " Haslam had told him. Kessler was prepared for skepticism among his new staff.

"I know many of you are wondering what a 3Com executive can bring to the table at Palm," he said now to the 500 incredulous people seated in front of him. It was exactly what the employees needed to hear. Many decided to give "the 3Com guy" the benefit of the doubt.

By his second day on the job, Kessler's extraordinary ability to communicate was becoming apparent. He sent a long, friendly message to all of the employees before noon. "It was about how I know everybody here thinks I'm sort of this cyborg, here to assimilate people," Kessler says. "I knew I had to build people's trust and confidence."

Over the next few months, the employees came to appreciate Kessler's straightforward style. They found it easy to approach him in the hallways, he seemed to listen to their concerns, and he responded within hours to every e-mail sent to him.

(A disciplined daily routine made such diligence possible: He awoke at 4:00 A.M. to exercise, put in a 12- or 14-hour day, then exercised again at night.)

Morale improved. "He just stabilized the whole ship because he has such an optimistic, open style," an employee says. "At first, everyone's impression was 'A 3Com guy got inserted here,' but he won people over pretty quickly."

But improving company morale with the strength of his personality was one thing; setting the direction for a handheld business was quite another for a man who'd spent the past 14 years in the networking industry.

Kessler needed to draw on the expertise of Palm's experienced staff, but that proved no easy task: Only four of the original VPs who'd worked for Dubinsky were still at Palm. Four months later, two of those had departed: Operations VP Jim Obot joined his former colleagues at OmniSky, and finance chief Bill Slakey became the CFO of a start-up company. Employee confidence in the company had crumbled long before Kessler's arrival, and Palm continued to lose workers at a furious pace.

"What I did the first two weeks was watch all of our best engineers line up, march into my office, and resign. You know, 'We want to go join a dot-com,' and 'We're never going to be set free to do our own thing,' " he says. "Two out of three people who tried to resign, I kept them here; every once in a while, I'd lose one, too."

Often, only the promise of a promotion and stock options would do. The irony was that, after a few weeks on the job, Kessler knew something that would have kept many of the exiting employees at Palm. But he wasn't allowed to utter the one sentence that would have done the trick. The time wasn't yet right.

TWENTY-ONE

ZERO TO SIXTY

In Handspring's offices above the coffee shop, Dubinsky, Hawkins, and Colligan had assembled a blue-chip product team that included every one of the people most instrumental in the Pilot's development

They had grand goals for their new company. "I'd like to get to a billion dollars [in revenue] as fast as anybody has ever done it," Dubinsky told *Newsweek*.

Handspring's goal, they soon stated in presentations, was to be "the leader in handheld computing"—never mind the fact that Palm, the incumbent, had nearly 4 million PalmPilot fans, or that Handspring was still a tiny company of only eight people.

When Lisa Lyons, office manager and general factotum, wasn't around, Donna rushed to pick up the company phone herself.

"I need to speak to Accounts Payable," a caller asked one day.

"Just a minute, please," Dubinsky said. She put the caller on hold, waited for a few seconds, and then picked up the line again.

"Accounts Payable, may I help you?"

Donna may have told the press that Handspring's goal was to become the "leader in handheld computing," but that was only a smokescreen. Within the walls of Handspring, Jeff maintained the real mission: to become the most significant personal computing company.

"I didn't say the largest or the most profitable," Hawkins points out. "I said the *most significant*. So, therefore, we are trying to do good things. We're trying to make great products. Bigness and success are subservient to doing significant things. And 'personal computing company,' because I think the future of personal computing is mobile computing. I want people to think big. You know, we're not just doing handhelds. We're doing whatever mobile devices people are going to carry in the future."

In fact, he thought he had a pretty good idea what these mobile devices would be. Like so many others, Hawkins believed that the future for handhelds was wireless.

"You could look at the analogy of what happened in phones, and how they all started out as wired devices," he says. "Then you started having cordless phones in your home, and then you have cellular phones. Today, the vast majority of phones have some sort of wireless component. You never see anyone with those big long spiraling cords that used to stretch all the way across the kitchen."

In Hawkins's view, handhelds were bound to follow a similar progression. "All computing and communication products need to have some sort of connection. And wireless is *the* technology for the last step, whether it's a mile or 100 feet. It's inevitable. You want to be able to move around."

The conventional wisdom held that customers wanted wireless access to the Internet. Most companies who rushed to cash in on the wireless boom were founded on this belief. So were Jeff's own creations, the Palm VII and Palm.net. Hawkins, however, had already changed his mind. It wasn't Internet data that the world wanted to receive wirelessly—it was phone calls.

To him, the logic was obvious. Even in 1999, hundreds of

millions of people were carrying handhelds—but they weren't organizers. They were cell phones.

Yet designing a cell phone/organizer combination device—a *communicator,* as Handspring would eventually call it—was an undertaking of staggering complexity, one that would involve technologies with which Handspring had little experience, not to mention the participation of carriers (companies like Sprint and Cellular One). "We had just done the Palm VII, and that was a really hard project," Hawkins says. "The idea of doing another one like that as a start-up company would be a killer."

In Palm's earliest days, the Zoomer had been a similarly unproven product concept—but Casio and Tandy had shouldered the financial risk. "We lived to see another day. If we had built our own hardware, we would have been killed."

The lesson seemed clear: Handspring's first product would not be revolutionary. Somehow, Jeff needed to find a way to create a traditional handheld computer—the kind that he, Donna, and Ed already knew how to build and to sell—that could also be turned into a cell phone.

Inspired by the game cartridges in the Game Boy machines, he retired to his garage and once again carved out some blocks of wood. When he emerged a few hours later, he held a PalmPilot-like shape with a tiny pinhole to simulate a microphone and a slot in the back that could accommodate a cartridge. Here was the solution: a handheld computer that could turn into a cell phone with the insertion of a module.

To test the concept, Jeff walked around for several days, answering imaginary phone calls on a block of wood. "It was sort of the ultimate weirdness," he says.

After several of these person-to-block conversations, he made his decision. Handspring's first product would have the traditional organizer functions of the Palm models—but could also be fitted with expansion modules.

This scheme would allow Handspring to tread conservatively, at first selling standard organizers whose success was almost guaranteed. The expansion slot would also give Handspring's product a feature that Palm didn't have. Best of all, it solved one problem of the wireless world: Handspring wouldn't have to gamble on a single technology or carrier. The company or its partners could develop different modules for different situations.

Dubinsky was sold. "The plan was to have this organizer business and then transition to the communicator business," she says. "The organizer business would get us in fast, gain brand [recognition], gain scale, build the infrastructure."

A cell phone module, however, was only the beginning of the possibilities. For years, customers, developers, and analysts had told Jeff, at trade shows and on the phone, to add this or that feature to the PalmPilot. "You should really put an MP3 player into it," one person had said. "How come you don't put a pager in there?" said another. The suggestions never stopped: A TV remote control. A digital camera. A GPS location-tracking system. With snap-in modules, developers could add any one of these features to the basic handheld.

The next evening, he sat down with the journal in which he kept his meticulous notes and began to list all the directions that expansion modules might take. What excited him most was the chance to "do expansion right": Each module's software would open instantly and automatically. The palmtop's owner wouldn't have to install, configure, or even tap anything. Simply inserting the module would take care of the dirty work behind the scenes—the ultimate in plug-and-play.

When he explained his Springboard slot, as Ed Colligan dubbed it, to the engineering team, Ron Marianetti pointed out a serendipitous, long-buried quirk of the Palm OS that would make Springboard much easier: He had designed the original Pilot to contain two removable memory cards, one each for read-only memory (ROM) and random-access memory (RAM). In the end, Palm abandoned the idea, but Marianetti had already developed the OS to handle an extra card. Now, years later, this long dormant feature would make it much easier for him to add expansion slot features without creating incompatibilities with existing software programs.

Over dinner one night, Jeff's 10-year-old daughter proposed a name for the new machine: Visor, a kind of shorthand for Advisor. The name immediately passed the first test: No consumer would be likely to confuse a handheld bearing the unusual name Visor with, say, a ballpoint pen.

Nobody outside Handspring knew of Hawkins's master plan for a vast communicator market. In fact, few knew anything about Handspring's plans at all.

At one point, someone heard Jeff, who likes to investigate all angles of an idea, discussing the potential that palmtops held for the education market. The rumor wound up in a *USA Today* article called "Tech duo's game plan: PalmPilot for kids," which appeared several months after Handspring's founding. "Officially, Dubinsky and Hawkins say their project is still secret," said the article. "But it's a decent guess that they're working on a version of the hand-held PalmPilot computer for children or families." Before long, the entire industry was convinced that Handspring was working on a handheld computer for kids.

The rumor suited Handspring, who was just as happy that outsiders—and Palm—didn't know what it was up to. "We fed that a little bit," admits Colligan. "Not too much, because we didn't want to feed it so much that people were disappointed." To help perpetuate the bogus rumor, the team chose toys as code names for its upcoming products: Lego for Visor, Risk for the Visor backup module, and Gumby for the VisorPhone module.

The Handspring trio watched the turmoil at Palm with concern. Palm employees called Handspring's offices in a steady stream. Some called to ask for jobs. Others just wanted to talk about being miserable at Palm.

"We knew from the Newton-Zoomer experience that your competitor failing is not necessarily good for you," says Dubinsky. "If they run into huge trouble, it's not good for us. We were worried." At the same time, the Handspring team knew that Palm's chaos also created a window of opportunity. "We certainly knew that they wouldn't be doing great products during that period. Any time a new CEO comes in, everything changes."

Handspring's team, on the other hand, was moving full-steam ahead. They had worked with each other for so long, and knew the job at hand so well, they were a well-oiled machine.

"The amount of work that we got done was amazing—everything just went flawlessly," says engineer Art Lamb. "We had functioning hardware and software by January, four months after we'd started. We were quickly approaching Alpha for our first product!"

At the project kickoff in October 1998, Rob Haitani had calculated that the engineers would have the product ready for manufacturing a year later, in October 1999. But shipping a consumer product into retail stores so close to Christmas is a recipe for failure; the logistics of manufacturing, delivery, and promotions during that crucial shopping time make success impossible. The Handspring executives decided to wait out Christmas and launch the Visor in January 2000.

However, the engineering team hit all of its milestones flawlessly. The Visor might be ready for production even earlier than they had planned.

Even so, a fall launch in the retail stores was out of the question. Investors Bruce Dunlevie and John Doerr, however, wanted the company to capitalize on the progress despite the constraints of a retail store rollout. During the next board meeting, they proposed an idea: Bypass the retail channel altogether. Sell the new handheld directly from the Handspring Web site.

More than a year before the bottom fell out of the e-commerce boom, *not* building a business around the Internet seemed crazy. For Handspring's particular investors, selling via the Web was an even more natural suggestion; both Doerr and Dunlevie had made fortunes backing Internet companies. Kleiner Perkins was behind some of the biggest dot-com names of them all, including Netscape, Google, and the granddaddy of e-commerce, Amazon.com.

Dubinsky was skeptical. She acknowledged the arguments that a Web-only business, without the intermediaries of the retail channel, could be more profitable than a retail operation, and would permit tighter control of inventory. But she was convinced that it would be a much smaller business. "I don't want a small business," she told them. "I want a big business."

The debate raged for weeks. "It was probably our biggest argument in the founding of Handspring," Dubinsky says.

Hawkins sided with the VCs. "I was much more interested in pursuing a direct-only strategy, the Dell strategy. At the time, everyone was saying, 'Dell is winning in the PC space. Direct is the way to go.' I felt that that was a good thing to try. Donna felt very uncomfortable with that, and we kind of got our way more than she did."

In the end, circumstances drove the decision. It became clear that the Visor would be ready for sale in the fall, but had no place to go. The Handspring executives decided to launch the Visor in the fall, to be sold at first only on the company Web site.

The decision would soon come back to haunt them.

In August, Tom Brokaw and NBC cameras came by the cramped Handspring offices to interview Dubinsky in the downstairs cafe. Due to its pedigree and the notoriety of its founders, the start-up with only 40 employees and no product to sell was already famous.

Even so, Hawkins looked ahead and saw danger on the horizon. To date, life had been almost too easy for Handspring. He wanted to curb the employees' expectations that times would always be good—especially now, a month before the launch date, when he knew from experience that grave last-minute problems always occurred. The time had come for one of his "fatherly words" talks at the company communications meeting.

"There will be problems," Jeff told his employees. "There may be problems in manufacturing the products, maybe problems with the Springboard slot, maybe other problems. Those are normal things—those things do happen."

When it comes to announcing new hardware products, the computer industry has an iron-clad rule: Never breathe a word about an upcoming product if it's designed to replace a model you're currently selling. However, when a company is new to the market, like Handspring, there's little risk in preannouncing. After all, it has no current sales to squelch—except those of its competitors.

Yet Colligan and Dubinsky held off on revealing the company's new product until it was ready; they had no interest in hurting Palm's sales. Furthermore, "we had this mantra of 'Underpromise, overdeliver,' " Dubinsky says. "We really didn't want to come out as our first introduction to the public with vaporware." When, in June, a *Wall Street Journal* journalist pressed especially hard for details of the product Handspring was working on, Dubinsky replied, point-blank: "Look . . . this is a market where there's been lots of hype, where people are announcing things and not delivering. We want to deliver a real product, not hype."

On September 3, ten days before the Visor announcement date, Hawkins and Dubinsky drove to the 3Com campus to meet with Eric Benhamou, Janice Roberts, and Alan Kessler, who was by now Palm's new president. It was a courtesy briefing about the new Visor and its announcement plans. After all, 3Com and Palm executives should be prepared to handle questions about their licensee when the product news broke.

Hawkins demoed the Visor to the executives, including its advanced datebook program, enhanced calculator, and USB connector. These were all nice features that would distinguish Handspring's products from Palm's.

Then he explained the Springboard concept. This feature was no longer a complete secret; despite Colligan's efforts to avoid leaks, a CNET reporter had reported on rumors about the expansion slot a week earlier.

Expansion in itself wasn't especially exciting. TRG (now Hand-Era), a small company in Des Moines, had been working with Mark Bercow's team for months to create a Palm OS–powered handheld with a slot for Compact Flash expansion cards. But TRG's expansion scheme was primarily designed for adding memory—an important feature in the corporate market. Hand-spring's scheme was far more flexible. Soon consumers would be able to turn the Visor into a phone, a pager, a global positioning system, an MP3 audio player, a voice recorder, game player, or a digital camera.

Donna closed the presentation by revealing the prices for the three Visor models. The Visor Deluxe would cost the same as the Palm III, but with four times as much memory and a choice of colors. The standard Visor would be $50 less than Palm's own lowest-priced model, the Palm IIIe. There was also to be an even cheaper model: the Visor Solo, which came without a synchronization cradle for use by people who didn't have computers. Any illusion that Handspring was not competing head-on with Palm had now been shattered.

The word that Handspring's new product was going to be a "PalmPilot killer" was spreading like wildfire. "If it's as good as it looks in demos, I can't imagine why anyone would want to buy anything else," *Time* reviewer Joshua Quittner wrote about the still unannounced Visor.

On Saturday, September 11, three days before Handspring's product launch, Janice Roberts called Dubinsky with dramatic news: 3Com was about to spin off Palm Computing. At last, the dream of an independent Palm would come true.

Dubinsky had no time to ponder her feelings about the belated spin-off; the immediate concern was the timing of 3Com's news. Eric Benhamou would issue a statement on Monday, and she knew instantly what would happen: 3Com's momentous announcement would push news of the Visor's introduction right off the front pages of Tuesday's newspapers.

"Janice, 3Com can't do that," she pleaded. "You know that this conflicts with our product announcement. It'll ruin our product launch. We are Palm's partner, for Heaven's sake!"

Over the weekend, Dubinsky repeatedly called Roberts and Kessler at their homes, pleading Handspring's case. "Delay the announcement until Wednesday," she asked, hoping to assure the Visor the full attention of the press for 48 hours. "Or even Tuesday, that gives us at least one day."

Like Donna, Ed was convinced that 3Com had deliberately timed its announcement to dampen the impact of the Visor launch. "It took them a year and a half to make the decision," he steamed. "You would have thought they could wait another three days."

Roberts and Kessler brought Dubinsky's plea to the 3Com board, but to no avail. "It really wasn't possible to change it. We had put together a full plan of communications," says Roberts. Benhamou was to make the announcements personally, and his schedule was booked solid for the rest of the week.

Colligan could do nothing to salvage Handspring's launch; it was too late to change the launch date. Frantic to find a solution, he even wondered if Handspring's announcement could run on Monday, preempting 3Com's news by a day—but it was too late. No newspaper could pull together an article overnight.

As soon as 3Com's announcement hit the wires on Monday, journalists began calling for comment. Until now, Donna and

Jeff had always maintained, in public at least, that they had left 3Com solely because they were entrepreneurs at heart and wanted to run another start-up. But when *Wall Street Journal* reporter Scott Thurm asked her that day, "Off the record, did you leave because 3Com wouldn't spin Palm off?" she shot back, "Yes. And you can consider that *on* the record."

Hawkins also was frank. "If they had spun us out, I'd still be there," he told a reporter from the *San Jose Mercury News*. They had no interest in prolonging the fairy tale about their pleasant departure. The cat was out of the bag.

On Tuesday morning, Donna, Jeff, and Ed pored over the newspapers. It was exactly as they had feared: Each paper ran prominent stories about the Palm spin-off, relegating the Visor announcement to a few paragraphs on inside pages. Worse, some of the Visor stories Handspring knew were already in the works got yanked. One in *BusinessWeek* never did appear, and one in the *Wall Street Journal* was folded into an article about the Palm spin-off.

Dubinsky was livid. "The fact that they decided not to spin [Palm] out, fine, I got it. In some sense it was the best thing for the 3Com stockholders at the time. And I wasn't angry when they decided [later] to spin it out, because I still felt it was the right thing to do. But I was very angry that they deliberately decided to take our headlines and tromp on our launch, and they did that, in paper after paper after paper."

Even some reporters wondered about the timing. *The Economist* noted in an article about Handspring later that week: "Given 3Com's paranoia about Handspring, it seems no accident that the day before, its chief executive, Eric Benhamou, announced that 3Com will spin off Palm Computing from its core computer-network equipment business."

Alan Kessler denies such talk. "It was not done maliciously. I know personally it was not done maliciously."

On Monday, September 13, a message from Eric Benhamou reached every Palm and 3Com employee's e-mail Inbox before 5:00 A.M. It told the employees that 3Com had at last decided to spin off Palm.

Alan Kessler called a communications meeting to share

more details. Well before the meeting started, the cafeteria was bursting with the company's 600 employees (plus over 100 contractors, who were filling in at jobs the company had been unable to staff otherwise). The excitement was palpable.

As they pushed through the crowd for a spot closer to the front of the room, high-fiving their teammates as they passed, most employees couldn't stop grinning. The nearly 300 newcomers who'd been with the company for less than 18 months were no less thrilled than the remaining original Palm employees—all five of them.

For those who'd hung in at Palm over the years, however, there was an extra bit of satisfaction. Over the past two years, they had watched colleagues leave for start-up companies and become overnight millionaires. It had seemed that the only way to get rich in the dot-com gold rush was by leaving Palm. Finally, Palm might make them wealthy, too. "It was a mixture of excitement and this feeling that we all deserved this because we chose to stay," says an employee. "We chose not to jump to Handspring and OmniSky. We had weathered this storm. We didn't bolt. We should feel good about this."

Kessler announced that an IPO would sell a small percentage of Palm's new stock; 3Com would distribute the remaining Palm shares to its shareholders. Until the bankers, lawyers, and management consultants completed their work on the IPO, however, he couldn't say when it might take place. Nor had it been worked out yet how many stock options in the new Palm employees would get.

The final piece of news prompted a gasp from the audience: 3Com was starting an executive search for a new Palm CEO. Kessler had seemed to bring stability back to Palm. Now yet another leader would be installed, bringing even more change. Employees and executives alike were tired of all the turmoil.

Somebody raised a hand and asked the question that was on many people's mind: "Will you be in the running for the CEO job?"

Kessler said that he was. "But if I don't get selected, I intend to stay on as president," he told the crowd, to a round of applause.

The question was: What happened to make Eric Benhamou change his mind?

Unbeknownst to anybody at Palm, the prospects for Palm's independence had actually looked bright at one point, during the fall and winter of 1998.

3Com seemed to be recovering from the disastrous merger with U.S. Robotics 18 months earlier. Though the company's sales were barely growing, its profits had been steadily rising, a sure sign that at least the company's operations had become efficient again. In December 1998, the company beat Wall Street's earnings expectations.

Benhamou had let Roberts run Palm as a relatively independent unit, much the way Dubinsky had. By the end of the year, only six months after Dubinsky and Hawkins departed, Benhamou had come to the conclusion that Palm would one day be spun off. "As we finished 1998, I was 100 percent sure we had to do that," he says. The only remaining question was when. "At the time, it was too early."

But 3Com's business renaissance quickly proved to be a house of cards. The bad news hit in February 1999. Sales of modems and computer connector cards were falling, and financial analysts warned that 3Com was losing ground even in market segments where it had been leading. 3Com's stock plummeted from $47 to $30 over the course of 10 days.

In March, Benhamou and COO Bruce Claflin explained their new plan to fix the company: They would shift emphasis from slow-growing or declining product lines to product lines that were growing quickly, such as cable modems and home networking equipment—and Palm.

3Com's strategy met with skepticism. By mid-April, the stock had hit $20. Benhamou repeatedly denied rumors that 3Com was ripe for takeover. He also insisted that "Palm has a very central place in the future."

The more 3Com's business spiraled downward, the tighter it seemed to clutch Palm to its chest. In May, Benhamou promoted a strategy he called *user-centric networking*. "The product that illustrates that mission the best is the Palm family of products," he told reporters. Rather than spin Palm out, "the thinking was to bring Palm closer in to 3Com," as one 3Com executive puts it.

But many financial analysts didn't see how handhelds could

be a logical addition to a networking company. Instead, they considered Palm a distraction that kept the 3Com executives from fixing the problems at the company's core.

All the attention to Palm also hurt 3Com's credibility as a serious supplier of networking infrastructure equipment. 3Com's customers began to wonder how serious 3Com was about networking—or was it now focusing on gadgets?

In June 1999, 3Com announced dismal financial results for the year. In a year when the networking market was booming (Cisco's sales soared by 43 percent), 3Com's total sales had grown by only $350 million, just 6 percent, over the previous year—and over $300 million of that growth came from Palm. In less than two years, 3Com really had become "a Palm Computing company," exactly as Dubinsky, Hawkins, and Colligan had only half-jokingly predicted.

The calls to spin off Palm became loud and frequent. Financial analysts and industry analysts alike argued that Palm should be spun off so that 3Com could unlock its value for its shareholders. "There seems to be no upside in the stock in the near term, unless they spin off the Palm Computing group," analyst David Takata told the press. Analysts who focused on the hand-held market agreed, but for different reasons. "There isn't one analyst who believed Palm didn't need to be spun off to be successful," handheld analyst Rob Enderle says.

Red Herring magazine published an open letter to Eric Benhamou. Under the headline "Palm it off," the magazine argued that PDAs and networking were "separate, uncomplementary technologies. Worse, the success of the Palm division could be spoiled by the sluggish performance of your networking business." At Palm, employees read the editorial's final demand with glee: "Sell off the Palm business, or sell off the data networking business. But split them up."

In July, 3Com's board reviewed two plans for the company. One strategy placed Palm dead-center in 3Com's future. The other proposed splitting off Palm. Benhamou's board, by now extremely concerned that Palm was a distraction to 3Com's top executives, voted for the spin-off. User-centric network visions aside, 3Com's shareholders would benefit far more from Palm if 3Com didn't own it.

Palm would be free at last.

Despite the loss of headlines to the Palm IPO, the Visor launch was a success. At the October Internet World trade show, Handspring's booth was packed. Instead of spending their tradeshow time in meetings behind closed doors, the norm for executives, all three Handspring executives shared booth duty, giving personal demos of their new baby to the public.

An editorial on the Motley Fool Web site summed up customer (and industry) impressions: "In my humble opinion, 3Com, which plans to spin off its Palm Computing unit, is in hot water. The Visor represents the biggest threat to Palm's grip on an overwhelming share of the handheld computing market. As a dedicated Palm owner and user, I see Visor as a better product."

Unfortunately, Handspring's period of smooth sailing was about to come to a miserable, crashing halt.

Dubinsky had been unable to fill one very important position, that of chief information officer (CIO). She made offers to people who turned her down and made offers to people who accepted but never showed up for work.

Without the crucial technology experience of a CIO, the Handspring executives decided to commission a massive Web site that they nicknamed Mother of All Web Sites (MAWS). It would take orders, process credit cards, track shipping, handle customer support requests, track repairs, permit internal and external electronic communications, and tie in the customer support and tech support reps—the works.

Unfortunately, the company Handspring hired to create this sensational system had never created a Web site of anything close to this complexity—in fact, had never created an order processing system of any kind.

Worse, the Handspring executives, focused on creating and launching the Visor and lacking Web expertise, didn't realize that MAWS was in trouble. "We had a few people who were trying to raise flags and say, 'I'm a little worried about this. I'm a little worried about this.'" But the executives dismissed the alarms, believing that, as Dubinsky put it, "We're going to pull it off. We're going to power through it."

A few days before Visor was to be announced, Colligan and his marketing team tested the new Web-based order entry system—and discovered severe bugs. By the night before the launch, the system still wasn't working.

That's when Colligan asked himself: "Would we ship a product if we were finding bugs the night before? No!" He pulled the plug.

MAWS, whose order taking mechanism Handspring counted on to see Visor's sales through the critical Christmas season, could not take a single order.

The nightmare had only begun. Predictably, the Handspring 800 number was immediately flooded with calls—thousands per day. The phone representatives, who had planned to type phone orders into MAWS directly, had no other computerized order taking system to fall back on; in desperation, they wrote down the orders on paper. It was a sure recipe for disaster.

To tide things over while they scrambled to get MAWS back online, Handspring's Web team whipped together a simple desktop PC database, so that the phone reps would at least have a computer system for taking orders.

The deeper the executives examined the Web site breakdown, the deeper the problems appeared to be. Panic set in. The executives and managers began holding crisis meetings at the end of each workday in Donna's office.

Ed, who was ultimately in charge of the site, searched for a solution. He uncovered a Canadian consulting firm who specialized in precisely this kind of work and hired its consultants on the spot to come to California.

It was just what Handspring needed. "The Canadians landed!" says Colligan. "It was like manna from Heaven. They looked at the system, and they figured it out."

In the meantime, something had to be done about the existing orders, and the thousands that would continue to pour in while the Canadians repaired the Web site. The solution seemed simple. Each night, Handspring would send the orders from its database to Logistix, the company hired to ship out the Visors, and let seasoned pros take over from there.

Then the situation *really* fell apart.

Dubinski and Colligan first realized that their troubles had just intensified when customers began to call. Some reported they'd received a dozen Visors. Others were furious about charges for multiple Visors on their credit cards. Donna ordered the processing of credit cards shut down and put a halt to the shipments while the Web team tried to figure out what was going on.

All clues led to the order data that was sent nightly from Handspring to Logistix. A few nights earlier, in an effort to simplify the order transfer, one of the outside programmers had written a program that would partially automate the process. The program contained the Mother of All Bugs: a glitch that utterly scrambled the data as it passed from the PC database into Logistix's systems.

"It was totally corrupt data!" says Dubinsky. "All these incorrect orders, which Logistix is happily shipping away. We're debiting people's credit cards twelve times! We're doing just dastardly things, just terrible, terrible things!"

It was a nightmare. Orders had been lost; Visors were stuck on the loading docks; Visors had been shipped to the wrong people. Meanwhile, with the process shut down, good orders were piling up.

For a full three months—October through December—Ed and Donna devoted much of their time to straightening out the mess.

With Christmas quickly approaching, and customers waiting for Visors they might have intended as presents, the Handspring executives and employees who had volunteered to assist with the crisis hunkered down in a downstairs "war room" filled with product packages and telephones. The mission was to ship a free Visor to every person for whom the company had any contact information at all. "There's now 1,000 orders left," says Colligan, "and we have no idea whether we'd shipped them or not. So we called every customer. We gave away probably five or six hundred units, because these people were so upset. We said, 'We're going to FedEx this overnight. Which one do you want? Keep it! And you know what? If you get another one, keep it! Merry Christmas twice!'"

Even so, some orders never did get fixed. Hundreds of people, having waited for months without receiving their orders, called Handspring to declare, "I will never do business with you again!"

The Handspring Web site never did become the mother of all Web sites, even though the two heroic Canadians became full-time Handspring employees. But through careful, phase-by-phase steps, it eventually did excel at taking customer orders, ultimately winning a 9.8 score (out of 10) from BizRate.com, a company that rates consumer Web sites.

Handspring's executives blame themselves for the meltdown. Dubinsky, for example, notes that she had had plenty of experience with distribution systems during her tenure at Apple, but the fact that this one was Web-based somehow made the task seem easier than it was. For Colligan, the critical error was biting off too much in conceiving MAWS.

Dubinsky estimates that between lost orders, the free Visors, and other costs, the meltdown cost Handspring $1 million. But the episode held some important lessons. "We could have done the best products in the world; we could have had the best marketing in the world; we could have the cutest logo in the world," she says. "If we couldn't deliver the product, we would fail."

TWENTY-TWO

IPO

When 3Com announced that it would spin out Palm, employee morale shot sky-high for the first time since Palm's founders had departed 15 months earlier. The company seemed astoundingly resilient, despite the damage that the desertions of Palm's key talent and the ever-changing leadership had caused.

Sales of Palm's products, especially the sleek Palm V, continued to grow by leaps and bounds. As the 1999 Christmas season approached, sales went into the traditional seasonal overdrive. Palm had zoomed to the top of the charts not only in the United States, where it had been the market leader within a few months of releasing the Pilot, but in Europe and Japan, where former market leaders Psion and Sharp fell behind. The Palm OS market share stood over 75 percent worldwide. The new competition from Handspring, while worrisome, didn't make a dent in Palm's growth. In the explosively expanding handheld market, there seemed to be plenty of room for more than one player.

At the same time, Palm hadn't made much progress toward achieving its long-term goals. "It wasn't a period of investment for growth, capturing the opportunity; it was a survival period to keep the teams and the company focused, to keep tension under control, to retain key talent and keep the ball moving," says product marketing VP Byron Connell.

One thing is certain: It was lucky for Palm that Microsoft hadn't been able to take advantage of the company's year of turmoil. Instead, Microsoft had itself hit a roadblock. In May, the company had told its licensing partners that it was working on a total rewrite of Windows CE, code-named Rapier, that would be easier to use (which industry observers took to mean "more like the Palm OS"). In other words, Microsoft was giving up on Windows CE 2.0, which had been a failure; all nine of the companies who had sold Windows CE 2.0 palmtops *combined* had not even gained a fifth of the market.

With a hefty $500 price tag and battery life even worse than in the black-and-white models, the new color Windows CE palmtops did little better. In the fall, discouraged by poor sales, Everex and Philips pulled the plug on their Windows CE products, exiting the market for good. "Is CE dead?" headlines began to appear.

Even as Microsoft's licensees dropped out of the market, new Palm licensees continued to join the party. For two years, Mark Bercow had been frustrated by an endless number of meetings with companies who didn't even bother to send senior executives with decision-making power. Palm had sold over 4 million handhelds; to many corporations, the handheld market seemed mere peanuts next to the more than 100 million cell phones or pagers sold each year, and simply didn't warrant the time of their top brass.

The tide turned when Finnish cell phone giant Nokia called. In October 1999, Palm announced that Nokia and Palm would work together on a Palm OS–based smart phone. Just one month later, Palm had more exciting news: Consumer electronics giant Sony had also signed a license for Palm's OS. "The Sony partnership is a broadside against an already weakened Windows CE," said industry analyst Tom Rhinelander. All of a sudden, the platform licensing business had gained momentum.

One fish was much harder to catch, however: Mark Bercow spent nearly a year trying to land a deal with old Palm acquaintance Motorola. The two companies had never quite lost touch since their ill-fated collaboration five years earlier.

Bercow badly wanted to close a deal with Motorola. Motorola had announced that it was to be a part owner of Symbian, a joint venture funded in the summer of 1998 by cell phone giants Nokia and Ericsson, British palmtop company Psion, and Motorola. Symbian's claims that its still unfinished OS would be the new standard for smart phones and wireless Internet palmtops created a stir in Europe.

Throughout the summer and early fall of 1998, Bercow's talks with Motorola proceeded well—so well that Bercow thought Motorola might back out of joining Symbian. Unfortunately, opposing political camps within Motorola stalled the talks, and in October, to Bercow's great disappointment, Motorola announced that it had joined Symbian.

For the first two years of its life, Symbian would be a darling of the technology press, even earning a spot on *Time Europe* magazine's list of 50 Hottest Tech Firms. At Palm, however, the old-timers were skeptical. The Symbian alliance was an almost perfect copy of the blueprint that had doomed the Zoomer— that is, it was a product designed by a committee of archcompetitors.

Sure enough, by the summer of 2000, Symbian's plans had stalled. Its EPOC OS drove fewer than 5 percent of the hand-held computers and smart phones sold. Losing faith, Nokia signed a licensing agreement with Palm; Ericsson joined Microsoft in a joint venture; and Juha Christensen, a high-profile cofounder of Symbian, defected for a job as a vice president in—of all places—Microsoft's mobility group.

Safe at Microsoft, Christensen complained that Symbian's unwieldy consortium structure had hindered the company's progress. "Something that set out to be a self-contained enterprise, driven by the paranoia and fear and entrepreneurship and opportunism that a company should be driven by," Christensen told the *Industry Standard,* "very quickly became what can best be described as a buyers' cooperative orchestrated by the device makers."

Finally, in September 2000, Mark Bercow's efforts to get a deal with Motorola paid off. To Symbian's dismay, consortium member Motorola announced that it would collaborate with Palm on a smart phone.

In Palm's hallways, though, only one topic of conversation rivaled the spin-off and stock option chatter: the Platform-Product breakup. In Alan Kessler's many conversations with employees and executives over the months, one thing had come through loud and clear: The division of engineering into platform and product groups wasn't working.

Palm had added enough engineers to make the two groups about equal in size now, but work on the OS and on new products was progressing far too slowly.

Under the split engineers arrangement, the Platform team could release a new version of the Palm OS only after all features that had been promised to all licensees were complete. The result was that all licensees, including the Palm Product team, had to wait much longer to get their hands on the OS and make progress on their own next generation of devices.

Furthermore, both engineering teams still felt understaffed. The split also resulted in vast duplication of effort—and to make matters worse, communication between the two groups was restricted by the Chinese Wall, which hampered their progress even more.

In February 2000, a full year after the stop-and-go engineering split was started, Kessler reunited the two engineering groups.

Despite the employees' excitement about going public, there were plenty of details still to be worked out concerning the Palm spin-off. One of the most important blanks left to be filled in was chief executive officer. Until 3Com had selected a CEO for the newly independent Palm, it couldn't file the necessary IPO paperwork with the Securities and Exchange Commission (SEC).

Finally, on December 2, 1999, 3Com announced that it had found the right man for the job: Carl Yankowski, billed in the press release as a former Sony executive. Yankowski had indeed been a Sony executive for five years, but had more recently completed a decidedly low-tech 14-month stint at Reebok. A self-professed geek with an electrical engineering degree from MIT, Yankowski's career had been a zigzag between technology and consumer goods at companies like Memorex and Pepsi.

As soon as the jovial, heavyset Yankowski arrived at Palm, he recruited an all-new team of senior executives, who would report directly to him. Palm was a company of 900 employees and close to $1 billion in sales, but Yankowski was clearly thinking big when he adopted the organizational structure of much larger enterprises, including a chief technology officer (CTO), a chief strategy officer (CSO), a chief operating officer (COO) for a new division Yankowski named Content and Access, and a chief marketing officer (CMO). Alan Kessler's title changed to COO of the Product and Platform division, and all of Palm's current vice presidents, now one more level down from the center of power, reported to him.

With Yankowski's name on the SEC documents and an organizational structure that suggested a multi-billion-dollar corporation, Palm's IPO could finally get under way. Bankers, management consultants, and the executives prepared the IPO road show, the grueling series of back-to-back presentations that corporate executives make for an audience of financial analysts, brokerage funds, and other money managers, in hopes of whetting their appetites for the new company's stock.

Even as the March IPO date approached, Palm's employees still were unsure about the size of the stock grants they would get. They did know one thing, however: Their options price—the price at which they could buy the stock—would be set at the IPO price, no matter how long they'd been employed by the company.

For old-time Palm employees, this news came as a big disappointment. In start-up companies, the stock option price is pegged at the stock's value when the employee joins the company. That way, an employee who joined the company in its earliest stages might have an option price of 10 or 20 cents. As the company's valuation climbs through successive rounds of VC funding, later employees' options might be priced at a few dollars. Then, if the company survives, becomes successful and goes public, the stock might trade in the tens or twenties of dollars—and the employee can pocket the difference.

In late January, 3Com and its bankers had set the price range for the Palm IPO at $14 to $16. But by late February, the company filed documents with the SEC raising the target price to between $30 and $32.

The market took the change as a signal that Palm's underwriters were being flooded with demand for the stock—that this IPO was hot. The hype around the Palm IPO, already at the boiling level, simply exploded. For investors, Palm seemed to be a software company that might be the next Microsoft, *and* a profitable hardware company that sold the hottest gadgets around, *and*—due to its (still tiny) wireless service revenues from Palm.net—an Internet stock, all rolled into one. This, said investors in online chat rooms, was a stock not to be missed. Individual investors revved up with orders to their brokers.

On March 2, a day before Palm's stock was to be publicly traded for the first time, the final price was set: $38, higher even than the price the bankers and company execs had set only four days earlier.

For the employees, though, the IPO price of $38 was bad news. An SEC rule prevents company insiders from unloading their shares within 180 days of the IPO; the stock would have to rise even higher—and stay there—in order for a Palm employee to make any money off the IPO. Few doubted, given the hype, that the stock price would rise—but few dared to hope that it would stay that high for six months.

On Thursday, March 2, 2000, all eyes in the financial world turned to Palm. About 23 million shares of Palm, fewer than 5 percent of the total shares in the company, had been allocated the night before to institutional investors; the rest would be distributed to 3Com's stockholders later in the year.

The laws of supply and demand did their trick. When the Nasdaq board lit up for the first time with a price next to the ticker symbol PALM at 11:20 A.M. EST, it showed an unbelievable $145. Soon after, PALM climbed to $165. Thanks to the three-hour time difference between the two coasts, most Palm staff listened to the reports on their way to work. "I remember being in the car listening to the radio, and I thought we were all going to be millionaires," one of the employees says.

Palm's executives had organized an employee meeting to celebrate. Long before the start of the meeting, the vans of national and local TV news crews were parked outside the Palm buildings.

The PR staff had set up the meeting room off the cafeteria for radio and TV interviews with the Palm executives who were in the building. In another room, a few executives watched Carl Yankowski's interview on CNBC, taping it for playback at the employee meeting that was to commence in minutes.

After CNBC announcers gushed over "the most talked-about IPO," the camera cut to Carl Yankowski in the Nasdaq studio. Usually a compelling public speaker, Yankowski seemed out of his element. When asked about larger screens for palmtops, he answered stiffly, "We are well positioned whichever way the market goes."

As the interview came to a close, the reporter said, "I've got to ask you about your suit." Yankowski smiled. He was wearing a very special suit, he let on, designed to satisfy the public's high expectations from Palm's IPO. The shiny pinstripes woven into the otherwise standard wool suit were made from threads of pure gold.

CNBC cut back to the studio anchor. "Was that for real?" he asked the correspondent.

The Palm managers assembled around the TV set looked at each other. "We're not showing this video," one of the executives decreed. Then they walked out to start the employee meeting.

Mark Bercow, the last executive from Dubinsky's original executive staff still at Palm, pushed through the throngs of employees to the head of the room to lead the rally. Every one of Palm's 900 employees seemed to be in the room, or at least listening to the meeting through conference phone lines that connected Palm's offices in Europe and throughout the United States. Palm VII handhelds flashed everywhere as their owners checked the latest stock price. "142 and 3/8ths," an employee would whisper to those around him—and the information rippled outward through the crowd until it collided with another, more recent quote.

Eventually, the stock started a slow decent from its high of $165; but the numbers were still so high, the crowd was giddy.

The employees still didn't know how many stock options they would be getting (and wouldn't for another two weeks), but they didn't seem to care. With a spread of $100 between their options price of $38 and the price of the stock, even 1,000 shares were worth $100,000.

When Bercow started his short speech, he asked that those employees who'd been with Palm since before the Pilot days stand up. Five people rose: Donna Gafford, Palm's first office manager, and four engineers. Their colleagues applauded as TV cameras circled the crowd. Those original Palm team members had waited a long time for this day.

The euphoria of the employee meeting held even when the stock eventually sank below $100. "Ah, there was tremendous excitement in the air," says Byron Connell. "A lot of people were watching the stock zoom to the ceiling, calculating their personal wealth and their date of retirement! And praying it would last."

Palm's stock closed its first day at $95, which gave the company the mind-boggling valuation of $53.5 billion. For the moment at least, Wall Street considered Palm Computing a more valuable company than General Motors, McDonald's—or 3Com.

Doug Haslam, Palm's HR director, had sent an e-mail to Jeff Hawkins, Donna Dubinsky, Ed Colligan, and others of the original Palm team that day. His note spoke for many who were still at Palm:

> While recent events may have had a bittersweet taste for some of you, I hope all of you feel a sense of pride and accomplishment at what you've spawned. In the euphoria and enthusiasm of late, I'm not sure many have stopped to appreciate those of you who set this in motion. I certainly do. Each of you and the many others who have helped make this such a success deserve a thanks from those of us who have benefited from your efforts.

"It was a difficult day for me," Dubinsky says. "I felt emotionally torn about it." Now that Palm had finally reached the independence she had fought for, other executives were center stage.

Since the day Hawkins and Dubinsky left the company, Eric Benhamou had been criticized for refusing to spin off Palm. Industry observers and Palm insiders alike pointed at the damage his refusal did to Palm: It resulted in both a harrowing brain drain and the creation of a formidable rival in Handspring.

But with the success of the IPO behind him, Eric Benhamou sees his decision vindicated. "With the benefit of hindsight, I'm just so glad I didn't do it [when Jeff and Donna asked for it]," he says. "I was under a lot of pressure to do it. It was a difficult decision, but I'm really glad that I decided not to do it then."

3Com board member Jean-Louis Gassée agrees. Benhamou's job was not to make Palm happy. For the CEO of a public company, Gassée says, "the only *raison d'être* is to make the shareholders richer. That mission was accomplished by Eric Benhamou."

Few outsiders watched the Palm IPO with greater interest than the executives at Handspring, who were readying an IPO of their own. After all, the frenzy over Palm's stock proved that there was a large demand for the stock of a handheld computing company.

From a business standpoint, Handspring was flying high. Once it finally began selling its Visors in retail stores, several months after the Handspring Web site meltdown, Dubinsky turned out to have been right: The overall volume of sales increased significantly. Handspring had followed the same strategy that had made Palm so successful at the launch of the Pilot: The company chose, and forged strong relationships with, only three large national retailers. In this limited distribution, Visors flew off the shelves. The retailers loved it. In its first week in stores, the Visor Deluxe model outsold all other handhelds, grabbing 27 percent of market share.

It was time for Dubinsky, Hawkins, and Handspring's bankers to pack up for the exhausting IPO road show, much like the one Palm's executives had endured two months earlier.

Jeff and Donna fought fatigue by taking catnaps in the hired car that ferried them from appointment to appointment; they fought boredom by playing Road Show Bingo.

Road Show Bingo went like this: Dubinsky knew that analysts at each meeting would ask many of the same questions. At Donna's request, Ron Marianetti had printed out randomized Bingo cards bearing these questions on their various squares. "Why did you leave Palm?" "Are you an acquisition target for others?" "How much do the modules cost?" To stay alert during the repetitive meetings, the Handspring executives quietly marked off squares on their Bingo cards as corresponding questions were asked.

Finally, the day of the IPO arrived. Little of the "Gee, I'm rich" mentality that pervaded many companies' IPOs was on display; a few weeks earlier, Hawkins, concerned about unrealistic expectations and emotional roller-coaster rides, had given another fatherly talk at the all-company communications meeting.

This time, he showed a slide that charted the stock price of an unnamed company. In the first five years of the company's life, the stock puttered along, well below $5, with small ups and downs. "Does anybody have a guess which company this is?" Jeff asked. Nobody volunteered a suggestion.

Then he showed the next slide, which covered the next five years; on this chart, the company's stock took off, zooming to $70. The company was Intel, and the point was clear.

"There are only two prices that matter in a stock: the price the day you buy it and the price the day you sell it," Hawkins says. "Everything in between is a total distraction. The fact is that none of these employees were going to be able to sell anything for a long time [because of the SEC's six-month holding rule]. You'll just get disappointed if you watch the stock and start dreaming about what this all means to you. I just didn't want people to get wrapped up in this."

Jeff also banned any of what he called "public display of stock affection." The stock price was not to be posted inside the building, and there was to be no stock-price ticker in the lobby, as was common at other newly minted public companies. "It's best to work here ten years," he told his staff. "Then sit back and see what it's worth. I bet you it's worth a hell of a lot!"

On the day Handspring was to go public—June 21, 2000—Handspring's entire executive staff, a few spouses in tow (including

Dubinsky's fiancé, whom she was to marry less than two weeks later), headed to the offices of a San Francisco investment bank, to watch as a new symbol, HAND, scrolled across the computer screens.

"We watched it on the computer monitor," says Hawkins, who'd brought his daughters. "You could see these trades being registered. Then they pull the trigger, and all of a sudden the buying and selling starts flying."

The stock price had been set at $20 per share; the company released 10 million shares to the public, hoping to raise $200 million. To the relief of the executives, the price didn't exhibit the rocketing up and crashing down behavior that characterized Palm's IPO. In fact, by the end of the day, it had seesawed gently up to about $27 at the closing bell.

Upon her return from the investment bank, Donna, still hoarse from her road show presentations, walked through the company from cubicle to cubicle, shaking employees' hands and thanking them for their contributions to Handspring.

Though their sudden wealth was purely theoretical—nobody could sell their shares for 180 days after the IPO—the promise of those future stock sales triggered a minor consumption boom at Handspring. Hardware engineer Karl Townsend bought a Ferrari; Ron Marianetti bought a Porsche.

Hawkins, on the other hand, was content to stick with his Volvo station wagon. But he couldn't entirely escape the effects of Handspring's sudden prestige. "Some guy [will walk up to me and say,] 'Where do you work?' And I say, 'I work at Handspring.' And he says, 'Wow! That's great. You got any stock in that company? You have any options?' So what am I supposed to say? I've gotten to the point where I try not to wear any Handspring or Palm clothing anywhere, because it just invites questions."

The company was now a living, breathing, publicly held corporation, but Handspring's mission was far from over. It wasn't yet profitable, for one thing. A long and challenging battle also lay ahead: competing with Palm and Microsoft to become the leader in personal computing that Jeff Hawkins envisioned.

TWENTY-THREE

MILLENNIUM

Independent at last, and with a billion dollars in the bank, Palm could say that the world of 2000 was its oyster. It didn't seem to matter that Palm had its fifth leader in only 17 months, nor that it had lost almost every one of the original creators of the handheld revolution. Hawkins and other old-timers had predicted that Palm would be running out of steam 18 to 24 months after his departure—but instead, Palm's success seemed simply unstoppable.

The reason was simple: Helped by the exuberant U.S. economy, the market for handhelds soared in 2000, and Palm, as the market leader, soared with it. At the buzzing PC Expo tech tradeshow in New York in June, people as far as the eye could see were promoting, selling software for, or using handhelds. "It should have been called PDA Expo," said one visitor.

Handhelds had entered the mainstream. As soon as inexpensive models like the Handspring Visor and Palm's m100 came on the market, students and women joined the PalmPilot-toting ranks that had previously been occupied by mostly male, high-income professionals. Oprah Winfrey discussed her Palm organizer on her talk show. The French couture company Hermès took orders for custom PalmPilot cases at its Paris flagship store.

David Letterman spoofed Palm's first TV ad, in which a young woman who's just boarded a train beams her phone number to a handsome stranger in an adjacent train. (In Letterman's version, she beams him a note that says, "Stop staring at me, freakshow.")

Making the job of Palm's marketing department even easier, the IPO hype had turned Palm into a known brand even outside the world of gadget lovers. In fact, two-thirds of the U.S. population had heard of Palm.

Even the Palm employees' joke that "Palm Computing, a 3Com company" would one day give way to "3Com, a Palm Computing company" took on a ring of truth. Once independent, Palm was worth far more than 3Com, its former parent—so much so that the S&P 500 stock index booted 3Com from its ranks and replaced it with Palm, triggering a wave of gleeful e-mail messages among former and current Palm employees.

At the end of its fiscal year in May 2000, Palm had reached over $1 billion in sales. During the next six months, it raked in another $922 million. It had taken Palm three and a half years to sell 5 million handhelds. The company would sell another 5 million during 2000 alone, not including the additional 1 million Visors that Handspring sold.

Despite Palm's hypergrowth, Carl Yankowski stepped into anything but a bed of roses when he arrived at the company. Outside Palm's headquarters, customers were snapping up handhelds at a record rate, but Palm's executives were grappling with business problems that would shape Palm's fortunes for years to come.

For starters, Palm was saddled with the conflicting forces it had unleashed by licensing its operating system to competitors. Satisfying the diverse feature demands of Palm's licensees—Handspring, Symbol, Nokia, Qualcomm, and Sony—had slowed down progress on the Palm OS; yet because few of the licensees' products had come to market, little revenue was coming in to compensate Palm for the effort. Palm employees and executives alike struggled with the paradox caused by conflicting objectives: making Palm's *own* handhelds successful even while assisting its licensee competitors.

A second challenge for Yankowski was sorting out a strategy for wireless products. By now, wireless connectivity was considered a must-have feature for handhelds. In predictions that sounded eerily like those made during the early pen computing days, analysts predicted that the market for such wireless devices would skyrocket. Investors were keen on stocks of companies that could make a claim to wireless developments.

On the advice of his IPO advisors, Yankowski announced that Palm would soon offer many more wireless options than just the Palm VII. A new wireless product was already on Palm's engineering schedule, he told analysts, slated to ship some time in late 2001. So was a $50 kit that would allow all other Palm models to make wireless connections using a cell phone as an intermediary.

Yankowski garnered a fair share of criticism for announcing the Palm VII's replacement well over a year before it was ready. How was the sales team to sell the Palm VII if customers were waiting for a newer version? When Yankowski got carried away and told a journalist that he didn't like the Palm VII, that it was "a brick" and "a lump of coal," a hailstorm of criticism broke out from developers who created and sold Palm VII add-ons.

Though Palm still stood as the undisputed leader in the handheld market, other players were nipping at its heels. Sony loomed on the horizon with a Palm OS–powered product slated for Christmas. Microsoft was gearing up to announce yet another new version of Windows CE. The greatest threat, though, came from Palm's own founders. Once Handspring finally began selling its Visors in retail stores, several months after the Handspring Web site meltdown, Visors promptly grabbed a quarter of the handheld market share from Palm.

Yankowski also found himself unable to defuse the press and analysts' notion that Palm was no longer a technology leader. Handspring, with the pedigree of its founders and the Springboard expansion slot, was touted as the true innovator.

"Right now, Handspring makes a better Palm than Palm," said a Microsoft product manager, happy for the chance to take a shot at rival Palm. "The brains behind Palm are those of Handspring CEO Dubinsky and resident technical genius Jeff Hawkins," pointed out *Fortune* magazine.

And analysts chided Palm for moving too slowly to upgrade its OS and therefore handing Microsoft the chance to catch up. "I just don't think the folks at Palm have a strong enough vision to continue moving the platform," said long-time industry analyst Ken Dulaney, echoing the thoughts of many.

Yankowski tackled his new job with full force, averaging 20-hour workdays and hiring new executives and a management consulting firm. His 1975 VW Beetle generally occupied the choicest parking spot right next to the building entrance—not because he was Palm's CEO, but because he was the first to arrive in the early morning. "I get up in the middle of the night and work again," he says. "Not because I want to or enjoy it, but because there's just a lot of work to be done."

Despite the hard work, Yankowski had a rocky start with his new company's rank and file. Though an inspiring public speaker, he was prone to gaffes when speaking off the cuff. Addressing the employees for the first time at the company communications meeting, Yankowski put both feet in his mouth: He proudly told the crowd that he had taken a $400,000 pay cut to work at Palm. He had meant to communicate how much he had wanted to run Palm, no matter the personal cost, but his new employees didn't view his $600,000 salary as quite the personal sacrifice he did. "We were all thinking, 'Your pay cut is more than anybody else in this room is even making,'" says one employee.

Shortly thereafter, at a meeting with Palm's engineers, Yankowski asked the female engineers, a small number scattered among their several hundred male colleagues, to rise from their seats, intending to praise Palm's diverse workforce. Many of the women were uncomfortable enough at being singled out simply for being female—"it would have been appropriate 20 years ago," a male engineer at the meeting says—but then Yankowski forgot to say why he had had them stand to begin with. He proceeded with his talk, leaving the women standing awkwardly, mystified.

With few exceptions, the new chief executives Yankowski had hired failed to impress the Palm rank and file. (One of them, Palm's chief technology officer, left the company only nine months later.) Shortly after their arrival, some sharp Palm tongue called the new executives the "C team." On the surface, the nickname was a nod to the new executives' titles: CMO, CTO, CSO, CFO, CHRO, and COO. But Palm employees understood the reference: These executives wouldn't have made the A or B teams. The nickname stuck.

Like many new CEOs, Yankowski ordered a sweeping reorganization of the company. In its new structure, the company consisted of two business units, each with its own COO. It was unusual for a CEO of a company of fewer than 1,000 employees to abdicate day-to-day operations to two COOs, but the scheme was designed to free Yankowski "to focus on big-picture strategy."

One of the two new units, led by Alan Kessler, was called Platform, Products, and Markets, and included most of Palm's current staff. The other, known as Content and Access, was run by Barry Cottle, a former Disney executive. Its mission was to develop Internet portal and access services (including the wireless service Palm.net) for customers with wireless handhelds.

Like the doomed Palm.net business managers before him, Yankowski believed that wireless services would become a key area of growth and high-margin revenue for Palm, and he wanted to invest in it. In the summer of 2000, he announced that Palm had acquired AnyDay.com, a Web-based calendar synchronizing system that could be accessed with wireless handhelds, for $85 million, as a means to improve Palm's revenue from service fees. Before long, the Content and Access unit grew to about 150 employees.

(The plan didn't work out. Nine months later, Yankowski dismantled the unit and wrote off $47 million from the AnyDay acquisition. "Revenue expectations associated with these Web services have come down in line with other Internet-based businesses," Palm CFO Bruner said. In other words, Palm experienced its own mini-version of the dot-com bust.)

Big-picture strategies notwithstanding, Palm had a short-term problem on its hands immediately after its IPO: a fourth version of Windows CE. Microsoft's latest handheld operating system would become the basis of devices that Microsoft shrewdly renamed Pocket PCs—a name designed to distance the new gadgets from their failed predecessors. Microsoft vowed to spare no expense in making Pocket PC a winner.

In early 1999, Robin Abrams had hired Michael Mace, who knew about competing with Microsoft first-hand from his 10 years with Apple, and had given him the unusual title of chief competitive officer. In Abrams's view, Palm's rank and file were too confident that the superiority of the Zen of Palm would carry the day. She gave Mace the marching orders to shake up the complacency and to prepare the company for a fight with the industry's fiercest competitor.

During his first months at Palm, the affable Mace toured Palm bearing a lengthy presentation, warning everyone in sight that Microsoft's strategy of "Windows everywhere" had not changed in the slightest. He flashed a chart from market research firm IDC that predicted Palm's sales growth would come to a grinding halt in 1999 while Windows CE sales nearly tripled. Worse, IDC forecast that Windows CE would overtake Palm's sales in 2001. (Despite IDC's grim predictions, Palm's sales doubled in 1999 and again in 2000, leaving Windows CE with little market share.) The time to ramp up marketing was now, Mace said, while Microsoft CE was weak and in transition.

His warnings fell on receptive ears—but then Abrams resigned, throwing Palm's staff into a holding pattern. Only months later, in the fall of 1999, did Alan Kessler convince 3Com to increase Palm's advertising budget. But soon the spin-off preparations took most of the Palm executives' time and focus. The compete-with-Microsoft momentum Mace had fostered gave way to other priorities.

So it wasn't until February 2000 that Yankowski and Mace gathered what Yankowski called a "tiger team" to deal with the new threat. The new Pocket PCs wouldn't be launched publicly until April; Palm's tiger team had a few months—and some funding—with which to steal Microsoft's thunder.

Microsoft CEO Steve Ballmer unveiled the new Pocket PC devices with a flashy show, staged on a balcony of Manhattan's Grand Central Terminal during the morning rush hour. But Palm's guerilla countermarketing team was ready: Over 20 Palm employees manned Manhattan's computer stores to demo Palm devices to customers, convincing many to leave the store with a new Palm model rather than a Pocket PC.

The new Pocket PCs were also on display at the Comdex tradeshow in Chicago. There, visitors were welcomed by Palm billboards, from the airport all the way to the convention center, that touted the 50,000 developers who'd signed up to write software for Palm OS devices.

By the time the first Pocket PC models from Casio and HP were shipping, press reviews judged them inferior to the Palm models. "New, Improved Pocket PCs Don't Capture Palm's Magic" wrote Walt Mossberg in the *Wall Street Journal.*

Michael Mace, and with him all of Palm, breathed a sigh of relief, and disbanded the tiger team in June. But they hadn't heard the last of the Pocket PC.

As Yankowski, his management consultants, and new chief executives settled down to long strategy sessions, it quickly became clear to Palm's middle managers that "it's less about devices and more about the other parts of the business for Carl," as one of the executives put it.

That meant less attention to Palm's products—Palm's primary source of income—and more on the Palm Platform and the "Content and Access" business.

Yankowski hoped that these initiatives would diversify Palm's income sources, a necessity in light of the profit squeeze that Palm's licensees were putting on Palm's hardware products. The inexpensive Handspring Visor had already forced Palm to cut its prices, and Sony's upcoming, high-end Clié would surely put pressure on sales of Palm's bestseller, the Palm V.

At the announcement of the Palm IPO, Eric Benhamou had predicted that, within two to three years, Palm would get most of its revenue from licensing its OS and other services rather than from its hardware sales. Unfortunately, reaching that point was easier said than done. (Even in the fall of 2001, two years after Benhamou's prediction, licensing and service revenue was still less than 8 percent of Palm's income.)

Instead, Yankowski found himself presiding over a hopeless catch-22: To get a large portion of its revenue from licensing, Palm would have to lose a huge portion of its sales to its licensees—yet the royalties from Handspring and Sony were only a fraction of what Palm could have made by selling one of its own handhelds.

The company became practically schizophrenic. Palm's sales and marketing people competed with Palm's licensees for customers—yet Palm's programmers were forced to write new features for the benefit of Palm's new rivals.

In any case, the Palm executives were stuck. The company couldn't very well get out of the hardware business—nearly all of Palm's revenue came from selling its handhelds. But Palm couldn't stop licensing, either. First of all, doing so would risk losing out to competitors like Microsoft or Symbian, the consortium of European cell phone makers. Second, Palm couldn't stop licensing even if it wanted to: Yankowski and Kessler had renewed Palm's contract with Handspring through April 2009.

The only change Yankowski and Kessler could make was to become more selective, granting licenses only to companies that were unlikely to compete with Palm's own products, much as Dubinsky had advocated when she was still at Palm. Samsung, for example, intended to develop a combination Palm/cell phone, and Acer would design a handheld for China, a market that Palm would have difficulty reaching itself.

In late 1997, while still at Palm, Jeff Hawkins had warned his colleagues of what he called "dangerous technologies."

One example was color. At the time, Palm had a handheld with a color screen on the drawing boards (the Palm IIIc), one that used a state-of-the-art screen technology—for 1997. But color-screen technology was still immature. The danger was that the technology would improve dramatically in the 12 to 18 months it would take Palm to finish designing its machine, opening up the possibility that Palm's effort might be trumped by a competitor.

The second danger, Hawkins had said, lurked in wireless technology. It seemed obvious that all handheld devices would one day have wireless connections. "It's inevitable, but I don't know how it's going to happen," he had said. "We don't know which technology is going to bring it to market."

Even in 2000, nearly three years after Jeff's "dangerous

technologies" talk, the designers of wireless devices still grappled with many unknown factors. The problems included not only choosing the right wireless network, radio, and battery, but also in determining exactly what consumers would want in the way of features. Did they want e-mail, Web, or access to corporate networks? All of these were pieces in the puzzle, all were interconnected, and all were moving targets.

Palm and Handspring were both at work on wireless products, though the difference in wireless philosophies between the two companies could not have been more stark. With product design centers in Chicago, Seattle, and Santa Clara, and with hundreds of engineers on staff, Palm started a number of wireless product developments simultaneously. Whichever technology and functionality emerged as the right one, Palm hoped to be ready for it.

In the meantime, the wireless model Yankowski was promising (later to be called i705) would offer Internet access along the same lines as its larger ancestor, the Palm VII, but it was smaller and better. A customer didn't have to explicitly check for e-mail, as on the Palm VII; e-mail was already downloaded and waiting whenever the device turned on. To Palm, Internet data was "the ultimate application for Palm Powered handhelds."

Over at Handspring, Hawkins's small engineering team was focused instead on the cell phone module that Jeff had planned since the founding of Handspring. Voice, not data, they believed, was the killer application that would create a mass market for wireless handheld devices. Called VisorPhone, the module would snap into the Springboard slot in every Visor organizer, turning it not only into a cell phone, but also a wireless e-mail terminal and Web browser.

Like the Palm engineers five miles away, Hawkins's team struggled in unfamiliar territory.

"We knew that that was a big project," says Hawkins, "because it's a very complex radio, it involves all kinds of new certification, it involves relationships with carriers, it's a whole different usage model and industry. We're competing against titans— Nokia, Ericsson, Motorola!

"But we had to do it anyway. We just had to bite the bullet. We had no expertise doing it, and, in the beginning, there was a lot of fumbling around. It took us a long time to get the VisorPhone done.

"And the idea behind it was, it would give us the knowledge to start doing integrated products"—including an entirely new product line that Jeff was already planning for late 2001, a product he felt could be as important as the original Pilot.

Though Palm's sales were soaring, employee loyalty turned fragile by midsummer. Through April 2000, morale had been propped up by the prospect of Palm's impending IPO and, immediately afterward, the temporary sensation of wealth. But that feeling didn't last long. The stock lost 50 percent of its value in the first month of its existence, and the cave-in of the Nasdaq in early April did the rest. Six weeks after the IPO, the employees' options were "under water," as Palm's stock traded well below the $38 option price.

The Internet boom of the past three years had created a culture of rapid job-hopping, and many employees' attachment to Palm was only paper-thin. About half of Palm's 1,000 employees had been with the company for less than a year—not much time to feel truly at home at the rapidly changing Palm. The other half had endured so many changes during their tenure that they would have found it hard to say which version of Palm held their loyalty. By May, another exodus of staff had started.

For weeks, a copy of an e-mail message from Microsoft CEO Steve Ballmer to *Microsoft* employees circulated at Palm, though nobody knew how it got there. The memo was written on April 25, 2000, within weeks of Judge Jackson's ruling that Microsoft violated antitrust laws. Ballmer wrote: "With the sharp drop in our stock price on Monday, and the government floating rumors that they may ask for a breakup of Microsoft, I want to address the concerns that I know you have."

Microsoft's stock had plummeted from over $100 to $66. Ballmer, acknowledging that "stock options are an important part of our compensation," granted every Microsoft employee additional options—priced at $66. Palm's employees, who had no such new grants in sight, heard the message loud and clear: Microsoft acts swiftly and protects its employees.

Ballmer's memo wasn't the only way Palm felt Microsoft's

presence. By July 2000, a month after the tiger team had been disbanded, a new Pocket PC model created a frenzy even before it was available in stores. The buzz among techies was that Compaq's sleek, silver iPaq was hot. Its bright color screen—one of Hawkins's two "dangerous technologies"—had trumped both Palm and Handspring. Gadget lovers rushed to stores to scoop up the earliest models as soon as they hit the shelves. Retailers quickly sold out. A few iPaqs soon surfaced on eBay, going to the highest bidders for hundreds of dollars over list price.

Consumers saw the shortages as a sign of overwhelming success, just as they had during the original Pilot shortages of 1996. And even though the far more pedestrian Casio and HP Pocket PC models outsold the iPaq month after month, the iPaq managed to hang onto its mystique of being the hottest gadget in the hearts of handheld enthusiasts.

Microsoft also applied skillful guerrilla tactics. In October 2000, it sent a unique invitation to influential Palm fans—software developers, Palm book authors, Web site hosts, consultants, and frequent Internet bulletin-board visitors. Microsoft would bring them, all expenses paid, to its headquarters in Redmond, Washington, for a personal demonstration of the Pocket PC's virtues.

The demo wasn't all they received: Microsoft gave each of the 35 attendees two Pocket PCs (including an iPaq), a modem, a memory card, headphones, and a gift certificate good for use in Microsoft's company store. The total value of the loot was $1,400.

Some of the Palm faithful became converts, raving about their new iPaqs. Others, like book author Rick Broida, were unimpressed. "It was a cheap tactic. And I think they did that because the device doesn't stand well on its own." (The following year, Microsoft repeated the invitation—and again gave away Pocket PCs—this time to the technical writers of major newspapers and magazines.)

By the fall of 2000, the dot-com boom was over for good. Most of the erstwhile high-flying Internet start-ups were struggling or dying. The U.S. economy showed early signs of a slump. Tech stocks crashed, and even the venerable Dow took a dive.

Palm's battered stock, however, staged a comeback. Handspring's stock, which hadn't lost any ground in the first place, went through the roof, making Dubinsky and Hawkins paper billionaires.

"The only time it really hit me was when I went to Yale in the fall for a couple of meetings," says Dubinsky. "I was wandering through the Yale Co-op [the bookstore], and they had terminals for Internet access. I walked up to one and plugged in our ticker symbol, and it was one of the days when it just had zoomed. It hit me when I looked at it, knowing my number of shares, that I'd just become a billionaire." Indeed, both she and Jeff landed on *Forbes* magazine's list of the 400 wealthiest Americans.

The trouble was, of course, that this wealth was purely theoretical; the Handspring executives, like their employees, weren't allowed to sell their shares for 180 days after the IPO. "I remember this CNN person interviewed me: 'What's it feel like to be a billionaire?' " says Dubinsky. "And I said: 'I'm not really! I know you think I am, 'cause the math works that way, but I know I'm not, because I can't spend it. It's just a theoretical exercise.' "

While his employees were jubilant, those who knew Hawkins well could see that he was worried. "Jeff wasn't happy at all," says engineer Art Lamb, who by now had worked closely with Jeff for 12 years.

"I kept thinking that all hell was going to break loose," Hawkins says. "I felt almost certain of it. I was kind of depressed."

Though Handspring's products (by now four models) were selling briskly, Jeff, Donna, and Ed understood well that at $90 per share, Handspring's stock price was just as much a bubble as the valuations of the dot-com companies had been the year before. When the bubble burst, employees would feel devastated.

Nor was that Jeff's only concern. He had also started to worry that handhelds would turn into low-margin commodities even sooner than Handspring had expected.

"The organizer business is going to be like calculators," he told his colleagues. "There is still a calculator business, but who wants to be in it? They're cheap, and sort of the backwater of consumer electronics."

If handheld organizers became low-profit goods, companies who specialized in low-cost manufacturing, not product development and innovation, could make a living producing them. Hawkins was eager for Handspring to get into the communicator business as soon as possible.

His feelings on this point struck many of his associates as premature. The handheld market was growing by leaps and bounds. Sure, organizers would one day become a commodity, but the other executives expected that selling them would remain a profitable undertaking for at least another year or two. By the time the organizer business petered out, Handspring hoped to be safely positioned in the wireless communicator market.

In fact, the company's first wireless product, the VisorPhone, was almost ready. When Art Lamb tried out the prototypes, however, he found them clumsy. "I didn't think it was going to be a huge success," he says. "You kind of sense a tangible line that separates products that sell 10,000 and products that sell a million."

Jeff, too, found the VisorPhone lacking. "On the one hand, we had all these people who were telling us how great it was," he says. "I was sitting there, thinking, 'Well, it's got its problems. It's big.' When I started using it, I liked it, but I could see why other people would pass on it. There were some things that were very frustrating with it. I felt kind of mixed—kind of like I'd felt about the Zoomer."

Sure enough, when the VisorPhone shipped in late 2000, consumers were indifferent, and Handspring's hopes for it faded quickly. By then, all eight of the original Pilot team members who were at Handspring compared the VisorPhone with the Zoomer: a product that taught them difficult but necessary lessons.

Some of those lessons had to do with the VisorPhone's seat in a boxy, three-by-five-inch pocket computer: The combined gadget simply made a large, ungraceful cell phone. Skin grease from the owner's cheek smudged the Visor's screen during phone calls—a phenomenon that Jeff's wood-block model experiments, of course, had failed to reveal. Dialing a phone number required both hands—one to hold the Visor, the other to tap the screen—which turned out to be surprisingly frustrating in daily use.

The team lost no time in factoring what it had learned into the VisorPhone's far more advanced successor, a device whose prospects excited the old-timers almost as much as the original Pilot had.

As 2000 drew to a close, the huge wireless market that industry observers had been predicting had still not materialized. After over a year on the market, the Palm VII had fewer than 150,000 customers. OmniSky struggled to sign up customers for its wireless service for Palm handhelds and Pocket PCs. Qualcomm's big, ungainly Palm-based cell phone flopped, and Handspring's VisorPhone had failed. A $500 e-mail pager called the Blackberry (from Canadian company Research In Motion) was a hit with stockbrokers and executives who couldn't afford to be out of e-mail contact. Even so, its customers numbered well under 200,000—scarcely the wireless megahit that analysts anticipated. The home-run product, the one that would create the wireless market the way the Pilot had created the thriving handheld market from the ashes of the Newton and the Zoomer, had yet to appear.

In fact, the only bona fide megahit remained the simple, elegant pocket organizer that Hawkins had invented. It had irrevocably changed American business life and become a ubiquitous sight in America's conference rooms, airport departure lounges, and commuter trains.

For the fifth year in a row, Christmas shoppers scooped handhelds up in record numbers despite the sinking economy. On the surface, only one thing had changed: For the first time, shoppers faced a profusion of choices. Four models from Handspring, five from Palm, one from Sony, and three from Pocket PC makers vied for their attention. In overwhelming numbers, consumers chose Palm or Handspring models.

No one, not even Hawkins, could have predicted the turmoil that 2001 held in store.

TWENTY-FOUR

UNCHARTED WATERS

"Jeff was ringing the alarm bells earliest, saying, 'I'm really worried about this,' " Dubinsky says. She, too, had noticed warning signs in the late fall. "Christmas was very, very late." Instead of buying the handhelds they intended to give as gifts in October and November, consumers had held off until December.

The U.S. economy was slowing, companies all around announced missed earnings and layoffs. Even though Christmas sales—once they came—were at a record high, Dubinsky, Hawkins, and Colligan reckoned that handhelds would not be immune to the slowdown they witnessed in other industries. The question was, how much of an impact would it have?

Certainly, the retailers selling handhelds were optimistic—and no wonder; palmtops were one of the bright spots of otherwise weak Christmas sales. Nor did Palm seem to expect a slowdown. Word from Handspring's parts suppliers was that Palm was purchasing components at an accelerating pace.

Donna wound up walking a path of moderation. "Look, I think [the handheld market] is going to keep growing," she'd say. "More slowly than we thought it was going to grow, but it's going to keep growing."

She reduced Handspring's manufacturing orders, preferring to risk product shortages to being stuck with too much inventory if the market cooled. The sales figures in February 2001 proved her right. The handheld market was still growing, but not as fast as the previous year.

Ever since Handspring had unveiled its first Visor models 18 months earlier, Palm executives had wearily fielded one question, over and over: When would Palm catch up with its younger rival and offer an expansion slot?

Now, in the spring of 2001, the Palm engineers were putting the finishing touches on two new models, to be called m500 and m505, which included such a slot.

The new product line was to be announced on April 10. As the months passed, however, rumors of new handhelds from rival companies began to circulate. HP might unveil a new Pocket PC in March. Sony planned new models for a summer release. Above all, a competitive threat loomed from Handspring, which was preparing to launch a sleek and upscale rival for Palm's high-end models.

It was a public relations crisis. If Palm were not among the companies showing off a new high-end model, the company would seem once again to be behind the times. Chief Marketing Officer Satjiv Chahil proposed a new launch plan to the company's chief executives and Palm VPs who were assembled for an operations council meeting in early March.

Under this proposal, Chahil's marketing team would announce the new m500 series models on March 19, before they were actually available. This would, of course, stall sales of Palm's existing products because customers would wait to see the new model. But at least the world would know that Palm, too, had updated its high-end product line. People who might have been attracted by Handspring's new models might decide to wait for Palm's. Barring any manufacturing glitches, Palm would ship 100,000 of the new models—just enough to provide small allotments to U.S. retail stores—by April 10, about three weeks after the announcement.

At a time when the engineers weren't even finished perfecting the new models, it was a risky decision. The plan would succeed only if all remaining work went off without a hitch. Yet all engineering projects, including Palm's previous models, require an unpredictable period of fine-tuning in their final stages. Worse, the m500 series contained a large number of new technologies and components. Each introduced an additional risk of delays.

Some of the executives privately doubted that this plan would work; in fact, some of their team members were sure it wouldn't. But solving Palm's PR problem overrode any other concern.

As Palm had expected, Handspring announced its new super-slim Visor Edge on March 12, 2001. It was a product clearly designed to compete with the sleek Palm Vx or the new m500. Colligan had campaigned hard for a color screen, but Handspring's engineers had their hands full with other projects, including the wireless communicators on which they pinned high hopes.

Even without a color screen, the Handspring executives expected the Visor Edge to succeed. The retail stores seemed to agree, too, and placed large orders.

A week later, on March 19, Palm made its own announcement. Though reviewers generally liked the fact that the m500 and m505 retained the Palm V's sexy shape, some blasted the m505's dim color screen. Unfortunately for Palm, the new products did nothing to dispel the perception that Palm had lost its innovative edge. "They do little more than add an expansion slot like the one Handspring has had for two years," *The Economist* reported. Jeff Hawkins's ideas, it seemed, were still piloting Palm.

By the time they made the announcement, the Palm executives had already lost all hope of shipping 100,000 units to stores by April 10. Instead of ramping up the manufacturing lines to crank out the thousands of units per day that were needed, the engineers were still fixing glitches in the test units. For now, all

Palm's execs could do was hope that the products would soon be ready for mass production.

In the meantime, Palm had caused itself a tidal wave of trouble that was now approaching from a different front.

For much of 2000, a worldwide shortage of key components had made life miserable for Palm in its efforts to feed the public's voracious appetite for m100 and Palm Vx models. Each month, Palm's manufacturing staff had ramped up parts orders, plied suppliers for a greater allotment of the components, and produced as many handhelds as it could. Even so, the m100 and Vx were always in short supply.

Then, in January 2001, the component shortage ended. Parts that had been badly needed a month or two earlier arrived at the plants and were quickly built into finished units. In February, Palm shipped half of that quarter's sales to stores, about a million handhelds—a daunting quantity that crowded retailers' shelves with models that would soon be obsolete.

Nor did the flood of handhelds stop there. Carl Yankowski and CFO Judy Bruner had told Wall Street analysts that Palm would end its fiscal year in May with revenue of $2 billion. To come through on that forecast, they would have to sell nearly 3 million additional handhelds to retailers during March, April, and May.

It was an ambitious estimate even in boom times. A million Palm handhelds on the shelves, and millions more queued up for production, meant that three times as many people would have to buy Palm's handhelds than had the year before. After more than a year of record sales, Palm's management was "driving with [the] foot all the way down on the accelerator," as one of its executives puts it.

But Carl Yankowski and his executives hadn't reckoned with the slowing U.S. economy.

The Palm executives noticed the first signs of the slowdown in March: The weekly sales reports from stores showed flat sales. The handheld market was growing more slowly than it had before, but what really hurt Palm was that it was no longer the only game in town. Sales of Pocket PCs and Sony Clié's didn't amount to much, about 12 percent in total, but Handspring had seized 28 percent of palmtop sales. While the handheld market was doubling and tripling, Handspring's share had hardly seemed to matter. But now, as trainloads of Palm models were rolling toward retail shelves already piled high with excess products, those were sales Palm could not afford to lose.

The situation worsened with the announcement of the m500 line in mid-March. Once consumers knew new models were around the corner, they stopped buying the old models. Palm urgently needed the new products in stores.

"Can we get the m500 line out in two weeks?" Yankowski asked his executives.

Unfortunately, they couldn't. When the first batches came off the assembly line in Hungary, Palm's testers immediately discovered problems. On some units, the screen showed a strange, subtle shadow. It took the engineers a while to ferret out the problem: A sticker on the built-in battery was a fraction of a millimeter thicker than it had been on the original prototype batteries. (Four of the original Palm old-timers were still around to remember that a battery sticker had also been the root of the original Pilot's shipping delays.)

April 10 came and went, but the new products were not ready. As one problem was fixed, new ones were found. Some of the devices shattered in the standard drop tests, thanks to faulty screens. On other units, the power button was sunken too low in the casing.

Although such glitches are par for the course in this stage in a product's life, waiting for the fixes was pure agony. "It only took two and a half weeks from the time we found the first problem to when everything was fixed, but those two and a half weeks seemed like an eternity," one executive says.

When the first m500 units finally reached the shelves in late April, Palm's sales increased modestly. But by then, the damage had been done. The handheld business was about to change radically.

In late March, while customers waited to see Palm's new product line, Carl Yankowski and CFO Bruner warned Wall Street analysts that Palm's revenue for the coming quarter would be only half of what they had previously predicted. The slowing economy was to blame for the steep drop in sales, they said.

Over at Handspring, the executives, unaware of the magnitude of Palm's inventory crisis, were scratching their heads. "We were perplexed," Ed Colligan says. "There was definitely softening [of market demand] but we didn't see it at the level that showed up in their numbers." According to the sales information from the stores, the same data that Palm had received, total handheld sales were still higher than the previous year. Indeed, Handspring's sales matched its forecasts.

Financial analysts lit up Dubinsky's phone lines, inquiring if Handspring's sales quarter would also be much lower. By the end of the day, she released a statement on the company Web site: "While no company is immune to current economic conditions, we see continued sales growth in our business at this time."

To cut costs, Yankowski slashed Palm's workforce, laying off 300 of Palm's 1,900 employees and contractors. To entice customers into buying the stockpiles of aging palmtops on the shelves and the millions more in its warehouses and cued up for production, Palm slashed its prices.

Dubinsky and Colligan watched with dismay as Visor sales dropped accordingly. Should they, too, cut prices beyond one long-planned reduction for the oldest model, the Visor Deluxe? A debate raged among the Handspring executives. Donna argued that Handspring price cuts would only force Palm to cut prices further, resulting in a stalemate in which both companies made less money.

Even without a price cut, Handspring's slowing sales brought in less income. Donna slowed, then stopped hiring in every department (except the team working on the wireless communicators), and began to scrutinize every dime of spending.

Colligan continued to argue for price cuts; Dubinsky continued to resist. Let Palm work through its inventory problem, she argued. Then we can both be back in business.

By summer, the sinking U.S. economy had finally caught up even with the handheld business. Market growth slowed to a crawl. Handspring was bringing in only half the revenue Dubinsky had forecast just four months earlier. In July, Donna laid off

40 people, nearly 10 percent of its workforce. "It was absolutely horrible," she says.

At the company meeting two days later, she had a surprise up her sleeve. "In times like these, it's important to hear from a customer," she announced. "So I found an average, loyal Handspring customer to come and share his experience with you. Please welcome—Sinbad."

The comedian Sinbad, a friend from her Benton Harbor high school days and a fan of high-tech gear himself (as well as a bona-fide Handspring customer), strolled up to the front of the room and launched into a performance of high-tech jokes. Dubinsky had hired him to cheer up the employees who were downcast from having lost so many colleagues and in shock to see their company in financial trouble. (Paying Sinbad's fee from Handspring's budgets was out of the question, so Donna covered it herself.)

Unfortunately, Handspring's troubles were not yet over. Even by August, five months after Palm's disastrous product transition, the flood of cheap Palm Vx handhelds hadn't abated. The sleek Visor Edge that Colligan had launched with such high hopes in March had stood no chance against the sexy Palm Vx, which now cost $100 less. Something had to be done to restart sales, or else Handspring, too, would start drowning in inventory.

Handspring finally cut prices across its product line in late August. Sales promptly improved, but the cuts triggered exactly the price war that Dubinsky had feared. Palm responded by cutting the price of its new m500; Handspring soon shaved $100 off its color-screen model; Palm dropped the price of its cheapest model, the m100, to $99.

Even the Pocket PC prices dropped. The Pocket PC vendors, too, needed to clear out inventory and make way for Microsoft's next-generation mobile design, called Pocket PC 2002.

The profits of all companies spiraled downward. The handheld industry was rapidly becoming a commodity business, just as Jeff Hawkins had feared.

In June 2001, Palm's CFO Judy Bruner declared a loss of over $150 million—and a write-off of $268 million worth of inventory stuck in Palm's warehouses. By fall, Palm would have little more than $300 million left from its $1 billion IPO war chest.

Wall Street analysts warned that Palm might run out of money. If Yankowski didn't stop the bleeding, Palm could be bankrupt soon.

A second layoff followed in late June. At a company meeting the day after, with the room packed to the gills, Yankowski attempted to give his employees a message of hope.

"My dog died," he began. On his flight to visit a breeder to buy a new puppy, he said, he had been reminded of a story. "A dog fell into a deep well. The farmer couldn't get him out." The farmer wanted to shoot the dog to put it out of its misery, but worried that the bullet might ricochet off the well's wall and hurt a human instead. So the farmer decided to bury the dog alive by shoveling dirt down the well.

The employees stood in stunned silence. This was supposed to cheer them up?

Fortunately, the story had a twist. As each shovelful of dirt hit the dog's back, he shook it off. As the level of dirt in the well rose, the dog was lifted closer and closer to the top of the well, until finally the farmer could help it out. Palm, too, would survive its current troubles, Yankowski concluded, despite—or even because of—the intense criticism from outsiders.

After the meeting, employees complained to their managers. "This was the most demoralizing communications meeting I've ever been to," said one.

By then, the events of the spring and summer had taken their toll. "Palm is just a paycheck now," one long-time employee says who remembers Palm in the days of Dubinsky, Hawkins, and Colligan. "I used to say, 'I love my job, I am so lucky to be here.' Now I leave at 5:00 P.M.—and most people around me do, too."

Unsurprisingly, the stock prices of both Palm and Handspring were dropping like rocks. By fall, both stocks had sunk under $2—a far cry from their highs of $165 and $99. Dubinsky and Hawkins had long fallen from the ranks of billionaires, and nobody on Palm's staff still dreamed of becoming rich based on their stock options.

Rumors circulated that Sony, IBM, and Apple were eyeing Palm for a possible takeover, now that the company could be considered relatively cheap.

Fortune called for a merger of Handspring and Palm "now—before it's too late." It was "the best way to prevent the two companies from killing each other." Handheld enthusiasts added their opinions on the Internet chat boards. At palmstation.com, one anonymous post read, "Carl Yankowski, Palm's CEO, has successfully lead Palm to the brink in his short tenure . . . only a takeover by Jeff and Donna at Handspring can save Palm now."

Many in the press and on Wall Street openly wondered if Carl Yankowski was the right man for the job. When he had taken over Palm, the company was flying high, and headlines had read, "Is Windows CE Dead on the Palmtop?" Now they said, "Has Palm Lost Its Grip?" The economic slowdown wasn't helping Palm, the analysts agreed, but the real root of its troubles was its mountain of inventory and bungled transition to the m500 product line. "Palm's management is under the gun to prove they should even be at the company," financial analyst Rob Cihra told the *Wall Street Journal*.

Microsoft, adroitly capitalizing on Palm's troubles, put out the word that there was no slowdown for Microsoft's Pocket PC models—that Pocket PC sales continued to grow, month by month. Compaq pointed out that demand for the color-screen iPaq Pocket PC still exceeded supply.

In May, Microsoft announced that 1 million Pocket PCs had shipped in just under a year. Of course, Palm and Handspring sold nearly that many at Christmas alone, and all Pocket PC brands combined still had less than 10 percent market share at retail. But Palm's management, focused on its still unfolding crisis, didn't have the resources to challenge the word on the street that Microsoft was coming on fast.

In June, research firm Gartner Dataquest only exacerbated Palm's public image crisis with a report on the PDA market. The firm estimated that Compaq would take in more money from shipments of its iPaq Pocket PC than Palm made on its handhelds during the current three-month period. In that calculation, Palm was at a statistical disadvantage: The iPaq cost, on average, twice as much as a Palm handheld, and Palm would be sending fewer shipments than normal to the retailers whose shelves were already stuffed with Palm models.

Nonetheless, the report caused a minor sensation with the technology and business press. Headlines like "iPaq Sales Overtaking Palm" and "Research Firm Predicts Palm Will Lose Top Spot in Hand-Held Market to Compaq" now added to Palm's headaches.

The report also made a very important point: Palm's handhelds were a hit with consumers, but Pocket PC seemed to be gaining momentum in corporations. Though a large enterprise market had still not materialized—few companies had placed bulk orders for even as few as 500 handhelds—most industry analysts agreed that the corporate market was poised to finally take off.

Unfortunately, Palm had little organizational bench strength to compete against Microsoft in this vital market. Recognizing the internal weakness, Robin Abrams had created a VP position to lead the enterprise effort in her last hours with the company. It was not an easy job to hold. Not only had the original VP left Palm, but his replacement had become a victim of Palm's layoff.

In March 2001, Yankowski had announced a remedy: the acquisition of an enterprise software company called Extended Systems, which was to become the enterprise business unit of Palm. Finally, Palm would have a large, focused organization to attack the enterprise market. But when Palm's stock cratered, so did the planned acquisition. Yankowski could no longer afford to buy the company, and Extended Systems didn't want to be paid in Palm's falling stock. The two companies severed their engagement. Palm's latest enterprise strategy had failed.

All spring and summer, the Handspring executives had watched Palm's high-speed unraveling with great concern. Palm's problems didn't just impact Handspring's sales and profitability; to the outside world, Handspring's own fortunes seemed indelibly tied to Palm's success or failure. By early October, Handspring's stock had fallen so low, the whole company was worth little more than the cash it had in the bank. Never mind the value of its management team, its patents, its brand, and its products.

"It's demoralizing," Dubinsky admits. It was a situation Dubinsky, Hawkins, and Colligan had encountered before. In 1995, months before the Pilot became the fastest-selling product in computing history, the only venture capitalist firm willing to invest in Palm at all had judged it to be worth a paltry $9 million.

Donna found herself remembering Palm's early days. "To every person who asks me, 'Aren't you getting depressed?' I say, 'Look, I'm the person who had to sell my company once. We'll get through this, just as we've gotten through other things. We have a good plan, we have plenty of cash, we just have to hang tight." What she couldn't yet say was that Handspring also had a secret weapon: its new line of communicators.

During one of the first presentations at Handspring's IPO road show, a fund manager had put her cell phone, handheld, and pager on the table in front of her and implored, "Can't you combine these? I need them all, but I'm sick of carrying all three with me all the time."

Adding paging and e-mail functions to a cell phone–palmtop hybrid wasn't a new idea. In the early days of the Pilot, when customers had beseeched Hawkins to combine the Pilot with a cell phone or a pager, he had always answered, "If I built it, you wouldn't like it. It would have to be too big. It would have a short battery life."

Now, however, technology had marched on, components had become miniaturized, and batteries had improved. The challenge was designing a single device that was a *good* organizer and a *good* cell phone and a *good* pager. A communicator that was a great organizer but a mediocre phone would never find a mass market, as the VisorPhone experiment had shown. During the daily design sessions for the new communicator, Handspring cultivated a new motto: "No compromises."

The resulting product looked like a small palmtop. But when its flip lid was open, it turned into a compact cell phone that could also send and receive text messages and browse the Web. Organizer, phone, and Internet features were all on hand in a single, compact device called the Handspring Treo.

It was obvious to Jeff that writing out long e-mail messages using the Graffiti alphabet was slow and inefficient. Because it would be used also as a pager and for e-mail, the Treo would become the first Palm OS–based handheld with a keyboard.

The tiny, thumb-driven keyboard Rob Haitani came up with would also solve the problem they'd encountered with the Visor-Phone: Unlike traditional cell phones, the VisorPhone couldn't be dialed with one hand. "It's the one feature that requires you to pull out the stylus and know Graffiti. It's always bugged me," Haitani says. The Treo, on the other hand, could be held and dialed with the same hand. In fact, Jeff designed a shortcut that made dialing names in the Treo's address book even easier: A Treo owner could type the first letter of the first name, then the beginning letters of the last name. Handspring's research found that this technique could zero in on a specific name in the average person's address book with only three "typed" letters.

Hawkins and Haitani grew increasingly fond of their clever little thumb keyboard, but Ed Colligan couldn't forget the customer research he'd done years ago. Palm had developed prototype Pilots with tiny keyboards, which focus-group participants claimed to despise. Had times changed, he wondered, or would people still be put off by having to punch little keys?

There was only one way to find out: He commissioned focus groups. Everyday consumers were asked to choose between a Graffiti-driven Treo model and one with the keyboard as Rob Haitani watched from behind one-way mirrors.

"It was all about personal preference," he concluded. "People would use the same reasons to argue for the exact opposites. Some guy would say, 'I want Graffiti, because it's simpler and faster and more intuitive,' and then the next guy would say he'd use the keyboard, because it's simpler and faster and more intuitive."

Colligan convinced Hawkins to develop both versions. The Handspring engineers had one extra project on their plate.

In the spring of 2001, Dubinsky had been confident that Handspring would be profitable by the end of the year. According to plan, Visor organizer profits would cover the costs of launching the Treo line and building a communicator market. Now, thanks to the price war, even the Visor line was still losing money.

The urgent question before the Handspring executives was how to make sure that Handspring was still in business when the organizer market staged a comeback—or when the communicator market took off.

Colligan suggested separating the financials of Handspring's Visor handhelds from those of the future communicator product line: "Let's invest in the future, but the existing business better carry its own weight." Department by department, the executives cut every expense that didn't directly increase sales of the Visors. Donna closed down Handspring's office in Japan, handing sales there to a distributor. Ed cut the company's advertising. "Brand building—gone!" Dubinsky says. "By doing broad, structural cuts like that, we could see our way clear to a profitable organizer business."

Where Dubinsky made no cuts, of course, was the budget for the Treo communicators, which would go on sale in early 2002. They, after all, were the future of Handspring.

While Palm's Product division struggled with its hardware sales, trouble was also ahead for the Platform group. Palm's licensing business showed signs of crumbling: Cell phone vendors Nokia and Motorola canceled the Palm OS–powered products they had been developing.

To help the Palm OS back to its feet, Carl Yankowski and Palm's board of directors came up with a radical plan. The Platform group would break off into a subsidiary with its own CEO, board of directors, and executive staff. This way, at least, Palm's schizophrenic years of splitting its loyalties between two competing business units would be over at last.

The employees, whiplashed by five months of unceasing corporate earthquakes, took the momentous news with surprising calm. "Morale is saved by the fact that we are emotionally worn out," one engineer says. This didn't stop them from speculating about the future, however. Once separated, might the Palm hardware company one day license another OS for its products? And would the Platform company permit even more direct Palm competitors to use the Palm operating system? The possibilities seemed mind-boggling.

More changes followed rapidly. Two weeks after announcing the Platform subsidiary, Palm acquired the assets of Be, Inc., the failed company of Eric Benhamou's friend and 3Com board member Jean-Louis Gassée, which had developed an operating system for Internet appliances. Among the Palm engineers, opinion about the acquisition was divided. Buying Be landed Palm some useful technologies and the expertise of Be's engineers. At the same time, integrating the new technology threatened to pull focus from the group's first priority—Palm OS 5.0, which Yankowski had promised for the second half of 2002.

Alan Kessler resigned the same day, a little over two years after he'd taken over the stewardship of Palm on short notice. He told his team that the Palm Platform needed someone with a deeper software technology focus and stronger connections in the wireless world than he could offer.

"You want to do the right thing. Sometimes the right thing is to make room," he says.

Palm still had one ace up its sleeve: its i705 wireless handheld. If the wave of the future were truly wireless communications, then at least Palm wouldn't be sitting on the sidelines. The i705, Palm hoped, would be in a class by itself—and therefore exempt from price wars with rivals.

Unfortunately, the i705's release date seemed to slip endlessly into the future. Yankowski had steadily promised its availability by the end of 2001. In a sobering analyst call in September, however, he announced that as a result of "economic uncertainty" in the aftermath of the terrorist attacks in New York and Washington, the i705 would slip to 2002.

Only seven weeks later, the beleaguered Yankowski resigned his post. Eric Benhamou, Palm's chairman of the board since the company's IPO, stepped in to lead Palm until a permanent CEO was found.

No wonder, then, that Palm loyalists began to worry if Palm's own missteps had handed Microsoft what it needed most: time to catch up.

Microsoft's road to market dominance is littered with the ghosts of once-leading companies like Apple, Novell, and Word-

Perfect. In each case, it wasn't Microsoft's brilliance or product superiority that permitted it to triumph. All Microsoft had to do was wait out its competitors' mistakes.

While Palm fans fretted, Handspring insiders believed that Jeff Hawkins was on the verge of changing the game—again. Once again, his mood seemed out of sync: He had worried during the go-go days of 2000, and now felt upbeat even as the handheld industry seemed to be collapsing all around him. "Everyone else is saying, 'Oh no, we can't make any money,' and I'm saying we're on the verge of a great success. Let's not forget the lessons of the past. I really do think we are onto something big here."

Within Handspring, Treo prototypes had made believers out of almost everyone who tried them. It made them gush to each other the way techies hadn't since they had used the first Pilot prototypes in 1995. The Treo was addictive. Even the cautious Hawkins says, "I love this thing."

The eight Palm old-timers at Handspring couldn't miss the way history was repeating itself. "This product could be the first real hit product of this new category, and that feels very much like the Pilot," says Colligan.

Handspring, of course, wasn't the only company to think of an all-in-one organizer/cell phone/Internet machine. In late 2001, Microsoft readied a variant of Windows CE, code-named Stinger, specifically for smart phones. Cell phone companies like Nokia and Motorola were tackling the problem from the other direction by adding organizer and Internet features to their phones.

Pundits predicted that the cell phone companies, with their massive clout and enormous research budgets, would win the smart phone market, but the Handspring trio didn't agree. Cell phone companies had little experience in handheld computing areas. They had never cultivated a community of software developers or designed an attractive, efficient user interface for handheld screens. Much like the rules of the PC business, the lessons of the cell phone industry didn't necessarily apply to the marriage of a handheld computer and a phone.

Dubinsky and Colligan had a hard time predicting in their business plan how many communicators they would sell. "It's just like [in 1995] when we said, 'The forecast is wrong. It's either going to be 10,000 or a million, we don't know which.' " The Treo felt to them like a blockbuster product, but until consumers snapped it up (or ignored it), they couldn't be sure. "We know there is no sure thing here," says Dubinsky.

Handspring's executives recognized that creating a thriving communicator market would be harder than it had been creating a handheld computing market. For example, carriers like Sprint, Verizon, and AT&T control which phone models actually reach the market. The wobbling U.S. and global economy also make it, as Joe Sipher says, "a tough time to introduce a new product."

On the other hand, the industry analysts who saw the Treo before its release were encouraging. "This is the first [communicator] that fits in your pocket. It's smaller than most men's wallets," one said enthusiastically. Rave reviews poured in hailing the Treo as "a triumph of design and functionality" (*Business Week*) and "a true breakthrough" (*Wall Street Journal*).

Of course, the opinions of analysts, journalists, and industry insiders are important, but they've been wrong before. So have the Handspring executives, despite their years of experience creating blockbuster products. Are Jeff Hawkins, Donna Dubinsky, Ed Colligan, and their team really onto something as innovative, powerful, and revolutionary as the original Pilot? Only one voice really matters. As Dubinsky puts it, "The customer will speak in the end."

EPILOGUE

I t's been more than a decade since the three-person firm called Palm Computing opened for business, but the handheld industry is still in its infancy. Handhelds will one day be as plentiful as cell phones—or even merge with them—but that's a long way off.

No matter what happens, Palm's position in history is secure. This was the company that turned conventional wisdom on its head, trumped Microsoft (at least so far), and changed millions of lives through its focus on simplicity and elegance.

The future, however, is still up for grabs. History books are filled with technology pioneers who created a market and basked in glory as market leaders—then were relegated to the sidelines by nimbler rivals, richer corporations, or the next turn of technology. With competitors crowding in on Palm from all sides, it's far from certain who the leaders will be when the market matures.

In fact, two battles rage in Palm's universe: one over hardware sales, the other over which operating system will dominate.

On the hardware side, the leader may well remain Palm—or, rather, its hardware business. Millions of people each year continue to fall in love with the convenience of a Palm handheld.

Any number of shifts in the wind direction could help put Palm's business troubles behind it: an economic recovery, a hit product, a merger, or a takeover. Palm is, after all, a corporation with massive customer loyalty, a strong brand, and, of course, the industry's centerpiece: the elegant little computers that Jeff Hawkins and his team of idealists brought to life against all odds.

On the other hand, the next leader may be Sony, with its global brand, manufacturing efficiencies, and track record of success in consumer electronics. It may be Handspring, which, though still the smallest of the major handheld companies, has enormous intangible assets that don't show up on a company's balance sheet: the quality of its executives, its speed of product development, and the intellectual capital of Rob Haitani, Joe Sipher, Ron Marianetti, Art Lamb, and many other of the industry's most experienced managers. And Handspring has Jeff Hawkins, in his garage, whittling down pieces of wood.

Then there are the cell phone giants like Nokia: By merging phones with organizers, they may ultimately carry the day in the handheld category. Pocket PCs and their successors, from companies like HP, Compaq, and Toshiba, could take over the corporate market. Or an unknown company with a radically new idea might come out of nowhere, the way Palm did in 1996, and reset the landscape of handheld computing.

As for the struggle for operating system dominance, Palm's OS Platform subsidiary commands an imposing lead. For entrepreneurs the world over, the lesson might just be that a small company can go head-to-head with Microsoft—and win.

But it's still early in the battle, and it's never safe to underestimate Microsoft. The company will continue to work on Windows CE, as it has now for seven generations of handheld operating systems—revise and advertise, revise and advertise. Someday, Microsoft may even force the Palm Platform off the road. It wouldn't be the first time Microsoft won a market by sheer force of will, stamina, and marketing.

Nor are the Palm OS and Windows CE the only contenders. Waiting in the wings is Symbian, the European consortium that's developing an operating system for smart cell phones. Like many corporate design collaborations, it has had its share of problems, but Symbian's backers include some of the world's

biggest cell phone companies, which gives it more than a fighting chance of success as smart phones become more popular.

But in the final analysis, the OS war may not matter as much
as Microsoft, Palm, and many analysts think. "Go around and
ask a bunch of people with Palm devices, 'What OS is in your
device?' " Dubinsky says. "I bet you anything they can't even tell
you. Customers want to buy devices that work and do the job for
them."

For puzzle lovers like Hawkins, figuring out the real rules for
success in the handheld market is a fascinating challenge. He
thinks Handspring is up for it. "There's a very simple formula to
get from any position to being number one: On average, be
slightly better on all of your decisions over time," he says. "That
doesn't mean we're going to do it overnight; it doesn't mean
we're not going to have some big falls in the middle; it doesn't
mean that everything's going to be peachy-keen. It just means
that if you persevere and you're a little bit smarter, then you can
outperform your competition over the long haul."

Palm old-timers often wonder: What if?

What if Psion, in 1994, had taken up Palm on its offer to
write connectivity software? Palm might have languished for
years, a tiny company, churning out PalmConnect packages
for keyboard organizers. What if Compaq had invested in Palm
in 1995, then crushed the Pilot with the market power of a
Compaq-labeled Touchdown—or abandoned Touchdown for
Windows CE to appease its PC partner Microsoft?

To this day, Donna Dubinsky wonders whether another CEO
in her shoes could have avoided the sale to U.S. Robotics. It's
unlikely. Palm needed $5 million at a time when investors were
gun-shy from the billion-dollar losses of failed handheld enter-
prises.

Of the many turning points, Eric Benhamou's refusal to give
Palm the hope of a spin-out had the biggest impact: a fracture of
the Palm universe into two pieces. Today, Handspring has the
brains, the soul, and the creativity that were the root of Palm's
success; Palm has the operating system, the well-known brand,
and the sheer size.

For its part, 3Com continues to struggle with the problems that have dogged it since the U.S. Robotics merger. Even as other networking companies were booming, 3Com executives spent much of 2000 dismantling product lines, abandoning markets, and selling off what was left of the U.S. Robotics modem business. Eric Benhamou no longer runs the company. In January 2001, he handed the reins over to former second-in-command Bruce Claflin. By then, 3Com's value had fallen below $3 billion, down from $10 billion when it merged with U.S. Robotics. Benhamou remains chairman of 3Com's and Palm's boards of directors.

Donna Dubinsky, newly married, still thrives on being the CEO of an independent company. "We are long-term players, and we haven't wavered from what we wanted to do," she says. "We're still working hard at it, trying to make it happen. It surprises people."

In July 2001, Ed Colligan became Handspring's chief operating officer. For years, the three executives had operated "like a three-legged stool," as Dubinsky puts it; Colligan's new title only formalized what has long been an equal partnership. "I have a bit of a dream that we can build a really significant, lasting company here," he says. "That someday we'll look back on this and we'll be like the [Intel founders] Andy Grove/Gordon Moore/Bob Noyce of the world, who stayed with those companies forever. It would be nice if we could somehow manage to be a part of this for a long time."

As for Jeff Hawkins, the unlikely master plan he formulated in 1987 has worked out beyond his wildest dreams. His success in the business arena has opened doors in the brain research world. Cold Spring Harbor Laboratory, a large research institution on the wooded north shore of his native Long Island, invited him to join its scientific board of directors; Hawkins accepted. "This is so much fun, you can't imagine!" he says. "These are really smart people, they all share a passion that I share."

Though passionate as ever about handhelds, he's carved out some time from leading Handspring's product design for meetings with neuroscientists across the United States. Discussing his ideas with these experts has strengthened Jeff's hopes that his dreams will turn into reality. "Maybe I'm deluding myself," he says. "But I've sat down with some of the most famous scientists in the world, and they've all been intrigued. None of them said, 'You're an idiot.' They all said, 'This is pretty good.' They invite me back. I take that as a positive sign."

Next, he'll set up a research organization. Years of exploration lie ahead. However, Hawkins is no longer sure that he wants to personally pursue Step Three of this master plan—the "brain business." Let other entrepreneurs try their hand at starting up companies. For Jeff Hawkins, the real thrill is putting together the pieces of the puzzle.

NOTES

CHAPTER 1

5. **Oracle was founded in 1977 with a mere $2,000:** David A. Kaplan, *The Silicon Boys and Their Valley of Dreams,* Perennial. An Imprint of HarperCollins Publishers, 1999.

7. **The founding of GO:** Jerry Kaplan, *Startup. A Silicon Valley Adventure,* Houghton Mifflin Company, Boston and New York, 1995.

9. **GRiD's corporate parent Tandy:** Although GRiD's innovative laptops had been successful in niche industrial markets, the company was perpetually hampered by a need for more capital. In 1988, GRiD sold itself to Tandy Corporation who allowed it to operate as a relatively independent operation. AST later acquired Tandy's computer division, and Samsung later acquired AST. It still sells the GRiDPad's descendants.

10. **VC industry investment totals, first half of the 1990s:** Jason Pontin, "What we believe: a Red Herring 100 primer," *Red Herring,* May 1 and 15, 2001.

11. **VC industry investment totals, 2000:** *The Money Tree,* the Mercury News/PriceWaterhouseCoopers LLP survey of venture capital, full-year 2000 and first-quarter 2001 results, *www.pwcmoneytree.com.*

CHAPTER 2

23. **John Sculley's prediction of a $3.5-trillion market for PDAs:** Sculley later asserted in a letter to *Red Herring* magazine ("John Sculley corrects The

Herring," *Red Herring,* November 1994) that the press had misinterpreted his comment. His estimate, he insisted, was based on a predicted convergence of several industries, including television, film, audio, publishing, the entire computer and telecommunications industries, and more. But his protests fell on deaf ears. After the speech in January of 1992, the computer industry commonly continued to refer to the expected trillion-dollar market for PDAs.

28. **Description of the Newton's announcement at a Chicago club:** Markos Kounalakis (text), Doug Menuez (photography), *Defying Gravity. The Making of Newton,* Beyond Words Publishing, Hillsboro, OR, 1993.

CHAPTER 3

34. **Apple HR manager's assessment of Donna Dubinsky:** quoted from Harvard Business School case, *Donna Dubinsky and Apple Computer, Inc. (A),* Rev. 11 December 1995.

42. **VC Barry Weinman:** quoted from Harvard Business School case: Professor Myra Hart, *Palm Computing Inc. (A),"* 22 January 1996.

CHAPTER 4

44. **Newton launches at CES in Las Vegas and Chicago:** Markos Kounalakis (text), Doug Menuez (photography), *Defying Gravity. The Making of Newton,* Beyond Words Publishing, Hillsboro, OR, 1993.

46. **Analyst Kimball Brown:** Barbara Bourassa and Mark Moore, "PDAs' momentum gathers steam at CES," *PCWeek,* 18 January 1993.

49. **Dataquest analyst:** James Coates, "High-tech device sends a note about the future of computing," *Chicago Tribune,* 3 June 1993.

50. **"They're not rushing the stage anymore":** quoted from Markos Kounalakis (text), Doug Menuez (photography), *Defying Gravity: The Making of Newton,* Beyond Words Publishing, Hillsboro, OR, 1993.

53. **Newton review in *New York Times:*** Peter H. Lewis, "So far, the Newton experience is less than fulfilling," *New York Times,* 26 September 1993.

53. **Newton review in *PC Week:*** Jim Louderback, "Newton's capabilities just don't measure up," *PC Week,* 13 September 1993.

53. **Newton review in *LA Times:*** Lawrence J. Magid, "Apple's Newton MessagePad—It's hardly as smart as its namesake," *Los Angeles Times,* 19 August 1993.

CHAPTER 5

59. **GO/EO's fate:** Jerry Kaplan, *Startup. A Silicon Valley Adventure,* Houghton Mifflin Company, Boston and New York, 1995.

61. **Zoomer customer survey data:** From an unpublished Zoomer Survey commissioned by Palm Computing, Inc., May 1994.

CHAPTER 6

80. **Apple spent $500 million on the Newton:** Jim Carlton, *Apple. The Inside Story of Intrigue, Egomania, and Business Blunders,* Times Business Random House, 1997, p. 235.

83. **the software version of the hardware miniaturization:** Eric Bergman (editor), *Information Appliances and Beyond,* Morgan Kaufmann Publishers, 2000.

86. **"Somewhere along the line, somebody has to be the bad guy":** quoted by Paul Kapustka, "Big Fish: Jeff Hawkins fights off feature creep," *Red Herring.com,* 28 October 1999.

CHAPTER 7

95. **Kraul's "instant messaging pager":** Doug Kraul remained with Motorola until 1997; in the meantime, he shepherded his two-way text pager, the PageWriter, into existence. It wasn't a hit on the order of the Pilot, but by 2001, Motorola had sold over 1 million PageWriters (including its descendants). An original PageWriter is on exhibit in the Smithsonian.

96. **Ted Clark of Compaq:** Ted Clark's career at Compaq stayed closely tied to handheld devices. In 2001, he was Vice President of Compaq's iPaq Mobile Solutions division, the group responsible for the iPaq, the best-known Pocket PC model.

99. **ice to Eskimos:** Pat Dillon, "The next small thing," *Fast Company,* June/July 1998.

CHAPTER 8

102. **"You can't row with one oar in the water":** quoted in Harvard Business School case Professor Myra Hart, *"Palm Computing Inc. 1995: Financing Challenges,"* Rev. 27 August 1998.

CHAPTER 9

118. *San Francisco Chronicle* **headline:** "Palmed Off," *San Francisco Chronicle,* 6 September 1995.

CHAPTER 10

142. **First press reviews:** Stewart Alsop, "The Pilot helps keep both your sets of data on course toward synchronization," *InfoWorld,* 29 January 1996.

CHAPTER 11

149. *BusinessWeek* **review:** Stephen H. Wildstrom, "The Little Dynamo," *BusinessWeek,* 25 March 1996.

149. *Wall Street Journal* **review:** Walter S. Mossberg, "A Palm-Size Computer That's Easy to Use and Cheap—Finally," *Wall Street Journal,* 28 March 1996.

CHAPTER 12

152. **Rave reviews poured in:** Rich Schwerin, "Portable Pocket Assistant," *PC Computing,* March 1996.

155. **Great press coverage continued:** Mark Gibbs, "Lead me to the office, take me to the pilot, I am but a gadget fan," *NetworkWorld,* 8 July 1996.

155. **"This is love":** "PDA goes beyond pure lust," *Boot* magazine, August/September 1996.

155. **"Envious attention from your friends":** "HotPocket," *Rolling Stone,* 22 August 1996.

166. **told the retailers what they already knew:** "Pilot has plenty of useful appeal," *Computer Retail Week,* November 1996.

166. **Palm market share of over 70 percent by Christmas 1996:** Palm Computing Market Research presentation, 1996–1998, based on data provided by U.S. retail sales researcher PCData.

166. **"God save U.S. Robotics":** "Mine Is Smaller Than Yours," *Forbes FYI,* 1 December 1996.

CHAPTER 13

167. **"People would ask me who I worried about":** quoted in Don Steinberg, "Hand-Me-Down," *Gentlemen's Quarterly,* November 1998.

168. **Toshiba and Compaq backtracked on their Pegasus plans:** Mark Moore, "Microsoft tweaks PDA plans," *PCWeek,* 19 August 1996.

171. **Windows CE mixed reviews:** Peter Wayner, "At last: Pocket PCs that run Windows," *Byte* magazine, January 1997.

171. **Windows CE mixed reviews:** Mike Langberg, "Windows CE not ready for public use," *San Jose Mercury News,* 8 December 1996.

171. **Windows CE mixed reviews:** Anne Kaliczak and Dylan Tweney, "Loved it! Hated it!" *Infoworld,* 18 November 1996.

171. **Microsoft and Palm market share:** Palm Computing Market Research presentation, 1996–1998, based on data provided by U.S. retail sales researcher PCData.

172. **"With Pilot, USR really taught Microsoft something":** *Windows Sources,* December 1996.

176. **"Palm had misled our customers"**: "Pilot Pen files lawsuit against U.S. Robotics," *Stamford Advocate,* 13 February 1997.

178. **"a kick-ass product"**: Brad Dosland, "U.S. Robotics PalmPilot: Love is in the air . . . again," *Boot* magazine, 1 April 1997.

CHAPTER 14

179. **Demo 97 press coverage:** Dan Gilmore, "Demo '97 provides a glimpse of the world according to Kai," *San Jose Mercury News,* 17 February 1997.

179. **"We were constantly struggling with the tension"**: quoted in David B. Yoffie and Mary Kwak, *Judo Strategy: Turning Your Competitors' Strengths to Your Advantage,* Harvard Business School Press, Boston, 2001, p. 111.

187. **"The integration plan was a disaster"**: Janet Kidd Stewart, "3Com-Robotics merger a lesson in frustration. Marriage yields turmoil, losses," *Chicago Tribune,* 22 March 2001.

CHAPTER 15

192. **"3Com was stuck inside the tent"**: Janet Kidd Stewart, "3Com-Robotics merger a lesson in frustration. Marriage yields turmoil, losses," *Chicago Tribune,* 22 March 2001.

CHAPTER 16

206. **Microsoft copied the PalmPilot's look:** "Windows CE Inside," *Wired,* 6 June 1998.

209. **Bill Gates quote "beyond bizarre":** John Markoff, "Microsoft, Accused of Trademark Violations, Is Sued in Europe," *New York Times,* 5 March 1998.

210. **"Microsoft's master plan is to control every access point":** David S. Jackson, "PALM-TO-PALM COMBAT," *Time,* 16 March 1998.

210. **Microsoft spent $250 million developing CE:** Andy Reinhardt, "Palmy days for 3Com?" *Business Week,* 16 March 1998.

212. **"The first palm-size PC to hit the streets":** Herb Bethoney, "Palm-to-palm combat," *PC Week,* 20 May 1998.

213. **"a major force in all kinds of new digital appliances":** Walter S. Mossberg, "The Palm Pilot Has Some New Rivals But No Competition," *Wall Street Journal,* 2 July 1998.

CHAPTER 17

215. **Class action suit against 3Com:** Complaint for Violation of the Securities Exchange Act of 1934 (*Reiver et al. v 3Com Corp. et al.,* Case No. C-97-

21083-EAI). The suit hung over 3Com for the next two years; it was finally settled in late 1999 in an unusually large settlement of $259 million cash.

216. **Deutsche Morgan Grenfell's recommendation of a spin-off:** Technically, the bankers recommended an IPO of a small portion of Palm's stock, followed by a spin-off of the remaining shares to 3Com's shareholders. For the sake of simplicity, we've avoided the morass of definitions and stuck to the easier but less correct layman's term *spin-off* to represent the entire process.

220. **Claris spin-off:** Shortly before Claris was to go public in 1991, Apple changed its mind and folded the company back in, buying the employees' Claris stock back at a much higher price than what the open market would have paid at the time.

221. **"Classic example of a young entrepreneur":** Kim Girard, "The Palm Phenom," *Business 2.0*, 3 April 2001.

221. **Eric Benhamou's decision to stay with 3Com:** Stewart Cheifet, "Computers, Communication, Compatibility." *San Jose Magazine*, March/April 1999.

CHAPTER 18

232. **Venture capitalists funding over 700 start-ups in 1998:** Scott Herold, "Class of '98," *Mercury News*, 14 February 1999.

234. **"the legendary Silicon Valley entrepreneurs":** Erin Joyce, "After the PalmPilot, What Do You Do for an Encore?" *BusinessWeek*, 28 August 1998.

237. **only opportunity to invest:** Handspring raised another $10 million in a second round of financing 10 months later. The lead investor was Qualcomm, who also licensed its CDMA technology to the company.

238. **Playing hard-to-get worked:** Handspring's $60 million valuation is described briefly in Randall E. Stross, *eBoys: The First Inside Account of Venture Capitalists at Work,* Crown Publishers, New York, 2000, pp. 120–121.

238. **"I can't build a good product using Windows CE":** quoted in "PalmPilot duo launch Handspring," *Infoworld Electric*, 6 November 1998.

CHAPTER 19

241. **whopping 73 percent market share:** Palm and Windows CE Marketshare, U.S. retail, in 1998 (annual), supplied by NPD INTELECT.

250. **"Beginning of the end for PalmPilot":** Jesse Berst, "Beginning of the End for PalmPilot?" *ZDNet.com*, 1 February 1999.

254. **Palm V reviews:** Peter H. Lewis, "Newest Palm models inspiring envy," *San Jose Mercury News*, 28 February 1999.

254. **Palm V reviews:** "This Palm Deserves a High-Five," *Newsweek*, 1 March 1999.

254. **Palm V reviews:** Stephen H. Wildstrom, "Give these Palms a big Hand," *Business Week,* 8 March 1999.

254. **Palm V reviews:** Chris Oakes, "Thinner, Sexier PalmPilots," *Wired News Online,* 22 February 1999.

CHAPTER 20

260. **OmniSky:** The wireless ISP business did not work out for OmniSky. By December 2001, the company had laid off most of its staff and was delisted from Nasdaq.

264. **Robin Abrams had resigned:** According to Abrams, 95 percent of the reason she left was simply the attractiveness of her new job offer. Internet start-up Chemdex, later renamed Ventro, was building online marketplaces, where buyers and sellers could trade specialized goods more efficiently than in the physical world. But 5 percent of her reasons for leaving, she says, were related to the stresses of operating inside a large company—such as the requirement for her to spend time attending 3Com's executive meetings, which, she says, "felt like a distraction." Chemdex/Ventro went public just weeks after Abrams arrived as the company's COO, and became a darling among business-to-business (B2B) Internet firms. Over the course of eight months, Ventro's stock zoomed to over $240, only to drop equally spectacularly during the next year. By February 2001, when Abrams and two other executives stepped down, the stock was worth only $1.68 per share.

CHAPTER 21

266. **"I'd like to get to a billion dollars":** quoted in Brad Stone, "It's a Real Handful," *Newsweek,* 20 September 1999.

268. **"It was sort of the ultimate weirdness":** quoted in Paul Kapustka, "Big Fish: Jeff Hawkins fights off feature creep," *Redherring.com,* 28 October 1999.

270. **rumor wound up in *USA Today:*** Kevin Maney, "Tech Duo's game plan: PalmPilot for kids," *USA Today,* 9 December 1998.

273. **journalist pressed especially hard for details:** Stan Sesser, "After Beating Microsoft, PalmPilot Inventors Plan Repeat with Handspring," *Asian Wall Street Journal,* 6 June 1999.

274. **"If it's as good as it looks in demos":** Josh Quittner, "A Palmy Import," *Time.com,* 23 August 1999.

275. **"if they had spun us out":** Deborah Clayman, "Palm is finally free," *San Jose Mercury News,* 14 September 1999.

275. **"Given 3Com's paranoia about Handspring":** "Palms together," *The Economist,* 16 September 1999.

277. **"Palm has a very central place in the future":** Ben Heskett and Wylie Wong, "3Com: It's a Palm, Palm world," *CNET News.com,* 29 April 1999.

277. **"The product that illustrates that mission the best is the Palm":** Tom Steinert-Threlkeld, "On the Edge with Eric Benhamou," *Inter@ctive Week,* 7 May 1999.

278. **"There seems to be no upside in the stock":** Om Malik, "3Com: Humbled by cheap PCs," *Forbes.com,* 23 June 1999.

278. **"Analysts who focused on the handheld market agreed":** Michael Lyster, "3Com Hands Palm Unit Its Freedom, Plans IPO," *Investor's Business Daily,* 14 September 1999.

278. **an open letter to Eric Benhamou:** "Palm it off. An open letter to 3Com CEO Eric Benhamou," *Red Herring,* June 1999.

278. **In July, 3Com's board met:** Andy Rheinhardt, "Why 3Com is handing off Palm," *Business Week,* 27 September 1999, reports about the July 1999 3Com board meeting. "As recently as July, 3Com Corp. CEO Eric Benhamou was still smitten with the Palm computer. At 3Com's board meeting that month, he floated a strategic vision that would have woven the popular handheld into every facet of the company's business. But the board didn't buy it."

279. **An editorial on the Motley Fool Web site:** Yi-Hsin Chang, "Visor Steals the Show at Internet World," *Fool.com,* 11 October 1999.

CHAPTER 22

283. **Palm OS worldwide market share:** Palm 2001 Annual Report, based on IDC July 2001 report.

284. **"The Sony partnership is a broadside":** Deborah Claymon, "Palm-Sony deal a slap at Microsoft," San Jose *Mercury News,* 15 November 1999.

285. **EPOC operating system drove fewer than 5 percent:** Based on research by the Gartner Group, reported by Sally Whittle, "The Symbian Alliance hits troubled water," *EONews.net,* 10 May 2000.

285. **"a buyers' cooperative orchestrated by the device makers":** Dominic Gates, "The Great Wireless War," *The Industry Standard,* 11 June 2001.

291. **Visor deluxe model outsold all other handhelds:** Jon Fortt, "Visor does Handsprings over Palm," *Mercury News,* 1 May 2000.

CHAPTER 23

296. **Yankowski calls the Palm VII "a brick":** Kim Girard, "The Palm Phenom," *Business 2.0,* 3 April 2001.

296. **Handspring grabs a quarter of the handheld market:** Stephanie Miles, "Handspring grabs No. 2 sales spot," *CNET News.com,* 22 June 2000.

296. **Microsoft product manager quotes:** Kim Girard, "The Palm Phenom," *Business 2.0,* 3 April 2001.

296. **"The brains behind Palm":** Adam Lashinsky, "Handhelds: Hold hands!" *Fortune*, 11 June 2001.

297. **"a strong enough vision to continue":** Stephanie Miles, "Majority of handhelds may be given away," *CNET news.com*, 10 April 2000.

298. **Yankowski motivation for appointing two COOs:** "Carl Yankowski Is Under Pressure to Turn the Ailing Palm Around," *Wall Street Journal*, 4 June 2001.

299. **Microsoft vowed to spare no expense:** Pui-Wing Tam, "Competitive Drive: Palm Puts Up Its Fists As Microsoft Attracts Hand-Held PC Market," *Wall Street Journal*, 8 August 2000.

299. **Michael Mace's efforts:** Pui-Wing Tam, "Competitive Drive: Palm Puts Up Its Fists As Microsoft Attracts Hand-Held PC Market," *Wall Street Journal*, 8 August 2000.

300. **Pocket PC press reviews:** Walter S. Mossberg, "New, Improved Pocket PCs Don't Capture Palm's Magic," *Wall Street Journal*, 4 May 2000.

300. **Benhamou predicts minority of Palm's revenue from hardware sales:** Deborah Clayman, "Palm is finally free," *San Jose Mercury News*, 14 September 1999.

302. **Internet data "the ultimate application":** Palm, Inc. 2000 Annual Report.

304. **Compaq, HP, and Casio market shares:** NPD Intelect.

304. **"It was a cheap tactic":** Richard Shim, "Palm Faithful: Can't buy Pocket PC love," *ZDNet News*, 19 October 2000.

CHAPTER 24

310. **"little more than add an expansion slot":** "One Palm flapping," *The Economist*, 2 June 2001.

311. **Palm ships 50 percent of its Q3 units in February:** Palm's executives told financial analysts this during the question-and-answer part of the Palm, Inc., Third Quarter, Fiscal 2001 Analyst Teleconference Remarks.

312. **Pocket PC market share in February 2001:** Cecile Barnes, "Handspring chips away at Palm market," *CNET news.com*, 19 March 2001.

312. **"Can we get the m500 line out in two weeks":** quoted in Pui-Wing Tam, "Pilot Error: Palm Tumbles from High-Tech Stardom," *Wall Street Journal*, 7 September 2001.

316. **a merger of Handspring and Palm:** Adam Lashinsky, "Handhelds: Hold hands!" *Fortune*, 11 June 2001.

316. **"only a takeover can save Palm now":** A. Nonymous, *Palmstation.com*, 5 May 2001.

316. **the company was flying high:** Barrie Sosinsky, "Is Windows CE Dead on the Palmtop?" *Windows 2000*, May 2000.

316. **Now the headlines said:** John Simons, "Has Palm Lost Its Grip?" *Fortune,* 28 May 2001.

316. **"Palm's management is under the gun":** Pui-Wing Tam, "Carl Yankowski is Under Pressure to Turn the Ailing Palm Around," *Wall Street Journal,* 4 June 2001.

316. **no slowdown for Microsoft's Pocket PC models:** Based on research by NPD Intelect reported by: Tish Williams, "As Microsoft Gains From Behind, Palm Gives Its OS a Push," *TheStreet.com,* 3 August 2001.

316. **exacerbated Palm's public-image crisis:** Todd Kort, Ken Dulaney, and Martin Reynolds, "Worldwide PDA Market Declines 21 Percent in 2Q01," *Gartner Dataquest.*

317. **report caused a minor sensation:** "iPAQ Sales Overtaking Palm," *Internet News.com,* 18 June 2001.

317. **report caused a minor sensation:** "Research Firm Predicts Palm Will Lose Top Spot in Hand-Held Market to Compaq," *Wall Street Journal,* 18 June 2001.

323. **a triumph of design and functionality:** Stephen H. Wildstrom, "Handspring's breakthrough hybrid," *BusinessWeek,* 30 November 2001.

323. **a true breakthrough:** Walter S. Mossberg, "Handspring expertly combines cellphone, PDA in New Treo," *The Wall Street Journal,* 29 November 2001.

EPILOGUE

325. **sheer force of will, stamina, and marketing:** Pocket PC 2002 is Microsoft's seventh attempt at the handheld market. The software company has already tried "Windows for Pen Computing," WinPad, Windows CE 1.0, Windows CE 2.0, Windows CE 2.1 ("palm-size PC"), and Windows CE 3.0 (Pocket PC).

326. **"What OS is in your device?":** Tish Williams, "The TSC Streetside Chat: Handspring CEO Donna Dubinsky," *RealMoney.com,* 4 August 2001.

INDEX